# Washing The Bones

**LOCAL
AUTHOR**

# Washing the Bones

## A Memoir of Love, Loss, and Transformation

Katherine Ingram

2013

*For W.D.*

# Acknowledgments

It would be impossible to faithfully and fully acknowledge all the persons and circumstances that contribute to the birth of a book. Everything that occurs in life is the result of a confluence of an infinite number of events and people. As the Tao Te Ching says, "The One begets the Two; the Two Begets the Three; the Three begets the ten-thousand things." That said, I do wish to offer the following, special thanks:

To the many teachers and friends who encouraged my writing and knew I was a writer before I did: your long-forgotten words stayed with me always and nudged me to this creation.

To my early readers, whose enthusiasm and support for this endeavor gave me much needed faith.

To the unexpected angels who stepped in and offered just the right help at just the right moment: Lou Haas, Rebecca Williams, and Patricia Cook—I blow you kisses and thank you for your support and for believing in me.

To Joanne Shwed for her editorial help and Anna Elkins for her creative ideas.

To my father, Charles Buford Ingram, who shared with me his love of words and books, and whose dream lives on in me.

To my late husband, whose life and death inspired this book and who gave me the peace and encouragement to share it with the world. Thank you for your courage, your love and your support.

To Dr. Naomi Lowinsky—teacher, poet, wise woman and analyst— who has journeyed with me for more than a decade and whose unfailing compassion, wisdom, support and counsel has healed and guided me. I am forever filled with love and gratitude for you.

To my guides and companions in Spirit who have been infinitely patient and gentle in showing me the way.

And finally, to my husband Michael, and to my beautiful, wondrous children, Aidan and Sophia, who brought me back to life and who continue to teach me the depth and breadth of love. You are the most unexpected and glorious gifts from my grief.

*"If you bring forth what is within you, what you bring forth will save you. If you do not bring forth what is within you, what you do not bring forth will destroy you."*

The Gospel of Thomas

"December 14, 1996, about 1520 Pacific Standard Time, N278ML, a Bellanca 8KCAB Super Decathlon [aerobatic aircraft], impacted terrain during an uncontrolled descent near Eagle Point, Oregon, and was destroyed. The certified flight instructor (CFI) was fatally injured. The student, who was a commercial pilot receiving aerobatic instruction at the time of the accident, bailed out of the airplane and suffered minor injuries. The wreckage was found in one piece, inverted, and with the rudder deflected to the right at maximum travel. The surviving pilot's parachute was found 50 feet from the wreckage. The CFI was found strapped into the rear seat of the airplane."

—Federal Aviation Administration Report

PART ONE

THE INCUBATION *or* HANGING BY A THREAD

*A caterpillar spends most of its life crawling on—and devouring—its food source.
But when it's time to become an adult, most caterpillars start to wander away from
what they've been eating. They find a sheltered, safe spot in which to pupate, or transform into an adult. Tenuously tethered, their body splits open, revealing a chrysalis.
Along with the ability to occasionally twitch in response to threats, this shell is
what protects the caterpillar
while it transforms.*

# 1

It was six o'clock. My mother had just shown up, unannounced as usual, lonely and bored since my stepfather's death ten months earlier. Her surprise visits usually annoyed me, but tonight I welcomed her company; it was good to have someone to talk to as I made dinner. I'd been lonely myself lately.

I fixed my mother a vodka tonic, made myself an Old Fashioned, and joined her by the fire. I had expected Andrew home an hour ago. He hadn't called, which was unusual. Even though we were having problems, he was always good about calling. He sometimes hung out at the airport after he'd finished giving a lesson; he loved it there, loved talking shop. These days, I imagined he preferred being there to being home. Still, I wondered aloud about him being so late.

"I always imagine the worst," I said, rolling my eyes at my own insecurity.

Then, my words still lingering in the air, there was a knock at the front door.

I froze in place. My eyes darted anxiously, meeting my mother's in a suspended second of timelessness. Her look reflected my fear. The blood drained from my head, leaving a profound ringing in my ears. My heart beat wildly. I stood, walked to the door, and opened it a few inches, trying to prevent the dogs from charging out.

There, on the concrete step, stood two uniformed men, harshly illuminated by the porch light against the pitch-black night. The man on the left had silver hair and glasses and wore a green jacket with a badge that read "Deputy Sheriff." Next to him stood a rotund, balding man in a black, collared shirt with a rectangular metal pin that read "Chaplain."

"Are you Katherine Alden?" the sheriff asked.

"Yes. What happened?"

The words came out quickly. They felt faint and taut as I spoke them. Strangely, all I could imagine in that moment was that Andrew had been in a car accident, and I wanted to get to the hospital immediately and not be standing here wasting time with unimportant details. Bella, my Rottweiler, was sniffing loudly next to me, her large head pushing to see who was there. I held fast to her collar.

There was what seemed to be a short pause, and then the deputy sheriff looked at me soberly.

"Andrew is dead," he said.

The door drifted open as I fell to my knees. I heard someone screaming "NO, NO, NO!" over and over, not recognizing my own voice. Bella was barking insanely, lunging outside. I heard my mother's voice over my right shoulder, repeating, "Oh, my God! Oh, my God!" The men were trying to pick me up off the ground where I had collapsed, screaming.

All at once, I felt a hot, searing pain cut across my skull behind my left ear. Instinctively, I reached up toward the pain. Blood covered my hand. Bella, smelling my distress and seeing the strangers pulling at my body, had moved to protect me. In full attack mode, she had torn into my cranium just behind my left ear. The pain of the incision brought me immediately into my body, pulling me down from the porch ceiling, where I had drifted in the first wave of shock.

There was a chaotic combination of hands grabbing at me, and a quick, muffled discussion, and then I found myself inside, sitting in our mostly empty front room on the blue-and-white striped sofas that Andrew's parents had bought for him before we met. I'd never liked these sofas; they were rough and uncomfortable. I sat, bleeding and sobbing, bent over double, reflexively jerking away from any attempts to touch me.

I heard the deputy ask my mother if there were someone they could call. I looked up through hair wet with tears and blood to see the chaplain paging through my address book, a smile pasted on his round face.

"Wow, you sure have a lot of friends all over the place!" he quipped cheerfully.

I hated him. I hated that he was voyeuristically going through my address book, hated that he was so stupidly cheerful, hated that he was here at all. Part of me—the small, coherent fragment still in tact—wanted to yell at him, "Get the fuck out of my house!" but too much of me was in agony to muster the energy to eject him.

He kept saying, "Bless your heart," and patting my knee. He was pissing me off. It was like something a grandparent would say to console a grandchild whose dead goldfish was being flushed to Kingdom Come; "Bless your heart," pat, pat. He didn't seem to grasp the horrible profundity of the moment. He appeared utterly unfazed by the reality of what had brought him to my door.

He stood up after I glared at him, angry and horror stricken. I saw him rub his behind, and heard him tell the deputy that Bella had bitten him in the ass. I was glad. She did what I would've liked to do. It confirmed my belief that she was not only a good guard dog but also an excellent judge of character.

My mother was examining the gash behind my ear and saying that I needed to go to the hospital. I pulled away, adamant that I would do no such thing. I wanted the blood. I wanted to bleed to death, wanted to die, *hoped* that I would die. My entire being was ruptured and hemorrhaging; there damn well ought to be blood. There ought to be some indicator to the world at large that I had been mortally wounded, that I was in grave danger of spilling out my entire life force—right then, right there—all over those blue-and-white sofas.

Keith materialized, seemingly out of nowhere, in response to my mother's call. He stood in the living room in the midst of the chaos, red eyed and stricken. His eyes were bleary, and I could see that he was trying to get his bearings through the alcohol and the shock. I stood and fell into his arms, sobbing into his broad, warm chest. He'd been out on the town drinking, as he usually did Saturday nights, but his strong arms felt safe and good and he held me tight.

Keith had been the older man and the love affair that I'd never gotten over until I met Andrew. We still loved each other, but it was a careful love now. He bore a slight resemblance to Tom Selleck and claimed to have been his double in Hollywood. He was strong and controlling and, when I first met him, married. Ours had been an intense, nine-month affair that had caused a divorce and had broken my naïve, twenty-two-year-old heart. That was ten years ago. Keith had welcomed us warmly when Andrew and I moved back to Oregon four months earlier. He and Andrew had even gone out and smoked cigars together, despite the fact that the only thing they had in common was me.

Brian arrived at the house shortly after Keith, and I moved into his arms where he held me gently. His was a very different sort of embrace, safe and sweet. I'd known Brian since I was seventeen. He was like a big brother to me; a long-time family friend whom my mother lovingly referred to as "an Iowa farm boy." Brian was responsible, solid, and perpetually, annoyingly cheerful.

Not now, though. It was the first time I had ever seen him unsmiling. He, too, had been a cigar buddy of Andrew's and a good friend to us both. He and his wife and Keith had all been at our wedding—our glorious, gorgeous San Francisco wedding—just seven months ago. Now they were in our dimly lit living room, tending to me the way that passersby help the victim of a car crash before the ambulance arrives.

After a short time, I took myself to a corner of the kitchen and sank down to the floor, hugging my knees, my back pressed into the cabinets. The swath of overhead fluorescent lights glared brightly. I was beginning to feel numb all over and, in that state, I began to think that the cops were wrong. They were terribly, terribly wrong. This was obviously an awful mistake. Andrew was still alive and trapped upside down, strapped into the five-point harness of the plane he had just purchased. He'd wanted that Decathlon so much. He'd been ecstatic about it, thrilled to at last have his own aerobatic plane.

They said that he'd crashed around three o'clock that afternoon. They said he had been killed on impact, that his student had parachuted to safety, unharmed except for a few scratches. I did not believe them; I could not accept it. In my mind, they had missed his pulse; they had not checked carefully. I imagined him still alive but left for dead in that airplane, way out in God-forsaken Eagle Point, Oregon, on a dark and freezing-cold December night.

My heart was breaking and I was worried sick about him. He was alone and hurt and needing help. What was wrong with these goddamned people? Why weren't they out there rescuing him? Why were they in my house looking so somber?

My mother came over and leaned down beside me. I looked up, eyes swollen, tears running down my cheeks.

"What if he's alive?" I whispered. "What if he's hurt and no one is there to help him?"

My mother looked at me with pained compassion, the way someone approaches a wild animal, caught in a trap.

"Oh, honey," she said, "he's not hurt."

In the corner of my consciousness, I knew there was no mistake. I listened, still coiled in a fetal position on the floor, as my mother phoned my brother. He was in California, making funeral arrangements for our stepbrother, who had just been found alone in his home—dead—two days earlier.

"Chris, Andrew has been killed." Her voice was breaking. "You have to come right away." She began to cry. I'd only seen her cry once before, under very similar circumstances. "In his airplane. I know. This is all unbelievable." She paused, listening. "You have to leave that. This is more important. Come now. Come as soon as you can."

She hung up, and the sheriff suggested that we needed to call Andrew's parents. My mother said she would do it, but I quickly told her no; it was my duty, my place to make this call. I sat looking at the phone and at their familiar number written in blue pen in my address book. I remembered writing it there after our first meeting, so I could send a thank-you note for the dinner, hoping to impress them. I knew the number by heart.

I stared at it, tears blurring my vision. I was trying to think clearly, trying to think how to say what had to be said. Slowly and carefully, I pushed the numbers. I squeezed my eyes tightly shut, trying to close everyone out. Richard answered.

"Oh, Kate. Hello! We just walked in from a Christmas party!" he shouted cheerfully.

I winced internally. The contrast between where he was and where I was about to take him crushed me.

"Hold on. Let me get Mumsie," he bubbled. It had not dawned on him that I was calling after midnight their time—something I would never do.

"Oh, Richard!" I interrupted. "Something terrible has happened."

"Oh?"

He stopped before getting Barbara and returned his attention to me. I could hear him becoming somber, his voice softening and growing faint.

"Andrew crashed his plane. Oh, Richard, Andrew is dead." I began to choke on my tears. "I'm sorry, I'm so sorry, Richard. I'm so sorry," I sobbed over and over. Sorry for everyone, sorry for everything: for Andrew, for me, for them, for this moment, for being the one to tell him, for shattering his heart into a million, irretrievable pieces.

I'd never before had to break such news to anyone, and this was not just anyone. I loved Richard deeply. His presence in my life—his sweetness and generosity and loving heart—filled an enormous void in me. To tell him this, to tear his heart open, to be the bearer of the worst of all possible tidings, was beyond horrible. As I spoke, my words felt like a dagger plunging into his heart. I felt his chest tear apart as I dragged the sharp edge down, flaying him open.

"Oh, Richard. I'm so sorry..."

"Okay," he whispered. "We'll be there."

# 2

There was a full two-second lull between waking and consciousness the next morning, two seconds of normal peace and quietude before the reality of the previous hours surged over me like a tremendous tidal wave, pulling me under, drowning me, the force of it crushing my chest. My heart began to ache as my grief erupted into a deep, mournful howl.

My mother held me as I moaned a choked, high-pitched lamentation against her chest. In a strong maternal move, my mother had stayed next to me in my bed through the night. She was always at her best when one of us was in acute crisis; the heady combination of drama and usefulness put her in her best form.

A protective cocoon of shock began to envelop me, holding and numbing me to the emotional and physical chaos. I felt like a caterpillar disappearing into its chrysalis, removed from its former life, from eating and sound and movement. The chrysalis was unbidden and unfamiliar. Inside of it, removed from my former reality, I was aware of everything but in a detached and dreamlike way. Sound and motion slowed dramatically. Time lost all meaning as hours and days moved and blended into one another. Images appeared in front of me like a life review just before death, but the scenes were all present tense.

Still in yesterday's clothes, I moved into the living room where I sat, shell-shocked. I watched Nicole's white Toyota Camry pull up to the curb. She was staring straight ahead and looking serious, her short, white hair pushed neatly behind her ear. I'd begun therapy with her just two weeks earlier. My mother had met her at her Symphony Guild group, and referred her to me in my quest for a therapist.

"Her name is Dr. Nicole Rothschild. She's a New York Jew," my mother had said, as though that were everything one needed to know.

I watched a different, unfamiliar woman arrive and listened as she spoke to my mother in the entryway. She was from the rental agency, and she had arrived at the most inopportune moment imaginable to inform me, sixteen hours into my widowhood, that I was to be evicted unless I got rid of one of our dogs. The neighbors, apparently, had complained.

My mother quickly ushered her to the door. "Her husband was just killed." I heard her say in a muffled voice. "You'll have to take this up later," and she shut the door behind her.

The interior of my chrysalis was a surreal swirling of images and sounds, all blurred and muted as though underwater. The thought of losing the dogs and maybe my house in the middle of this unspeakable loss completely overwhelmed me. I sat, small and scared, on the sofa. Everything was being torn away. In a matter of only a few hours, my entire life had been swept away forever. I could not absorb it all.

As the afternoon unfolded around me, I heard someone quietly announce that Barbara and Richard had arrived, having flown in overnight on a red-eye from D.C. I both dreaded and longed to see them. I had no idea how to greet them, what to say. I walked slowly to the door and then outside to meet them.

Their rental car was parked in the driveway. I stood numbly on the walkway and watched as Barbara opened the passenger door. Her glasses were black, hiding her eyes. I watched her step out of the car. She wore a black skirt and jacket and dark green opaque hose, like the green hose that shopping mall elves wear at Christmas. I stood for what felt like many long, quiet seconds musing about the hose when it dawned on me that green and black were Dartmouth colors: Dartmouth was Andrew's beloved alma mater. It was a very conscious tribute to her son; I was astounded by her composure.

I don't know if I embraced them, or if we spoke, or what I said if we did. I don't recall seeing either of Andrew's parents cry that day or any other day after that, although I was certain that they did. The Aldens epitomized the White Anglo-Saxon Protestant stereotype, which is to say that there was no visible emotional life or public discussion of difficult topics—certainly not from Barbara, at any rate. One did not vent anger or sadness or even display overt joy in these circles: "It simply isn't done," as Andrew used to say in his clenched-teeth impersonation of East Coast snobbery. Crying, the urbane Dr. Rothschild once admonished me, was something one did in private.

Not I. Emotion is something I've never been able to hide; further, and more to the point, I see no need or value in hiding it. Hiding emotion is what fucks us all up in the first place. And at this precise moment in my life, there was nothing whatsoever left to hide. I was hollowed out, transparent; a neutron bomb had been dropped in a strategic, surgical strike to my heart. My body was still more or less in tact, but my spirit—my life force—was gone ... completely and utterly vaporized.

Friends and family began to arrive over the course of the next few days. Ainslie, my best friend, immediately came up from San Francisco and spent the week caring for me, wordlessly standing by my side. Andrew's younger brothers, James and Stephan, came with his Uncle Pierce. Chris and his wife Linda arrived and set about taking care of insurance and legal matters. Barbara stoically handled all the funeral arrangements. Her face appeared ashen and somber, but she seemed in total control of herself, just as she was on every previous occasion I had witnessed: completely contained and in charge.

James and Pierce quickly disappeared into Andrew's office to go through paperwork and organize everything, making themselves hugely helpful even as they dodged the emotional black cloud drifting through the house. I wondered, in a distant sort of way, what they might discover in Andrew's private affairs, and if I should care; but on the heels of that thought a morbid awareness arose that it didn't matter anymore. Andrew was dead now.

His brothers brought his car back from the airport where he had left it for the flight lesson that day, parking it in front of the house. It was painful to see it parked there; it made the horror seem more real. They busied themselves by cleaning it out, in the process discovering two airline tickets and a hotel confirmation in the glove box, where Andrew had hidden them.

They were to have been a surprise for our first wedding anniversary, which was not for another four months. James handed me two tickets to Zihuatinejo, Mexico. I had always wanted to see La Casa

Que Canta—a tiny, romantic resort overlooking the Pacific Ocean. I'd wanted to go there ever since we saw the movie *When a Man Loves a Woman* and watched Andy Garcia and Meg Ryan swimming in the blue infinity pool, pink bougainvillea framing a cloudless horizon.

I looked at the tickets, reading and rereading everything in slow motion. There was my name, his name, and our would-be anniversary date of April 20. Standing there on the sidewalk, fingering the slips of paper, I disappeared into the Buena Vista Bar on Fisherman's Wharf in San Francisco.

It was Christmas Eve. We'd ridden a cable car down the hill in the fog to this place: my favorite bar in my favorite city. Meg Ryan and Andy Garcia filmed a scene for that movie here. It was packed tonight: wall-to-wall people, five deep at the bar, everyone festive and happy. We pushed our way through the throng and shared a table with ten other people, joining in the mayhem and carols, drinking Irish coffees.

One of the women at our table, fairly sodden at this point, stared intensely at Andrew and then shouted to him over the din, "You look just like Andy Garcia, from that movie!" which he sort of did, and then to me she yelled, "And you look like Meg Ryan!" which I only vaguely did if you were drunk and crossed your eyes. "Look everyone," she howled, "it's Andy Garcia and Meg Ryan!" and everyone whooped and we all drank a toast to us: The Beautiful Couple.

As my reverie retreated, I found myself back on the sidewalk in front of the house, shivering in the cold, holding the itinerary in my hands, overwhelmed by the magnitude of everything that was now lost to me: the shared memories, the love, the future.

"We'll take care of this," James said, gently taking the papers out of my hands. Later, I would hear him on the phone down the hall, canceling the hotels and the flights. He cancelled spring in Zihuatinejo and the Christmas we had planned in Santa Fe. Bit by bit, my lovely future disappeared, snatched away before I could even touch it, the beautiful dream shaken out and emptied as I listened, mute and helpless to stop it.

My sister Connie arrived somewhere in the midst of all this quiet busyness, looking—as she always did—as though she just stepped off Rodeo Drive. I was standing in the front room when I saw her come through the door and beeline straight toward me, looking a little blurred somehow. She grabbed me, sobbing and saying something that I didn't quite understand. Her bright red lipstick was slightly smeared around her mouth and she smelled of alcohol and heavy perfume. An aversive feeling washed over me and I peeled myself away from her grasp; I didn't need someone holding me unless they could offer some desperately needed strength and love. She was falling apart, and she didn't even know Andrew; she hardly knew me.

My sister and I were separated in age by almost thirteen years; she married when I was still in grammar school. But even beyond the chasm in age, we were photo negatives of one another. She was Dolce and Gabbana to my Levi Strauss. She was a born-again Christian and a devout materialist with a white-hot temper; I had left Christianity in a search for something more, and I tended to internalize my emotions, covering them with a cool blanket of isolating depression.

From the moment she arrived on the planet she had, to her great misfortune, been the black sheep of the family, or as my mother so delicately phrased it, "a bad seed." Her birth was difficult and had been very traumatic for my mother both physically and emotionally, and that, compounded by the unfortunate circumstance of Connie emerging looking exactly like our paternal grandmother (a woman whom my mother despised because she despised my mother), had created a convoluted psychological mess—a mess that my mother chose not to address.

I moved away from Connie to sit by myself, looking out the picture window in the living room. I heard my mother and sister talking in the kitchen, discussing the chicken that I had been making when the sheriff arrived. I found it repugnant that they could even think of eating, that they had an appetite. I watched people driving to work as though nothing had happened, as though the world had not stopped when, quite obviously, it had. How could all these people dumbly drive off to their meaningless jobs, so unaware? How was it that they did not seem to have the slightest idea that my world had imploded? Couldn't they hear it? Couldn't they feel it? A phrase from one of W. H. Auden's poems kept running through my head: "Stop all the clocks."

The traumatic blow had shattered the illusion of time, returning me to the primordial eternity of the omnipresent moment. *Stop all the clocks.* Time had stopped. The world had stopped. I became aware that I was in an alternate reality, a different galaxy. I was spinning off in a sort of out-of-body experience, looking at what used to be a solid world, a world of continuity and garden-variety problems; that world appeared small and distant to me now. I looked around our living room, which seemed strange to me: odd and meaningless.

Inside my protective cocoon I was dissolving, floating, removed from life, from sensation and sound and consensual reality. The feeling of existential aloneness was all encompassing. The world at large could not see me floating there, did not know that I was dying. No one could enter the realm I now inhabited. No one could hold me as I quietly, painfully deliquesced. I was in a distant limbo: no longer what I was, not yet what I would become. I floated, tenuously, in this liminal reality.

Muffled in this quiet netherworld, I wondered what had happened to the funeral rites that people used to observe. Where were the black wreaths on the doors, the draped mirrors, the black armbands signifying to the world that your life had been sliced open and emptied out? Why had all the indicators been removed? Why were we all ignorant of one another's suffering, going about our business as usual and crying in private? It was a shame. It was a stupid, goddamned shame. I wanted to scream out to everybody up and down the street and to the people driving blithely by in their cars that I was in mourning. I wanted to scream, "See me! Help me!"

Instead, I sat silently. The house was muted and silent, even as people came and went. I told Ainslie that I wanted to go outside, so we walked, arm in arm in slow motion, moving at dream speed up the sidewalk in the sharp winter air. I shivered as the cold penetrated my coat. We walked in silence, stopping every few feet. Movement seemed foreign and oppressively demanding.

We turned after a few yards and headed back. I stopped in front of the house, watching a redheaded woodpecker hanging on the trunk of the tree in the front yard—the tree that had split in two during a recent storm. I thought about how Andrew had identified with the woodpecker, and how he said that, if he ever died, he would come back to me as that bird. Was this Andrew? Or was this a message from Andrew, telling me that he was still with me? Had that woodpecker always come to that tree? I couldn't remember. I watched his shiny red head and black body hopping about on the white trunk: so bright and beautiful. Ainslie and I looked up, watching the Red-tailed Hawks circling together in the winter sky.

Later in the afternoon, my mother came into my bedroom where I was lying down and sat on the end of the bed. The room was dark.

"I need to ask you something," she said. It was extremely quiet. She waited a few moments before she spoke again. "You need to decide whether you want to go to see his body."

I looked up at her without lifting my head, unsure of what to say, uncertain, even, what to think. It took a few moments for the words to form a cohesive meaning in my brain.

"You have to go now if you want to see him," she continued after a pause. She was unusually careful and maternal in her wording and behavior. Tears came slowly to my eyes; they came constantly now, with each person's arrival, each thought. I felt slightly unreal and floaty and quiet. I went off into some middle distance.

"You won't be able to see his face," I heard her say. The full implication of this did not immediately take hold. "You can hold his hand." I imagined his hand, blue and cold and heavy, hanging out from under a white sheet. I did not want that to be my lasting memory of him. In my mind's eye, he was still alive.

Slowly, I formed a reply. "If I can't see him, if I can't kiss him good-bye, then I think I don't want to go."

"I think that's a good decision," she said gently.

I asked Barbara and Richard to wait for a few minutes before they went to the mortuary, to give me some time to compose a letter to Andrew to be burned with his body. I had done the same when my father died twenty-four years earlier. I shook with convulsions of sadness as I wrote, tears dropping onto the card, blurring the ink. I told him how much I loved him, how lost I was without him, how I hoped that he now realized how many people loved him, and how much. I thought he would be surprised and deeply moved by the amount of love and heartache his death had engendered.

I sealed the small note card and handed it to my mother. Before his family left for the mortuary, I asked them to bring back the Dartmouth jacket he was wearing when he crashed—the one he loved, the one he always wore. I desperately wanted to hold and touch what he had been wearing; it would still have his energy, have *him* on it.

When they returned some hours later, they had the jacket with them. They handed it to me, dry-cleaned and encased in a plastic bag. I was horrified, dismayed beyond words. I desperately did not want it cleaned and sanitized; I wanted his smell, wanted it just as it had been on his body when he left. I was angry.

"We thought it would be too hard for you to see the blood," someone said.

*Blood?* I thought. I had not yet taken in the violence of the accident. Well, if there *were* blood, I wanted to see it. I *wanted* his blood, wanted something solid of him to hold, to wear. It was the coat he lived in, the coat he was wearing when I saw him drive off to that lesson. I didn't want the sanitized version: I wanted the *real* version. I needed it. I needed him. I needed to feel the reality of it all.

I lifted the filmy plastic and looked at the green wool, the white letters curving across the back spelling "DARTMOUTH." There were small holes in the back at symmetrical points, puncturing the heavy fabric. I touched them carefully with my finger. I knew that was where the five-point harness had punctured the coat, punctured him when the plane hit the ground. That was real at least.

I pulled the plastic down, hung it in the coat closet, and closed the door.

# 3

My mother sat on the end of the bed, watching me putting on my makeup before the service. I was moving very slowly and deliberately and I felt strangely calm. I put on the black suit with the velvet trim that Andrew had given me last Christmas and the pearls that had been his wedding gift to me. He had always been loving and lavish in his gifts, buying me clothes and jewelry and even the full-length blue fox coat I had admired at a charity auction last summer. I was wearing it all as I made my way into the miniscule, wooden 1800s Anglican church, unaware of how oddly Cruella de Vil I must have appeared, subsumed in that coat. In my state of mind, however, it made perfect sense: I wanted to be completely wrapped in Andrew.

I'd asked Keith to find me a bagpiper to play for the service. Murray, arrayed in his full dress kilt, was now warming up on the snow-flecked museum lawn across the street, waiting for the service to begin. I walked over and introduced myself.

"You're playing this for my husband," I said, looking right at him. He nodded, respectfully. "I want you to make everyone cry." I strongly believed that the Episcopalians needed some help. He nodded his head again, looking at me sadly.

I walked back to the church and joined my tiny family in the crowded anteroom, which was the size of a small closet. My coat took up most of the space in the tiny vestibule. I held a dozen red roses, which I intended to lay on the altar. The priest, whom I had never met, asked me for the roses, saying that he would have to place them for me. I clutched them to my body, staring at him.

"You can't approach the altar," he stated.

"I think God will understand, don't you?" I asked. It wasn't really a question.

The priest stood, speechless. His hands fidgeted. I imagined that he was weighing out the potential wrath of his god with that of the widow standing unwaveringly before him. An intense moment of silence ensued. Then he bowed his head, turned, and walked away.

The service began in the little wooden church. Green wreaths adorned each tall, rectangular window. We entered from the front, near the altar. I was surprised to see that the church was packed. I could see our realtor in the back—how did he know?—and Aunt Brooke's face in the middle of the small crowd, somber and drawn. Richard stayed close, sitting next to me in the front pew while Barbara and the boys sat across the aisle. The fact that he sat with me surprised and moved me to tears. I wanted to curl up in his arms and cry until no tears were left.

I could sense Andrew's presence in the church. I looked up, half expecting to see him, and I half did. In the upper left corner of the church, behind the altar, I sensed what felt like his energy—hovering, watching. It could have just as easily been a figment of my rapidly disintegrating sanity, but to me it was very real. I liked it. I felt as if we were together again, a couple again, sharing this moment as we had shared so many others. It felt like being at a cocktail party when we would catch each other's eye across the room and know exactly what the other was thinking; it was that sort of connection. I now inhabited the liminal space between the pew where I sat and the ceiling where my spirit wandered. I floated briefly there, hovering between the living and the dead.

Steve, Brian's friend and pastor, began to speak. He had met me only two days before, when he had arrived at the house in the late afternoon and sat with me for an hour as darkness descended. In that brief interlude with a complete stranger, I had shared our love story. I'd smiled as I recounted some of it, even laughed a little at the quirky bits, like how Andrew taped every episode of *Star Trek* and how sick I got the first time I flew upside down with him. I shared how we adopted our first dog, Beau, a Doberman puppy, outside the grocery store on Christmas Eve and the way Andrew would sit with one ankle on his knee when he drank his vodka gimlets. Steve had sat, quiet and relaxed, watching me as I spoke. He took no notes at all.

Now I sat in grateful amazement as this man, who had never met Andrew and who had only spoken to me for an hour, began to describe Andrew as though he had known him for many years, as if he were toasting us at our wedding.

When he finished, I rose, glanced toward the priest who did not look at me, walked to the front of the church, and set the roses gently on the altar. I looked up toward the corner to see if Andrew were still there, but I couldn't quite tell. I whispered my love into the space between us, and then turned, walked to the lectern, and opened my journal to the place where I had pasted two poems. My mother had asked me earlier if I was sure that I wanted to do this, thinking, quite fairly, that I might not get through it—or that I might collapse—but I was undeterred. I wanted to do this more than almost anything I had ever wanted in my life. I wanted to share with the world what this man meant to me.

I began to read the W. H. Auden poem that had been running through my mind all week:

> *Stop all the clocks, cut off the telephone,*
> *Prevent the dog from barking with a juicy bone,*
> *Silence the pianos and with muffled drum*
> *Bring out the coffin, let the mourners come.*
>
> *Let aeroplanes circle moaning overhead ...*

With this line, the full force of my grief came pouring out. Tears flooded my eyes and rolled down my cheeks. Stephan, seated two feet away and directly in front of me, stood and handed me his handkerchief. I took a deep breath and continued.

> *Let aeroplanes circle moaning overhead*
> *Scribbling on the sky the message He is Dead,*
> *Put crepe bows round the white necks of the public doves,*
> *Let the traffic policemen wear black cotton gloves.*
>
> *He was my North, my South, my East and West,*
> *My working week and my Sunday rest,*
> *My noon, my midnight, my talk, my song;*

18

*I thought that love would last for ever: I was wrong.*

*The stars are not wanted now: put out every one;*
*Pack up the moon and dismantle the sun;*
*Pour away the ocean and sweep up the wood.*
*For nothing now can ever come to any good.*

I sat down to profound silence. Steve stood again and asked, at my request, whether any of the attendees would like to share their memories of Andrew. After an interminable silence, Brooke spoke up.

"He was always good with the children."

There was another uncomfortably long silence.

I was disappointed. I'd wanted a wake, wanted remembrances. But this gathering of WASPs was not prone to publicly sharing their intimate feelings about a person. My West Coast, therapy, let's-share-our-feelings style wasn't going over with the Georgetown crowd. Besides which, everyone was just too damned sad.

The bagpipe began its doleful wheeze in the back of the church, softly at first and then louder and louder. The resonance of the pipes in the small space was deafening. Murray walked slowly up the aisle, playing *Amazing Grace*, to the front pew where Richard and I were seated, then turned and looked me in the eyes as he played, tears rolling down his face. Tears rolled down Richard's cheeks as well, and mine. Murray turned again and walked stoically back down the aisle and outside, where he finished his dirge. We were all undone by the deafening sound of the bagpipe, the intensity of the experience, the expression of love and longing. It was cathartic. I got my wish: the Episcopalians cried.

I enveloped myself in my coat and made my way outside where I stood on the sidewalk and shivered. One of my classmates from grade school appeared in front of me, one I hadn't seen for twenty years. He hugged me, crying.

"I'm so sorry," he said.

I wondered how he knew, why he was here. A car pulled up to the curb and my brother Chris helped me into the back where I sat, feeling completely emptied and vacant. We drove the half-mile back to the house for the reception.

I walked in the front door and saw Andrew's handsome face, smiling out from his wedding picture atop a small table in the living room. The paucity of furniture compelled the plethora of flowers that had been sent to spill over the one, small accent table onto the carpeted floor, where they formed a pool of color. I marveled at the abundance. I crouched down and looked a the card attached to a vase that held two dozen, long-stemmed red roses; they had been sent by my brother's best friend from high school. I was completely confounded and taken aback by the outpouring.

"Look how he was loved," I said to my mother.

"They aren't for him. They're for you."

Family and friends—and even some people I didn't recognize—filled the house. My sixth-grade teacher, Mr. Elam, was there. Brian was out on the patio, smoking a cigar, slightly drunk, and singing something incomprehensible. I wandered onto the concrete slab in the backyard and asked him what he was singing.

"A song to the fallen warrior," Brian replied, his words slightly slurred, "in Scottish."

I smiled and kissed him. I wrapped my arms around myself against the cold and went back inside. Spotting Richard across the living room, I made my way through the crowd of people and chaos of chairs and sat on the arm of the sofa next to him. I didn't want to mingle or to talk. Richard stood beside me, and I leaned my head over and rested it against his arm.

Richard was poking all of his fingers into enormous black olives and thrusting his hand toward my face, wiggling the round black tips, trying to encourage me to eat them. Andrew would have been mortified; he was frequently embarrassed by his father's slightly odd behaviors, though he himself was quirky as hell. I wondered where Richard's suffering was, how he could nurture me when his own heart must be crushed under the weight of unspeakable grief.

Slowly, after a couple of hours, the gathering dwindled. Andrew's best friend, our best man, hugged me good-bye. He and one of my bridesmaids had flown together from Philadelphia and then driven for hours through winter storms to be here. Final condolences were offered as guests departed. The house grew quiet.

Then someone—I have no idea who; I recall no face—spoke to me as I stood in the little hallway near the front door.

"Remember," the voice said, "energy cannot be created or destroyed. It only changes form."

Then the voice—and the body it came in—left, and it was just my mother and me. She hugged me and made me promise to call her for anything, she would come, and then she, too, left.

I stood in the absence of sound, listening to the hum of silence. *It only changes form.* If this were true, then perhaps Andrew wasn't gone at all, not really; he was just in a new form. I liked this thought. It made sense and it comforted me. In the far future, it would become the foundation for a whole new life, but that would not be for some time. I had a long, long journey ahead.

# 4

Seven days had passed since the accident; everything was done and everyone had left, returning by car and plane to their old, familiar worlds. I remained in my new, unfamiliar and insufferably uncomfortable one, more alone than I had ever felt, more alone than I could imagine surviving. A week had passed and with it all the chaos and commotion that beginnings and endings engender. Now it was silent and dark in the house, and there was nothing left to do.

Beau sat staring at the front door, waiting. His big, brown Doberman eyes glanced over at me, then back to the door; he was looking for Andrew.

"Oh, honey," I said, "he's not coming back."

I sat down on the floor beside him, wrapped my arms around his sleek, muscular body, and wept. Beau could still smell Andrew, but where was he? That's what I imagined him wondering. I was wondering it too. If he had indeed just changed form, was he still here somehow? Was he hanging around, making sure that we were okay? I wanted that to be true.

Big Dave, a friend of Keith's, came over the next day to take away all the trash. Big Dave lived and worked at the dump. He had his own corner stool at the Bella Union Bar, where he could be found most any given night. He liked to refer to me as "Katie May."

I opened the door to greet him; his usual loud exuberance and crooked-toothed grin were gone. He stood, speechless, his large, heavy frame filling the front door. His face was red and bloated from years of alcohol and days of sadness. He looked straight at me, shaking his head, tears welling in his eyes.

"This is just shit," he announced.

I liked his honesty. It was the most honest thing anyone had said to me, and it pretty much summed it all up. He wrapped his big arms around me, pulling me into his enormous frame. I felt dwarfed by his body. He held me for a few seconds and then, uncomfortable all of a sudden, he dropped his arms. I pointed him toward the garage door where the extra bags of trash were stored. He walked heavily into the garage, picked up the bags, and then silently lumbered out to his waiting truck.

I turned and went back inside. I paced around the house, thinking and crying and wondering what on earth to do, how to be. The darkness of the hallway scared me, just as it had when I was a child. I felt afraid to walk down to Andrew's office, afraid that I would see him at his desk, afraid that I wouldn't.

I wandered into our bedroom, opened the dresser drawer, and took out Andrew's polo shirt—the green one he had worn the day before he died. It still smelled of him, of his cologne. I stared at our wedding picture sitting on the dresser, the dresser we had just bought together. I held the shirt to my face and buried myself in it, closing my eyes. His smell was still alive and he was gone: how completely incongruous, how impossible, how fucking bizarre! How could he be dead when I could smell his aliveness? How could that be? I folded the shirt carefully and placed it back in the drawer, trying to protect and preserve his scent as long as possible; I knew this, too, would disappear.

I flopped down on the bed and picked up one of the paperbacks on life after death that Brooke had given me and glanced through it. I supposed that it was intended to give me hope, to make me feel better, but it didn't. It didn't speak to anything that I was feeling: to my pain, to my fear, to the ache filling my heart. I tossed it aside and picked up Sogyal Rinpoche's *The Tibetan Book of Living and Dying*—a book that, coincidentally enough, Ainslie had given me right before the accident. I paged through it slowly, looking for something helpful.

I discovered that Tibetans believe a violent or accidental death is very difficult for the one who dies (the "di-er," I suppose? God knows, it's hell on the "di-ee") and that apparently it helps the soul to become oriented to the fact that they have left their incarnation if you pray for them, sending them love and encouraging them to accept and complete their transition. So I sent Andrew my love and told him it that was okay to move on.

I waited. Nothing.

I turned to another smallish book in the pile beside my bed, one someone had left for me, by C.S. Lewis, titled *A Grief Observed*. I began to read, and could not put it down. Here was someone I could identify with, someone who expressed the multitude of feelings and thoughts swollen up inside of me. Here was someone who told it like it was, unvarnished and devoid of trite aphorisms like "time heals." The Lewis I communed with on these pages felt as I did: mad as hell, confused, and pained beyond description, beyond reason. His outpouring laid bare the pure torment and indignation that death leaves in its wake. Lewis' pained and angry thrashings as he attempted to find meaning spoke to me—to my anguish and confusion and sense of unmooring.

"Yes!" I kept saying aloud as I read, "Yes, yes, *yes!*"

His words did not provide solace exactly, but rather companionship in suffering; to know that someone else felt as I did and could articulate it so precisely was tremendously comforting.

Ultimately, Lewis found some sort of resting place within the context of Christianity. I, unfortunately, was not so lucky. I wished I could pray. I wished I believed in something that would give me some answers and tell me what to do. I had been a devout Christian in my adolescence, my faith holding me together through some difficult years. These days, though, I couldn't reconcile the idea of an all-loving male deity who could turn around and banish the vast majority of his own creation from his presence, dooming them to famine, fire, and general unpleasantness. Bad people I could understand, but *Buddhists?* Buddhists are some of the nicest people on Earth. It didn't make sense. I mean, what sort of god would do that? A mean and narcissistic one; one that I had no interest in talking to.

My more immediate spiritual concern, however, was making sense of Andrew's sudden death and my exile to this personal hell. None of it made sense to me. I had no context, no understanding; it all seemed utterly random and Job-like. The more I thought about it, the more questions I had.

Frustrated and overwhelmed by the inundation of pain and confusion, I crawled off our bed and went into the bathroom. I stood for a while, not sure what I was doing there. I opened the top drawer and saw Andrew's hairbrush. I picked it up and looked at it. Strands of his hair were in the bristles. I put the hairbrush back, closed the drawer, and looked at myself in the mirror. I looked like I felt: tired and irretrievably sad.

*Who would possibly want me now?* I wondered. *What possible life could be left for me?*

I undressed, started the shower, and got in. I turned my face to the water and stood, motionless, leaning against the plastic wall and letting the water beat down on me. Tears mixed and flowed with the water as I cried and told Andrew how much I missed him, how much I wanted him back. Then, hearing nothing but my own voice and the sound of the water, I became painfully aware that I was in this alone, and for a long, indeterminable run, and I became angry.

"Thanks a lot!" I yelled as I cried. "Thanks for leaving me with all this *crap* while you are out there, somewhere"—I gestured wildly above my head—"I have no idea where, free from all this *shit* while I am stuck here with this mess to clean up!"

Then I felt guilty for being angry with him when, after all, he did not ask to die. I stood there, sobbing and apologizing. The horrible awareness dawned on me that I could do anything I wanted, say anything I wanted, and it wouldn't matter. No one could hear me. Nobody was here with me. It all felt futile and slightly crazy. Everything I thought I believed, everything I thought I knew, everything I had, was slipping away. I stood in the tears and the water, watching it all wash down the drain.

# 5

I met Andrew in the fall of 1993—9-3-93, to be exact, which made it easy to remember. My brother Chris had just relinquished the apartment he'd lived in for more than a decade in order to move in with his girlfriend, and I had slipped in surreptitiously to take advantage of a $500 rent-controlled opportunity.

The apartment was on the second floor of a circa 1911 building across from Golden Gate Park; it had originally been a trio of Victorian-era flats but was now a carved-out collection of six smaller units managed by what could only be called a slumlord. Most mornings I had to step carefully over one of the legion of homeless people who had camped overnight on the dirty, black-and-white tiled front entryway. The place was run-down and perpetually cold. The sole source of heat was a small, old, ceramic, gas fireplace; the back bedroom, a former laundry room with a slanted floor that used to allow the water to run off, was completely uninsulated. There were large spaces between the old boards that my brother had stuffed with newspaper to keep out the drafts.

I'd spent most of the day repainting the living room, covering over the dingy yellow with what was drying to a sort of Pepto-Bismol pink. At least it was pretty and clean. It was my fresh start. I had the radio on and I was listening to music and enjoying the odd juxtaposition of feeling both lonely and happy. Everything had fallen back together a few years after it had fallen apart. In the previous seven years I'd graduated from college, been through a messy, heartbreaking affair, held three crummy jobs, and endured one abusive, alcoholic marriage and divorce. I had moved three times, had my car stolen, and gone through graduate school. My body and spirit felt like I'd just been spit out of a long, terrible ride at some dark amusement park. Now, I was free and on my own. I had my own place, gotten the position I wanted at a wonderful counseling center, and was officially a practicing psychotherapist. My parents had helped me buy a used, silver Volkswagen Fox, making me mobile once again.

Sick of painting, I walked down the stairwell, which had not been swept or vacuumed for a decade, and out into the fresh air, smelling the eucalyptus trees. I ran across the street toward Golden Gate Park, squeezing between the parked cars, crossed through the Panhandle, and walked up past the corner of Haight and Ashbury, where a new Gap store had just opened. Someone had already thrown a rock through its brand new plate-glass window.

I walked up two more blocks through the blowing fog until I reached Jammin' Java. Warm, coffee-infused air rushed out to greet me as I opened the door. The place was full, even mid-afternoon, and most of the customers were wearing successive layers of black. Local, questionable art hung on the walls and it was loud. All in all it was the perfect antidote to all my quiet aloneness. I ordered an almond latte, found a seat against the wall, and opened my journal, but I didn't write; there was too much to see.

Hat Man was sitting across the street on the concrete steps of an old Victorian. He was there just about every time I walked by: a large, heavy black man, perhaps twenty-five, or he might have been forty; it was impossible to tell. He loved to wear costumes. On any given day he might be a cowboy; resplendent royalty in a Burger King crown and robe fashioned from an old blanket; or a Viking with a gold, plastic, horned helmet. He threw out cheerful greetings to everyone who walked by, enjoying the exchanges he elicited with childlike delight. He seemed—and this was, for me, the most intriguing and wonderful thing about him—utterly joyful.

As I continued staring out the window, sipping my coffee, Chicken Man rode by on his bike, cloaked by the swirling late-summer fog. It was a seminal experience to see both of these characters on the same day. Chicken Man was clad, as he always was, in a worn, black leather jacket and black rubber scuba pants. His feet were bare and dirty; on his head, he wore a wide-brimmed leather hat, replete with a peacock feather, which fluttered behind him as he rode. His thin, bearded face was lined and weathered and his hair was long and scraggly, pulled into a ponytail. He rode an old, one-speed bicycle with a basket on the front, in which sat a large, plumed rooster that cocked its head from one side to the other in a jerking motion, attempting to discern where it was going.

Chicken Man and Hat Man were emblematic of what I loved about San Francisco: The great mixed bag of cultures and personalities, coupled with an unprecedented attitude of tolerance and incredible beauty, made it unique in all the world. I'd been in the city for almost seven years, and I loved it. The presence of these characters made me exceedingly happy. Being in San Francisco made me happy. Being free of a life-sucking relationship made me happy.

I sat, sipping at my drink, trying to make it last, and breathed deeply. I felt very much at peace. Peace was not something I'd felt for a long time. It was an amazing feeling to be happy and single with nothing burdening me. I had been on an emotional jag for five years—a self-induced, albeit unconscious, juggernaut of epic proportions that began under poor conditions and went rapidly downhill from there.

It had all begun at the gym. Satele was six feet tall, Polynesian and muscled, with enormous dark, round eyes and a quick smile. He appeared, on first meeting, to be kind and protective, with the added allure of seeming slightly exotic. He was flirtatious and soft spoken; I believed him when he told me that he was unhappy in his marriage. I wanted to believe him.

My attraction was, in part, a reaction to Keith's infidelity and inability to commit to a relationship. His philandering had wounded me, breaking my naïve little heart and spurring a desire to wound him in return. Partnering myself with Satele, a man in many ways identical to Keith, served my desire for a quiet sort of retaliation, and it fed my need for a strong, male figure in my life.

Satele was also attractive because of, and not just in spite of, his past. He had lost his mother to cancer while he was in college and his father in a car crash a few years later. His childhood had been filled with physical violence, abandonment, and alcohol-induced trauma. The damage he had suffered triggered a rescue reaction in me. I felt a deep, only partially conscious desire to love him back to wholeness, to heal his hurt and win his gratitude. Unconsciously, I was searching for the father figure I desperately wanted. The fact that Satele was loving, protective, and generous of spirit led me to imagine—and it was only imagining—that he would fiercely love and protect me. I could not have been more wrong.

As with many wounded creatures, Satele was almost primal in his emotionality. He could shift in an instant from easy warmth to dark anger, and frequently did; alcohol only exacerbated this tendency. He drank frequently and heavily. He could disappear for hours or even days, resurfacing in the middle of the night, incoherent, unable to negotiate the furniture, trying to force himself on me or making an offering of a puppy or some flowers in an attempt to mollify my anger.

When he was sober, Satele could be extremely loving and generous, even complimentary. But gradually, as the drinking and the relationship went on, his jealousy and attempts to control me increased: what I wore, who I saw, and where I went were all fuel for incendiary arguments. And Satele was a cop—an emotionally labile, alcoholic Samoan with a gun. As time went on, he became increasingly violent with me and others: beating a suspect in custody, tearing off the bathroom door to get to me at my firm's Christmas party, holding a gun to his own head and threatening me with it as well, brawling while gambling on a booze cruise and being dumped, bloody and unconscious, in our cabin in the middle of the night.

Three years of steadily swelling abuse and violence took its toll. I became increasingly depressed and demoralized, ashamed to tell anyone what was happening, ashamed that I was even involved in such a relationship, but terrified to leave. Years of being told that I was fucked up, that I was both frigid and a whore (an intriguing combination), years of drunken arguments a host of communicable diseases had all conspired to wear down what little esteem I had to a tiny nub.

I tried everything I knew to make our relationship work. I tried badgering him and loving him into sobriety. I went to Al-Anon. I tried counseling. I begged and wrote letters and asked his family to help. Finally, I suggested that we separate while we "worked things out" which, strangely, I believed we actually could.

At Satele's suggestion and with his promise to support me, I had left my job as a paralegal for a full-time graduate program in psychology exactly one month before he left. Returning from class late one afternoon, I opened the door to the apartment to find it completely emptied, save for the green and yellow Formica kitchen table, the green shag rug the table sat on, and a mattress on the bedroom floor. There was a note on the windowsill. I picked it up and opened it. It said, "I love you."

I stood in the middle of the empty room and took a deep breath. Satele hadn't told me that he was leaving—or when—and although we had talked about separating, the emptied apartment took me by surprise. Usually after a fight, he would come back soft and supplicant, begging my forgiveness. I dropped down on the rugless, hardwood floor in the living room and leaned against the wall. No tears came; instead, a deep, hidden spring of resolve and determination bubbled up inside of me. I had one overriding thought: I would not quit school. That degree was my ticket to independence.

Two weeks later, I moved into my friend Marcia's house, occupying her daughter's old bedroom for a hundred dollars a month. My mother loaned me $5,000 for school and I applied for student loans and a work-study position. When my car was stolen from the front of Marcia's house a week after I'd cancelled my insurance to save money, I walked the two miles to school.

For a year I lived as a starving student, sharing a home that was not mine with a teenage boy and an incontinent Cocker Spaniel, attending classes while holding two unpaid internships and a work-study job. On Saturdays, Satele and I went to marriage counseling. He would often walk out in the middle of our sessions, leaving me looking weakly at Dr. Bob who, chin in hand, looked tiredly back at me. Sometimes he didn't show up at all. But I still wanted to believe there was something to save.

When I graduated two years later with my master's degree in psychology, Satele was there with a dozen red roses. He asked me to move back in with him and I did. Three days later, as I was unpacking my things, the phone rang. It was Satele, calling me from work to say that he wouldn't be home for dinner. He was going out to eat with some fellow cops and his old girlfriend, the one he'd carried a torch for since high school, the one whose father wouldn't let him near his daughter.

I stood, stunned and speechless in his tiny kitchen. I thought about moving all my things up four flights of stairs by myself because his back hurt. I thought about the couple's counseling. I thought about what had undoubtedly been happening all along. I thought about what a bastard he was, and what a complete, stupid ass I was.

"That's okay with you, isn't it?" he asked. I realized that the receiver was still in my hand.

"No, that's *not* okay with me," I said—a mind-numbingly mild response.

Satele swore something at me and hung up.

I lay on the hideaway that night, sick to my stomach and feeling unbearably stupid. Satele came home around midnight. He stood at the side of the sofa bed in the living room, looking at me.

"Don't ever do that again," I said, tearfully.

He laughed. "I told the guys at work that my wife's a nice person, but she has no spine. You'll never leave."

I stood up, looking at him as he spoke, letting it sink in. He spoke of me in the third person, as an object of disdain—not his wife, not even a person.

Maybe it was the years of fighting, of being threatened, of being left stranded. Perhaps it was the buildup of his drunken disappearances or the litany of demeaning remarks about my body and my Caucasian inferiority. Maybe it was the stark realization that he had been sleeping with another woman while going to therapy with me. Whatever it was, his taunting this time came up against my fiercely won self-esteem: esteem gained through countless hours of hard work and sheer tenacious survival. Whatever it was, at long last, I was finished.

He pushed harder. "You don't have the guts to leave."

"Watch me," I said.

That next morning while he was at work, I repacked everything, loaded the boxes and my few clothes into my VW Fox, and drove north to Oregon.

⁀⁀

I'd struggled with leaving my marriage to Satele because I believed that divorce was unacceptable. Marriage for me had meant doing everything you could to save even the unsavable, even the never-should-have-happened-in-the-first-place. The stigma of divorce had held me back from what I knew I needed to do: even on our honeymoon when he disappeared into the Balinese jungle all night, reappearing the next morning drunk and forcing himself on me; even as he'd degraded me verbally; even as he'd left me stranded on street corners, driving away; even as he'd moved out, taking everything with him; even as my therapist literally held his head in his hands as I repeated the same, tired story week after week.

Now, with the emotional fog dissipating, I had a new vision. I had made a mistake and I could rectify it. It was just that simple. I would not be my mother or my grandmother, hanging on for decades to a sad, flimsy marriage with an unloving, unhappy alcoholic. I was going to break out of that mold, a victim no more.

Going back home was the best move I'd made in a long time. The physical distance from Satele cleared away the emotional debris that years of abuse and fear had deposited. I took long walks in the early mornings before the summer heat became too intense, looking at the calves in the pastures and listening to the Red-winged Blackbirds call from the rushes. I gratefully ate food prepared for me by my mother and soaked up the loving, peaceful presence of my stepfather. I poured out the whole story to them, most of which they did not know. I sat and read. I went out with Keith, now divorced for the second time. We danced and drank and laughed, and I began to remember life outside the confines of a stifling, abusive marriage.

And then, while I was recuperating, I got a phone call offering me the counseling position I'd interviewed for in the city, followed by a call from my brother offering me the apartment he was vacating. As if on cue, things began to flow and with the movement came clarity. A strong wind had blown away all my mental fog, and I felt strong and solid for the first time in a long time. I felt whole.

I called Satele and told him that I wanted a divorce. He cried. I cried, too—from relief. The next week I returned to San Francisco and moved into my brother's rent-controlled flat. I felt scared, exhilarated ... and free.

I'd survived it all somehow—a bit worse for wear—and here I sat, drinking my coffee and feeling very good about myself. I was finally finished with that crazy, painful odyssey: no more school, no more insane relationship. Life spread out in front of me, full of possibility. I was single and newly professional, with a new apartment and a new job and a new life.

I sat back in my chair at Jammin' Java, my hands wrapped around my mug, warming myself. I was enjoying the unfamiliar new reality of having nothing in particular to do and nowhere in particular that I had to be. I sat, relaxed and unencumbered, my hands flecked with pink paint, watching the wind blow the gossamer fog in swirls outside. Across the street, Hat Man was in his Viking helmet, waving and shouting out his greetings. I picked up my pen, smiled to myself, and began to write.

In front of my table a couple sat, engaged in relaxed conversation. The man had long, dark, shoulder-length hair combed straight back. He wore jeans and a magenta-colored fleece jacket over his T-shirt. The shape of his nose and brushed-back hair and dark, long-lashed eyes suggested Italian heritage. The young woman he was with had curly, short, dark blonde hair and a perky nose. She wore a coarse, bright Mexican serape and no make-up. The two of them spoke loudly over the din of the café, and I could easily overhear their conversation.

Hearing the man mention the name of a professor I knew from the university, I listened more closely. It sounded as if he were in the same counseling program from which I had just graduated and, interested, I used this coincidence to interject myself into the conversation.

"I couldn't help but overhear," I said. "Do you go to USF?"

"Yes," he replied, and then added, "I remember you. You were on a panel of speakers in my sex therapy class."

I smiled, remembering sitting in front of the class at a table with a woman who was bisexual and one who was lesbian. I had been the "straight" speaker on a panel discussing sexual orientation. Strangely, or perhaps not so strangely, given life in San Francisco, I seemed to be the central curiosity of the bunch.

"Well then, you know a lot more about me than I do about you!" I replied, smiling.

"You were going through a separation from your husband," he continued. "How did that turn out?"

"We're divorced," I replied.

"Oh," he said, "I'm sorry to hear that."

The smile on his face said that he was not at all sorry to hear that. My heart felt a little twinge of pleasure.

"Thanks," I replied. "It's okay. It's a good thing."

"I'm Andrew Alden," he said. "This is Emily."

Andrew gestured toward his serape-draped companion, who smiled and told me that she was a nursing student. They invited me to join them and I happily moved my chair to their table. We slipped immediately into an animated conversation that stretched into the late afternoon and ended with a plan to all meet the following night.

We met the next evening for dinner at a colorful Caribbean restaurant called Cha Cha Cha! The line snaked out the door where Andrew, Emily, and I stood waiting for a table. I was delighted to have met some new friends and to be out. We ordered sangria to enjoy while we waited. Music erupted each time the front door swung open to the street. When we were finally seated at a small table with a fruit-covered vinyl tablecloth, we ordered more sangria and an array of small plates of food to share. A large, black, ceramic voodoo priestess stared down at us from a candlelit alter high above our heads.

Somewhere early into our dinner, Emily quietly slipped out of focus for me as Andrew and I offered one another bites of food and laughed about our school experiences. I became happily lost in the sensuality of the evening as the music and the voodoo wove a passionate mutual attraction. Andrew, who was a pilot as well as a psychology student, invited me to go flying, and I excitedly accepted.

After our dinner that night, I returned regularly to that café on the corner in hopes of running into Andrew again, which I frequently did. Soon I began to receive odd little notes written on small, two-inch scraps of paper stuffed into the vents of my mailbox. Some of the notes were smartly illustrated, usually with airplanes. Others were sweet and some were suggestive, like the one in which he playfully rhymed my name: "expli*kate*; communi*kate*; impli*kate; forni-* ... oh that's naughty." I began to look forward to checking my mail.

A few weeks later, I was reading at the café, happy to be out and hoping to see Andrew. Emily appeared out of the crowd and approached me at my table. I looked up and smiled. We exchanged pleasantries. She looked nervous and a bit awkward. She hesitated, listing slightly back and forth, clearly wanting to say something. I lowered my book and looked at her expectantly. Then she crouched down and got very close to me. Her serape pooled around her on the concrete floor. She began to speak *soto voce*, choosing her words very carefully.

"Are you still seeing Andrew?" she asked.

"Yes ..."

I wondered where this was going. I began to suspect that she felt herself a woman scorned, and I became suspicious of her conspiratorial crouch.

"You know," she said, glancing around as though she were delivering a secret message, "Andrew has ..." (and here a large pause) "... sexual issues."

This was not what I had expected.

"Don't we all," I quipped, attempting to summarily abort the conversation.

Emily stood and glanced around the café. She seemed uncertain of herself and of me, but she continued.

"He likes to wear women's clothes," she said flatly and looked at me knowingly.

I put my book down and looked up at her, trying to ascertain whether this were true or a desperate move born of jealousy. Was she warning me, or trying to get rid of me? It was a completely off-the-wall, bizarre thing to say if she were making it up.

My mind raced. I had no idea what to make of this bit of news or how to assimilate it, or if I should, or even what it meant.

Very obviously uncomfortable now and not sure what to do with my silence, Emily said good-bye and left the café. I waited until she was out of sight, and then gathered my things. I hightailed it back toward the park, waited for a lull in the traffic, and then ran across the street, up the stairs and unlocked the opaque, glass door to my flat.

Still wearing my coat, I picked up the phone and punched Ainslie's numbers, impatiently anticipating her pickup and hoping that she was home.

Ainslie and I had the sort of friendship that required no formalities or explanations. We called four or five times a day and launched right into whatever we had to say without bothering with hellos. We laughed a lot. She thought I was funny, which immediately classed her as my Very Best Friend Ever. We called each other "Pea," as in "peas in a pod." I couldn't wait to tell her the newest bit: the seemingly ubiquitous, obligatory snag in an otherwise promising relationship. I knew she would howl with delight.

"Hello?"

"He's a transvestite."

"No ... he's ... NOT!" she screamed into the phone, erupting with laughter. "Oh, Pea, that's just perfect."

"What the hell?" I asked.

"You know how to pick 'em, girl," she said, still roaring with delight.

"I know, I know. Shit."

We hung up and I slipped off my coat, hanging it on the back of the kitchen chair. *I still like the guy,* I mused, as I picked up the paintbrush and resumed painting. He was smart and funny and interesting. We could be friends. We lived in San Francisco, after all, where the unusual was commonplace. So it wouldn't be a romance. So what? Besides, I still had the flight scheduled with him in a few days and I was really looking forward to it.

The following Saturday, Andrew picked me up at my place and we drove across the bay to the small airport where he practiced. I kept looking at him in profile, thinking about what Emily had said. He looked and acted like a normal guy, maybe a little quiet and nervous as we made conversation alone in the car for the first time. We talked and laughed and flirted. He was a slightly sturdier version of Andy Garcia: broad-shouldered, thick, dark hair and a five o'clock shadow. His nose was prominent and very Romanesque. He wore jeans and a

Dartmouth sweatshirt and walked with a heavy, forward motion—not the least bit feminine. He was Ivy League educated, multilingual, well traveled, and from a blue-blood East Coast family. Whatever a cross-dresser's profile looked like, I had a hard time placing him in it.

We arrived at the airport and Andrew went through the half-hour preflight. Once I finally climbed into the cockpit, all of my thinking and wondering was suspended as fear consumed me. I couldn't even muster a flirtation as Andrew strapped me into the five-point harness of the tiny red-and-white biplane and instructed me in the proper technique for using a parachute, should the need arise. I attempted to calm myself by thinking that if I had to go, this was a good way to do it: quick and dramatic.

He lowered the clear bubble of the cockpit dome over my head, and I heard a muffled roar through the headphones as we taxied down the runway and then soared straight up into blue sky and blinding sun. Once at altitude, we stalled and rolled and spun until my stomach was teetering on the edge of rebellion. I focused all my thoughts and energy on breathing in and out with regularity, desperately trying to keep the threat of a bilious accident at bay. Andrew's head was just a few inches in front me in the tiny tandem cockpit; getting sick now would be eight kinds of horrible.

Andrew was enjoying himself tremendously. He obviously loved flying, loved showing off his skill. I was incredulous that his stomach could be so unaffected. We'd been at it about forty minutes when I knew I'd hit my wall. I was miserable and on the verge of something terrible.

"I'm done," I said into my microphone. "I need to go down ... *right now.*"

I heard Andrew's voice in my headset say, "Okay."

We turned and headed back. All of a sudden, we lurched straight up and then into a loop. I wanted to yell "Son of a bitch!" but I couldn't. As we leveled off and headed down, I heard Andrew suppressing his amusement.

"Sorry," he said, stifling his amusement.

Once the tiny plane came to a full stop, I clamored out and plopped down on the warm tarmac a few feet from the plane, praying to God that the roiling in my belly would abate. I breathed deeply, marshaling a concentrated focus. I had never felt so sick in all my life. I wanted desperately to look collected, to be able to say, "Wow, that was great! When can we go up again?" But I couldn't. I could barely summon the steadiness to speak.

"How in God's name do you not get sick?" I asked, irritated by that last loop and his total composure.

"You get used to it."

I doubted that. I wasn't going to try. I never wanted to get near that plane again as long as I lived.

It was a subdued hour-long drive back to San Francisco. My thoughts alternated between the state of my stomach and the state of Andrew's proclivities. I'd promised to take him to dinner that night in exchange for the flight, a promise I was now regretting.

Five hours later and still queasy, I met Andrew at his flat. We were headed for sushi, although the prospect of eating raw fish this particular evening sounded singularly unappetizing. I had the distinct impression that he was running a dating racket, trading flights for food and trolling for dates in the process. I was getting the short end of the stick in this exchange.

Andrew was very quiet during dinner, his demeanor completely different from our date at Cha Cha Cha! and from what it had been earlier in the afternoon when he was all confidence and bravado. He now seemed rather shy and nervous. There were periods of quiet awkwardness during dinner, to the degree that I began to wonder if perhaps this would be the end of things.

But after dinner, we took a walk up the hill to the crest of Broadway and Fillmore. It was an unusually warm, breezy night. We stood with our arms around one another, looking out over the blackness of the bay, feeling the beauty of the city. It felt good to stand there, to feel his arm wrapped around my waist, to feel the quiet excitation and anticipation of what was certainly coming next.

A tired, calm happiness wrapped itself around me—the same feeling I'd had at the café a few weeks earlier. The thought *I'm free* drifted through my mind; I was free of a frightening marriage; free of a crazy, spirit-crushing life. I could make choices without fear of retribution. My future had become as open and as full of possibility and beauty as the vista sweeping out in front of me. I could carve out an entirely new life for myself.

I closed my eyes to the breeze, and then I felt a kiss on my mouth, warm and soft, followed by an odd little nip on my nose. Andrew laughed a little, the way he had earlier when he made that final loop in the sky. It was the kind of laugh one makes when reading something amusing in a book, a private laugh to oneself. I liked it. I liked him. He was handsome and quirky and intriguing.

Later that night, alone at home, I thought again about what that irritating little Cassandra, Emily, had said. I cautioned myself to wait, to be careful. Whatever, whomever else he might be, he was a friend, and a friend was something I welcomed.

As if to underscore my newfound happiness, my ex-husband called a couple of days after my date with Andrew, saying that he wanted to drop off a few of my remaining things. We'd been separated for over a year and I was more than ready for our relationship to be formally finished. We had been legally married for all of nine months before we had separated, and had very little common property and no need for attorneys. I had filed divorce papers five months prior and, in a few weeks, everything would be final.

I met Satele on the sidewalk in front of my place; I wanted him nowhere near my apartment, did not want him to see it or for us to be out of public view. I had placed a restraining order on him, not that it would help all that much. Cops, I had discovered, stick together like glue; they're always ready to protect and defend one another. I'd seen him get away with any number of improprieties because of his exclusive membership in this club. I was at a serious disadvantage should he decide to act on his impulses; no cop was going to take my side over his if something happened. I was on my own. I just wanted something on record, in case it did.

I watched Satele get out of his brand new, white pickup truck and walk across the street toward me. Seeing him made my stomach turn, and I could feel the anxiety swarming inside my body like bees in an overturned hive. He seemed bigger than I remembered, having not seen him for a few months. In both appearance and demeanor, he reminded me of O.J. Simpson, who, at that particular moment, was occupying the news for allegedly—and most certainly, in my book—murdering his ex-wife Nicole Simpson and her companion, Ron Goldman. The parallels were not lost on me. I couldn't watch any of the trial; it made me sick to my stomach. I was grateful that I'd gotten out in time and in one, mostly whole, piece.

Satele stood in front of me, his large, round, Polynesian eyes difficult to read. He almost looked sad, but then he spoke.

"You bleached your hair."

I chose not to take the bait, loath to engage in yet another round of vituperation. He looked down at my new, black, I'm-not-taking-any-more-shit cowboy boots and snorted. I stared back at him, waiting, glad that I was wearing them, glad that I no longer cared what he had to say about what I wore or who I was.

He stared hard at me. My body felt tense and rigid and I could feel myself shaking a little; I hoped it didn't show. Then his face suddenly morphed from a sarcastic expression to one of what appeared to be honest hurt.

"Why are you doing this to me?" he asked, plaintively.

"Why am I doing this to *you?*" I replied incredulously.

Stunned by the comment, I almost laughed; surely he must be joking. Yet there he stood, looking seriously wounded, as though he had no memory of everything that had transpired, as though the fights and the drinking and the affairs and the threats and the failed couples' therapy had never happened.

"*You* did this," I replied. "*You* did this to us."

I should have kept quiet, but I couldn't help myself. I couldn't stand not speaking up. As quickly as it had arrived, his hurt suddenly—but not surprisingly—shifted to rage. He moved right up on top of me and pointed his large, brown finger in my face. His face had the look that always scared the shit out of me. It was hard and intense and threatening.

"You'd better not get an attorney," he warned in a low voice, "or you'll be sorry."

I had no doubt whatsoever that he meant what he said. I stood, silent. He turned to leave, walked a few steps, and then looked back.

"Fuck you," he snarled.

I stood frozen in place for a few moments, reeling internally, my head buzzing, watching him peel off down the street. Then I turned, walked up the stairs, and called an attorney.

# 6

Despite Emily's cautionary pronouncement, and despite our first date, and most especially despite my severe emotional exhaustion, I found myself spending more and more time with Andrew. It was refreshing to be with a man who was in every manner the opposite of Satele: sweet, gentle, intelligent, funny, psychological. He made me laugh. He was warm and witty and cultured. He was handsome. We talked Jung and Freud, flying and families. It felt like what I imagined "normal" to be: easy and lovely.

A week after our first flight together, Andrew asked if I would join him for dinner with his parents, who were coming into town from Washington, D.C. I was both happy and nervous to meet these people who, by all accounts, were from old, East Coast money, cultured and connected. Boarding schools, vacations in Europe, and summer houses were things that I'd only ever heard about, the way one hears that there are multiple universes or that Tom Cruise is gay: you can't prove it, you've never experienced it, but you accept it on hearsay evidence. As far as my naïve, unsophisticated, middle-class self was concerned, boarding schools were for poor little rich kids, a place that parents who didn't love their children could send them under the guise of providing a top-notch education.

I confessed this particular perception to Andrew, whose quick retort was, "That's what I thought, too."

As it turned out, Barbara and Richard were not snobbish or cold or any of the things I imagined and feared. They were kind and warm, and I felt mostly at ease as we met and then drove down into the Financial District to One Market, which had just opened across from the Ferry Building. The new restaurant was all glass with an easy elegance; white-aproned waiters moved decorously through the loft-like space and enormous spays of flowers reached up toward the vaulted ceiling. I had watched the well-to-do eating here from the other side of the glass when I worked as a paralegal across the street, never imagining that I would be on the inside.

Drinks were ordered and we began to chat easily. I examined Barbara as we spoke. She was a smallish woman with a narrow, angular face and a sharp, birdlike nose. Her hair was short and light brown and feathered back on the sides. She wore glasses and very little make-up, a tweed suit à la Jackie Kennedy with a blouse that buttoned way up the neck, and flat shoes with flat bows on top. She had just published her first book, a scholarly work that had already garnered a great deal of media attention and a number of awards. Before we even met, I had seen her interviewed on *The Today Show*.

Richard put me at ease immediately. He was affable and effusive, the least likely incarnation of a career government man that I could imagine, although that's what he had been until his recent retirement. He looked like a character straight out of Central Casting; the rumpled tweed blazer, tortoise shell glasses, disheveled gray hair, and wild, Andy Rooney-esque eyebrows gave him the appearance of the quintessential absent-minded professor.

He was telling me a rambling, disjointed story about his youngest son's troubles in boarding school. (*What did I tell you?* I thought, triumphantly.) I didn't know why he would be sharing this in the first five minutes of our dinner, but it had the effect of making me feel more, not less, comfortable.

It did the opposite for Barbara, who hit his arm and said, "Richard!" clearly indicating her displeasure at his public airing of family laundry.

Richard was unfazed and continued cheerfully telling his tales of family happenings. I quickly realized that he had the slightly disorienting habit of jumping into the middle of an ongoing, interior stream of consciousness assuming that his listener, in this case, I, would know what he was talking about, which I did not. Andrew was obviously embarrassed by this and seemed to share with his mother what I viewed as a certain disdain for Richard and his ramblings.

Except for raised eyebrows and heavy sighs, Andrew, to my consternation, seemed to be shrinking and disappearing as the meal went on. He was almost completely silent, answering his mother's queries monosyllabically, his irritation and discomfort barely contained. I had the distinct impression that I had been invited to this dinner to be his foil, and I kicked him under the table to signal my displeasure. He glanced up at me and I gave him a "what-are-you-doing?" look, which he ignored, glancing away.

After dinner, we drove back to Andrew's flat where we said our good-byes. Richard and Barbara both embraced and kissed me, a gesture that took me totally by surprise, particularly coming from Barbara who, with her high collar and intellectual bent, did not seem at all the huggy type. I felt honored, as though I had somehow just received their blessing.

They waved and smiled as they drove off, and Andrew asked if I would come over to his place for a bit. As we walked in the dark and up the block to his flat, I felt Andrew re-inhabit his body. It was as though he finally exhaled, and he resumed being the person I knew. He began fuming about his mother's criticisms of his long hair and nagging questions about work; Barbara did not think flying was much of a career. (In the world Andrew came from, connections are everything. When Andrew had told his mother that he wanted to fly for a living, Barbara had replied, "But we don't know anyone.") I said very little, interested by the family dynamic and glad that he was back to being the Andrew I liked so much.

We greeted his roommates in the hallway and then excused ourselves to his room. I had never been to his place. As I looked around the small space, I noticed an unusual array of objects strewn around: a bike, two pairs of skis, women's shoes, a *Glamour* magazine addressed to one Sonia Alden, clothing on the floor—both male and female— and a row of photographs artfully hung opposite the door. I sat down on the bed and drew in a long, quiet breath. *Damn that Emily*, I thought. Andrew remained standing in front of me, watching me look around, slightly anxious.

"I need to tell you something," he said.

He directed my attention back to the series of large, framed, black-and-white photographs on the wall. I glanced at them again, and then looked back at him and waited. The photographs were of a man scantily dressed in women's clothing, draped in sexually provocative poses on a bed. It was obviously Andrew. Dressed as a woman, he bore a remarkable and disturbing resemblance to Barbra Streisand.

"That's me," he said, in case there was any confusion.

The look on his face was watchfully expectant. I sensed a certain pride in the pictures; I, however, had a hard time looking at them. The subject of the photographs was not the person I knew, not someone I had ever met. *Damn it*, I thought. Emily had been telling the truth: Andrew was a cross-dresser.

Preempting my musings, Andrew hastened to explain the images. The person I saw in those pictures—"Sonia"—was no more, he said. He no longer wished to live a double life, and he had recently stopped cross-dressing entirely. He told me about his years of psychotherapy, assuring me that he liked women, and that he was not gay. He told me that his family knew, which explained a great deal about the dinner we had just had and the warm reception I received from his parents. I imagined them whispering to each other as they drove back to their hotel: *Thank God that messy business is over with.*

The truth was, Emily's divulgence weeks earlier had given me time to think, long before Andrew revealed his secret to me. I had already decided that I didn't care if Andrew were gay or a cross-dresser or whatever; he could dance naked on the balcony for all I cared. He was my friend. I liked him.

Being lovers, however, was another story altogether. I know that there are women who can deal with this sort of thing, who accept and even enjoy their boyfriends or husbands dressing up. They go shopping together and have a high old time. I am not that woman. If Andrew wanted or needed to dress as a woman or pretend to be a woman or become a woman, our relationship could continue, but it would remain strictly platonic, and I told him as much.

"I'm done," he reiterated. "The last time I dressed up, it took me four hours to get ready and when I was done, I looked in the mirror and saw a man in drag. It just became too painful."

I felt sorry for him and simultaneously relieved. I was glad he had told me so early in our relationship and glad that he wanted to tell me.

"I really like you, and I'd like something more. I needed to be completely honest. I'm done with it," he said.

I liked his courage and his honesty. I liked that he was in analysis, that he was dealing with his demons, and that he had the capacity and desire for introspection. That sort of self-awareness and intelligence was extremely rare and very compelling. Coupled with his kind nature, charm, and good looks, I was hooked.

The mood in the room was intensely intimate; I'd never heard anyone confess anything this vulnerable before. I felt a pressing compulsion to drag out my skeletons as well, sort of even the playing field a bit. I told him about my relationship with Satele, about the abuse and the alcohol and the various and sundry diseases that he had imparted. I was still very ashamed to confess the truth of that relationship, ashamed to admit that I had put myself in such a position, that I had invited insanity into my life, participated in it even. I was equally ashamed of being divorced—that title was something I never imagined putting on my personal résumé, and it made me feel equal parts stupid and a failure.

Andrew sat beside me, listening quietly to my whole story, in the end saying simply, "I'm so sorry you went through that. You deserve so much better."

We were two people wanting to carve out new lives. Our personal histories couldn't have been more different, yet here we were at a strange and compelling crossroads.

I stayed the night.

# 7

In the course of the next few months, Andrew and I became a couple. We spent all of our free time together, making frequent pilgrimages to Napa and Sonoma on the weekends, stopping afterward at the Buckeye Roadhouse at the foot of the Golden Gate Bridge for cocktails and dinner before heading back over the iconic span and through the fog that rolled under the bridge and into the city.

Throughout the days and weeks of long conversations I heard about living in Europe, about being raised by a Guatemalan nanny, about ski vacations in France and photographic safaris in Botswana. I waxed indignant upon learning that he had gone to Dartmouth—a school I'd very much wanted to attend—despite horrific grades, all because a relative sat on the college's board of directors. He made fun of his elitist life and relations, but he clearly loved the perks such a life afforded.

But I also saw that Andrew was not a vacuous, disconnected scion; he had a very strong ethic of *noblesse oblige.* He worked for a parental help line where he volunteered many hours every week, talking to parents on the verge of abusing their children, getting them connected to educational and support services. He volunteered his time and plane to fly cancer patients to hospital appointments when travel by car would be too onerous.

I accompanied him to New York for the Thanksgiving holiday to meet the rest of his family. We flew to New York City and then drove through an ink-black night to a beautiful 1700s farmstead located in a remote and rural part of upstate New York, where his Uncle Pierce and Aunt Brooke had a weekend house. We were greeted jovially at the door with warm embraces from both Barbara and Richard and then ushered out of the cold and into the warm, bright kitchen. I was handed a glass of wine and everyone gathered around the big, wooden table.

I met his younger brothers James and Stephan; his grandmother, who went by Margaret because she despised the idea of being called "grandma"; Uncle Pierce and Pierce's wife Brooke, and their two little boys, whom Andrew and I anointed Squirmy and Spud.

Brooke's father, Ben, was also present but unaccounted for, tucked away in his room, busily writing a memoir. Ben, as I quickly learned during Thanksgiving dinner the following day, was an outspoken, extremely intelligent, old school Associated Press journalist. I managed to endear myself to him by recognizing his father's name, my history degree finally making itself useful. ("Sumner Welles?" I had exclaimed enthusiastically. "Secretary of State under FDR?") Over the course of Thanksgiving dinner, I learned that the upper class is alive and well; I also learned their names and occupations—extremely important facts in this milieu. Pierce (also called "Skip") was an investment banker in South America and very bright, much like his older sister, Barbara. He reminded me of Warren Beatty both in appearance and demeanor: handsome and suave. He often seemed to be winking at me, though I was never exactly sure. I could easily imagine a beautiful girl in his every South American port.

Skip's wife Brooke was a lovely, blonde, forty-something, who seemed slightly frayed around the edges: a little defeated and windblown somehow. She had recently left her position as an editor of a financial magazine and was rapidly losing her mind staying home with their two little children. She had a slightly British accent, inherited, I surmised, from her now-deceased English mother. She had grown up in Spain and England and gone to all the right schools yet somehow maintained a very down-to-earth quality. Unlike the rest of the family, she seemed very open and slightly vulnerable, and was more inclined to speak candidly. I was grateful for her presence.

James, Andrew's middle brother, was a sailing enthusiast, busy at Yale, Richard's *alma mater*, and soon to be heading off to Stanford for his MBA. Stephan, the youngest brother, had left college temporarily to work in Alaska with the titleholder for the Iditarod sled race. This was not a family of lightweights. I listened attentively, feeling outclassed and out of my league, yet deeply enjoying the good-humored and intelligent conversation.

During the days that followed we took long walks and looked for wild turkeys, tasted wine in a large, centuries-old barn, and went for lunch at an old stage stop. We pulled the nephews around on a sled, swung on the tire swing, and sat in the kitchen at the long farm table, getting to know one another. This, for me, was an entirely unique and wonderful experience of family. I had grown up mostly without my siblings and without any extended family whatsoever. Being with the Alden tribe was like slipping into a warm tub with a drink and a good book: relaxing, entertaining, and interesting all at once.

On the afternoon of the third day, Andrew whispered in my ear, "They all love you."

Life was getting really good.

When we returned to San Francisco, Andrew divested himself of all vestiges of Sonia—the photographs and the clothing—and moved into my new flat with me. I accompanied him to a salon and watched as he had his shoulder-length, dark hair cut short.

At Christmastime, we drove up to Oregon. Andrew was quietly apoplectic at the prospect of meeting my diminutive family: he broke out in a dramatic, red rash that covered his face, and repeatedly mentioned the desire for a martini upon arrival.

I found his anxiety both touching and amusing, given the daunting task I had surmounted in meeting his illustrious brood a month earlier. He would only have my mother, stepfather, and brother to impress. If anyone had reason to be anxious, I thought, it was I. I wondered what he would think of my middle-class town and my middle-class home with the spray-on sparkle ceilings—a town and home that suddenly looked very paltry and slightly embarrassing to my newly opening eyes.

Once introductions were made and drinks were in hand, however, the visit turned into a great success, made memorable mostly by our adoption on Christmas Eve of a four-pound, black-and-tan puppy that was being given away in a box in front of the market where Andrew and I had made a run for eggnog. Andrew immediately wanted him, begging and cajoling me to take him home with us. My logical and adamant arguments about living in an apartment in the city that forbid pets notwithstanding, the warm little handful, whom we named Beauregard—Beau for short—came home with us for Christmas.

By all accounts, life with Andrew and Beau moved in a seamless rhythm. I'd never been so happy. I loved my clients and my colleagues. I saw adults at a counseling center in the Marina District three days a week and children at a private elementary school the other two days. I liked the challenge of therapy, liked seeing my clients improve, liked working for myself, and loved coming home to Andrew and Beau.

Andrew decided at the end of the year that he'd rather be flying than be in graduate school and returned to full-time flight instruction, his mother's career concerns notwithstanding. In the evenings, when we returned home together, we talked and drank the wines that we had discovered on our weekend forays while I made dinner. Andrew was affectionate and romantic. I'd never met a man so soft, so gentle and soulful. Loving him was easy.

It appeared that he was making peace with his male self as we fell more deeply in love. From time to time, I would check in with him about how he was feeling. I understood his "problem"—if that was the right thing to call it—as something not unlike alcoholism, a condition I understood all too well. Now that Andrew was "on the wagon," life seemed utterly normal. It was better than normal: it was wonderful.

One afternoon as I sat in the backseat with Beau, Andrew driving us over the San Francisco–Oakland Bay Bridge on our way home from a day of flying, I asked Andrew how he was doing with the gender struggle. Nothing in particular had prompted my question; in fact, everything seemed fine. From time to time I would check in with him. Andrew paused, becoming quietly thoughtful. Sitting in the backseat of his old, dirty, dog-haired Saab with our now ninety-pound Beau, I could see his eyes in the rearview mirror. They looked large and sad.

"I just want to be happy being a man or happy being a woman, one or the other," he said. His response took me by surprise; he usually would say "fine," and nothing more. I remained quiet, stroking

Beau's side. "No matter what I do," Andrew continued, "I will never look like a real woman. I'll always look like a man trying to be a woman, and I can't live with that."

He sounded defeated and very, very sad. What he had not exactly said, but I inferred, was that he was not fully happy being a man. He was trapped in a netherworld feeling neither male nor female. The insurmountable problem was that he would never have what he longed for, what he needed, which was inner acceptance and peace. No amount of surgery or manipulation or smoke and mirrors could make it right, not in this lifetime.

Even with this honest, painful admission, I did not fully grasp the depth of what he was telling me, the depth of his dilemma and suffering. Had I been less in love, had I known more about gender disorders, had I possessed greater perspective, I might have been able to piece it all together and really hear what he was saying.

I might have thought, for instance, that if, as a little boy of five, you begin to play dress up in your mother's clothing, and if, in college, you relish the thought of fraternity hazing because you will be asked to shave your legs and wear a skirt, and if you move to San Francisco in order to have the freedom to express yourself without overwhelming judgment—you are not simply a closeted cross-dresser.

When he told me that he took "girl lessons" to learn to move like a female, and that he took an initial round of feminizing hormones, I might have thought, *Hmmm, that doesn't sound like a transvestite. That sounds like a man who wants to be a woman.* I would have seen that this was an inborn, immutable condition.

But I did not understand this, not fully, not completely, not then. What I heard was that Andrew had been sad and unhappy for much of his life, and that is something I understood all too well. He had deep, unresolved issues with his mother, which I also understood. He'd been working for years with a Jungian analyst, an expert in the field of gender issues, and if he had decided of his own accord and with expert analysis to let go of all the striving to be Sonia, I embraced his decision as a move toward self-acceptance. I believed, as he wanted to believe, that this behavior was transitory, a result of poor bonding in childhood.

*People can grow and change*, I reasoned. That was my belief and my mantra as a therapist. I knew that he loved me: he said it and he showed it. Certainly I loved him, like no other love I had ever felt. I deeply believed that my love could heal him and that he would, quite literally, become more comfortable in his skin as I continued to express my love and appreciation and acceptance for him. *Perhaps*, my reasoning went, *I could give him the validation that he had never felt, and with that acceptance and love he would blossom into the man that in every outward respect he seemed to be.*

These were my thoughts as I sat silently in the backseat.

# 8

June arrived, and with it came our first joint pilgrimage to Andrew's family summer home in Cape Cod. Winslow Cove is a large peninsula of some six hundred acres that is privately owned by the family and its familiars. Andrew's Great Uncle Malcolm had bought the land decades earlier and, over time, the family had built a large compound, a summer retreat, in the beautiful Cape Cod forest. Although not technically an island, it was referred to as such, being almost completely surrounded by the sea. It was private and serene with miles of beaches and large, brown shingled houses with white trim tucked among lush swaths of coastal vegetation.

The Kennedy compound in Hyannis Port was clearly visible just across the bay, and members of that clan could often be spotted out for a sail. Family legend had it that then Senator John F. Kennedy tried to buy some of the land from Great Uncle Malcolm but was turned down; the family didn't want all the chaos that having a Kennedy there would entail. More recent lore had Arnold and Maria Schwarzenegger arriving on the beach only to be asked to leave by Winslow Cove security. Andrew loved to tell that story.

The island had an elfin-like chapel called "Sing." Sunday services consisted of three hymns and a short reading by one of the growing gaggle of Winslow Cove children. Over time, the generations had grown exponentially, so half of the island's population stood on the padded forest floor outside of Sing while the early arrivals squished themselves inside the rough, hand-hewn chapel.

The eldest member of the clan was a white-haired, swift-moving matriarch, who was just shy of a hundred. The ancient widow of the founder of Winslow Cove, Great Aunt Betsy was wizened, almost skeletal, and had a frightening habit of popping up, literally and unexpectedly, apparition-like. On my first trip to Sing, while standing in the back against the far wall, I looked up to see the specter of Great Aunt Betsy's ghostly visage pop up in the window. I watched her face, framed by shoulder-length, white hair and oversized black sunglasses, as she peered through the glass for thirty seconds before disappearing as quickly as she came.

I was enchanted, if slightly overwhelmed, by Winslow Cove, a place inhabited by what can only be described as old money. Families here still used their social registers. Unlike the new-money Hamptons, everything on Winslow Cove was understated, imbued with a pervasive sense of simplicity, style, and grace. This was the summer refuge of the quietly privileged.

The Beach Club, which was open for lunch and special events, was filled with pastel painted wooden benches and tables that overlooked the sound. Most of the island chose to eat lunch here, rather than at home, for the convenience and conviviality, but also because the food was so darned good. ("The best hamburger you will ever eat," Andrew informed me with complete conviction.) Mr. and Mrs. Green, former public school employees, served as the proprietors, congenially cooking and serving ice cream cones to the privileged population of the island.

Up a half mile from the Beach Club, an iconic, old lighthouse— the emblem of the island—stood vigil on the point overlooking the sound. The whitewashed walls and spiraling wooden staircase formed a sensual, curvaceous line that lifted the eye to the apex where the wooden beams of the turret met in a serene gesture. I loved how warm and windy and desolate it was, and how I could squint and see the Kennedy compound across the water. (In my childhood memory, Jesus may have sat at the right hand of God, but JFK sat at the left. Over my crib, in place of a crucifix or a picture of bunnies, my mother had hung photographs of Jackie and the Kennedy children. They were family.)

The entire population of the island—save me, it seemed—swam and sailed and played tennis. They hired instructors to make sure that when the children were not with the nannies, they were learning the finer points of affluent downtime; it was the Kennedy's without the fame and football. There were annual clambakes and lobster feeds, private parties, and cocktails at five. Cooks and housekeepers and nannies took care of the more mundane exigencies of life, a radically new experience to which I took an immediate liking.

It was here on the island that I met Richard's extended family. His sister Caroline, whom everyone called "Poppy," had been married twice, both times to well-to-do men with famous last names. The middle sister Julia had been widowed young when her physician husband drowned, leaving her with three small boys. Richard's youngest sister Jane was married to a Greek named Stephanos, and they divided their time between Cambridge, Massachusetts, an apartment in Paris, a home in the Greek Isles, and their place on Winslow Cove. The children of all three of Robin's sisters were either in or bound for the Ivy League. None of the sisters worked.

One thing was immediately apparent: Richard and his sisters adored one another. I had the impression that they had banded together for comfort and companionship during a childhood of great privilege but with little emotional expression or affection. Having an affinity for psychology and storytelling, I was deeply curious to hear about their lives and background; I found it all fascinating. Richard was quick to share pieces of the historical puzzle, but early on Barbara had commented to Andrew, in a warning sort of way, that I "asked a lot of questions," which caused me to temper my enthusiastic curiosity in an effort not to alienate myself.

All of the homes at Winslow Cove had names: the Alden's home was called the Marsh House. Built by Richard's parents, it was a classic, weathered, gray saltbox on a largish scale. Sailing memorabilia, old pictures, and an abundance of seashells and books filled the large rooms. It smelled of a musty humidity. The enormous, wood-paneled living room centered around a large fireplace, where an array of various chairs and sofas invited conversations or reading or lolling into a nap. Outside, blueberry bushes lined the walkway and pink marshmallow flowers poked majestically out of a lushly vegetated pond in front. A road with two dirt tracks wound behind the pond and disappeared into a cool, verdant undergrowth and canopy of trees.

In the back of the house, an enormous salt marsh reached almost up to the back lawn, the sandy beach and ocean lying just beyond. A long, thin, wooden bridge—really just a series of planks with a rickety handrail—zigzagged across the marsh to the beach where giant horseshoe crab shells could be found, looking like creatures from prehistoric times. Baby blue crabs scuttled to hide at the sound of footfalls, and Andrew and I fished for them like little kids with pieces of bologna tied to a string. We kayaked in the marsh and swam in the ocean and took walks or rode bicycles to the Beach Club. We watched graceful white egrets flying overhead. Unable to stay away from an airplane, Andrew rented a small Cessna and gave me an aerial tour of their island and all of Cape Cod. Other sultry summer days, we took the ferry to Nantucket and Martha's Vineyard, enjoying the ocean breezes and diversions of the islands. Richard joyfully took me sailing with his boys, and as I sat on the deck of his sailboat, looking out at the blue water and white clouds and the faces of this family, I fell euphorically in love with my new, sophisticated, and reassuring life.

In December, Andrew took me to dinner at the Lark Creek Inn, across the Golden Gate Bridge in the small, forested enclave of Larkspur. Inside the iconic home-turned-restaurant, we were taken to our table, upon which a dozen red roses sat in a vase. Andrew ordered a bottle of Iron Horse Wedding Cuvee. After we toasted, he came to my side, got down on one knee, and—offering a diamond and sapphire ring—asked me to marry him. Although I knew it was coming, the reality of it left me lightheaded and uncharacteristically speechless. We called his parents immediately upon arriving home, both our ears bent to the receiver to hear their response.

"It's about time!" Barbara exclaimed joyfully.

"Well done," Richard chimed in, their mutual delight over the first engagement in the family palpable.

Barbara began planning a celebration the very next day, and three weeks later, in January, we flew to Washington, D.C., for an informal engagement party in Andrew's Georgetown home, where a small group of family and very close friends gathered to fête us. One of the attendees—a pasty, white, balding man in his fifties—approached me, drink in hand, and looked at me over his glasses.

"Congratulations," he said loudly and flatly. He stared at me unsmilingly.

"Thank you." I replied, waiting to see what he was about.

"I hope you like being a widow."

I stood, shocked. "Pardon me?"

"I said I hope you like being a widow. Having a pilot for a husband."

Was this a friend of Barbara and Richard's? A relative? I hoped he wasn't family because this man was clearly an insufferable prick. Despite my inner horror, I managed a reply.

"I'm not worried." I tried to be as pleasant as possible, given that I wanted to tell him exactly where he could go. "Andrew's an amazing pilot."

I excused myself, hoping that this was not a person with whom I would be required to interact on a regular basis. When I told Andrew about the exchange, he rolled his eyes in disgust.

"He's an asshole," he said.

Three months later, in mid-April, we again stood in the enormous Georgetown living room for our formal engagement party. My parents and my brother and his wife had flown out for the occasion, my sister choosing not to attend. Barbara had invited one hundred and fifty of her closest friends, including a Supreme Court justice—a fact that had my brother Chris, an attorney, aflutter.

Though extraordinarily expert at party throwing, Barbara was pacing fretfully, pausing to stand with hands on hips, a frown creasing her face. Descending the stairs, I saw Richard, James, and Stephan standing at the ready, waiting for further orders from Barbara, who could not seem to find a satisfactory arrangement of the furniture.

"It looks beautiful," I said.

Barbara's head shot up. "No, it doesn't," she replied tautly.

She commanded another furniture arrangement and then, thoroughly irritated, she ordered everyone out of the house to the great relief and happiness of all present.

"Barbara," I said before I left, "could you give me the address of your hairdresser? I wanted to put my hair up for the party."

Barbara stopped moving around and stared at me briefly. "Your hair looks fine the way it is."

I smiled and then, attempting to be as deferential as possible, pressed a bit harder. "I just want to put it up in some nice way, nothing too elaborate. If you could just tell me where to go." I grabbed my ponytail with my hand and showed it to her, imagining that we were just being girls together.

"No," she said. "I think it's fine. Wear it like that. You don't need to get dressed up."

I stood at the wide pocket doors that opened to the now emptied living room, flummoxed. No? No, she wouldn't tell me? What was she talking about? She'd had her hair done that morning, ordered hundreds of dollars of flowers, hired caterers, torn the house to shreds—and I shouldn't do my hair?

Andrew appeared and escorted me into the hallway, out of Barbara's sightline. He found the salon's number, called and made me an immediate appointment, and took me there to have my hair done, an act that placed me in direct defiance of my soon-to-be mother-in-law. This small, quiet skirmish left me slightly shaken: It was a no-win scenario, foreshadowing the confusing and frustrating relationship that was to come.

After I had dressed and just before the guests began to arrive, I walked downstairs from my third-floor bedroom to the cramped, L-shaped kitchen on the first floor. It was an old, fifties-style kitchen, with yellow walls and a swinging door that led to the formal dining room. There was no table; it was far too small for that. No one in the family cooked, or made anything other than toast and coffee. This was the domain of the help.

There was scarcely room for two people to move comfortably, yet four or five ladies, dressed in black-and-white uniforms, now stood at the counter. They were headed by the Alden's former, longtime housekeeper, Nana, who had raised Andrew and his brothers from the time that Andrew was six weeks old. She was Guatemalan, small and soft and pleasantly round with beautiful, wrinkled brown skin and large glasses. She was the sort of person into whose warm embraces and loving nature I could easily imagine wanting to run as a child.

I stood there in my little black dress and heels, clutching a glass of champagne. The ladies all smiled at me, nodding their heads deferentially. I was uneasy. I was the one who usually occupied the kitchen. During my early days in San Francisco, I had worked as catering help for wealthy socialites. I loved to cook and spent much of my time in the kitchen wherever I found myself, particularly at parties, which usually bored me to tears. For me, this was the most comfortable place to be.

What had not occurred to me, but what was slowly dawning, was that I was in an entirely new milieu. I had entered the world of class structure and hierarchy. Although I felt more akin to these ladies than to the family that employed them, I was not; they knew this and they were flummoxed by my loitering presence. I was flummoxed, too, not at all at ease with being seen as someone from a different station. I wasn't. I was an impostor; Cinderella fancied up for the ball.

It felt wrong that this woman, who had raised my husband and been his surrogate mother, was bowing her head deferentially to me, calling me "Señora." In her lovely Spanish, Nana told me that she was honored to meet me and that she was looking forward to raising our babies. I stood slightly stunned, having difficulty not with the Spanish, which I spoke fluently, but with the idea that she was speaking to me as a new mistress of the house—not to mention the polite but ridiculous notion that she would, at her advanced age, raise the babies I had not to that point even considered having. It was a gesture of polite, Old-world servitude. I wanted to kiss her cheek, to escort her to the sofa, bring her a drink, and listen to her stories about Andrew. But I couldn't do that. So, instead, I began to speak with everyone in Spanish.

They were surprised and delighted that we could communicate and that I even wanted to. Immediately the atmosphere in the tiny kitchen became relaxed and happy. We chatted and laughed, and the ladies told me illuminating things about themselves and about my soon-to-be in-laws. I was gratified to discover that I was not the only one who had difficulty with Barbara's demeanor and relieved that a simple conversation could place us on par with one another—sort of. I wasn't "the help," but neither could I treat the help like the help.

Twenty minutes later the Georgetown crowd filled the enormous living room, with its two fireplaces and multiple love seats, to capacity. Barbara was deftly working the room, greeting her friends, and making introductions. All traces of her afternoon unhappiness were gone. She was a master of the social grace of party giving, skilled from her many years entertaining government officials in Europe when Richard had been stationed in Brussels and from her volunteer work organizing social events at the National Gallery.

Barbara directed Andrew and me to the center of the room where we stood in a formal receiving line to greet each guest and exchange pleasantries, a process that took an hour and a half. From this singular experience, I learned a number of important, if nuanced, social graces. For example, one never congratulates the fiancée; it's considered gauche. Instead, I was offered multiple "felicitations." Along with other archaic Victorian practices, such as who is seated next to whom at the dining table (Rule: Couples may be seated together only when engaged but never when married) and to whom one speaks first and for how long during the meal (Rule: You may speak to the guest on your left, for three to five minutes, no more), this became part of my early indoctrination to D.C. society.

Strangely, this code of conduct did not seem to extend to thank-yous. The flowers and gifts that I sent the family were never acknowledged. This sort of cherry-picking of the rules of etiquette was exceedingly frustrating, leaving me feeling as though I were perpetually trying to grab the last seat in a game of musical chairs and never succeeding. I came off appearing totally inept and unsocialized or as though I were just trying too hard. But I gave it my best shot. When in Georgetown, sit where you're told and go with the flow.

But now, standing next to Andrew, who was whispering funny things in my ear as we greeted and smiled, I mostly felt a lovely, floaty sort of ephemeral joy. From time to time, I glanced over my left shoulder where my stepfather David, drifting into the early stages of Alzheimer's disease, sat a few feet behind me on a stool, smiling broadly. I smiled back and winked, re-centering myself as I looked at his beaming, contented face. I couldn't tell if he understood what was happening, but I could see that he was happy and that made me happy, too.

When the receiving line was finally finished I bee-lined to the dining room for a drink; I was worn out and not a little overwhelmed by excitement and the entire experience. The house was hot and packed with people, the cacophony of the multiple conversations filling the rooms. The large, French doors to the diminutive backyard opened to receive the spillover. It was an unusually hot April evening in Washington and the cherry blossoms were in full bloom. I stood at the hors d'ouvres table, enjoying a few moments of quietude amidst the happy chaos.

I heard Margaret's subtle, southern accent coming from somewhere nearby. "I had a nice talk with your stepfather."

I looked up and saw Barbara's mother standing a few feet from me, plate in hand. Margaret was old school. She liked to know what your surname was and to whom you were related. She was round and graying and the spitting image of Barbara in thirty years: they had the same, small eyes and slightly beaked nose and the same hairstyle. She was a very sharp woman, in every sense, and she dominated the family with her tremendous force of will and intense narcissism. Everyone placated her, walking on eggshells so as not to incite a protracted, internecine feud.

I privately imagined that Barbara had escaped her critical and supremely self-absorbed mother and absent, military father by becoming an academic, but she was still tied to her mother—tied in knots. Although Barbara was the most emotionally buttoned-up and intellectually intimidating woman I'd ever met, I saw her reduced to a slightly agitated, small shadow in the presence of her mother. Barbara was forever trying to cajole Andrew to appease Margaret, to call her or talk to her so that Barbara would not have to deal with the fallout.

"Oh, I'm so glad," I said, and turned back to fixing myself a plate of food.

Margaret stood coolly, staring at me, her small eyes narrowing. "I *said*," she repeated, "I had a nice talk with your stepfather."

"That's lovely, Margaret. I'm glad," I said again, wondering what more I was supposed to say.

As I looked back to the table, I could feel her standing, eyes fixed on me, calculating. Once again I had the sinking feeling that

I was doing something wrong, or not doing something I should be doing, but for the life of me I had no idea what that something was.

Then, loudly and more emphatically, I heard Margaret's voice again.

"You ... are ... *cold*."

I stopped and looked up at her. "Pardon me?"

"You are a cold girl," she declared, staring at me with squinted distain for a moment before she walked off into the crowd, smiling and nodding as she balanced her plate and glass.

I stood frozen for a moment, unable to comprehend what had just transpired. I felt a rush of heat rising inside of me and the noise of the room grew muffled. And then, standing there at the hors d'oeuvre table in the middle of my engagement party in my beautiful dress with my beautiful hair and at the height of my bliss, I began to cry. All of my pent-up energy and emotion was punctured by this unexpected comment, and it began pouring out.

I made my way through the crowd, looking for Andrew, fighting my tears. I saw him standing below in the garden, laughing and talking with his brothers. I went down the steps, hiding my face and dabbing my mascara with a napkin. I took him aside, telling him through my tears what had just happened. His face took on a look of determined anger. He left me with James to compose myself and strode determinedly into the house.

What happened next must have been a supremely satisfying moment for Richard, or so I imagined. My fictionalized backstory was that Richard had been waiting for years to have his say about Margaret, and this confluence of events finally galvanized him. I had little idea what sort of hornet's nest was being shaken by this small event; I was, in a sense, an innocent bystander in the long-running drama that was Margaret.

Richard shot like a heat-seeking missile in search of his mother-in-law, whom he found mingling in the living room, and told her, in no uncertain terms, to leave his house. Margaret, self-righteous and seemingly unaware of her bad behavior, did not believe him. He reiterated his demand.

Incredulous, she gathered her coat and loudly proclaimed to no one in particular but everyone in earshot, "My son-in-law is throwing me out of his house!" She then made her way toward the door. As she passed by my brother, she said, "I can see where your sister gets her coldness ... from your mother," and indignantly walked out the front door.

I had inadvertently wandered into the middle of a minefield, having traipsed in quite unawares. Although my brothers-in-law and Aunt Brooke assured me that none of this drama was about me, I knew for a fact that this would not prevent certain parties from holding me responsible. I imagined that all the sparkling diamond and sapphire rings, which Margaret had indicated to me would one day be mine, were now going with her to the grave.

But, even in the midst of the chaos I had unwittingly unleashed, I felt tremendous gratitude for Richard's defense. Once the initial storm calmed, I made my way into the house to search for Richard, and found him in the kitchen, speaking with an animated Stephan. I sidled up quietly and gave him a hug.

As I embraced him, I whispered in his ear. "Thank you."

Barbara approached from behind as the family gathered near the swinging door of the kitchen, away from the guests. It was not Barbara's way to speak about any of this—certainly not around me.

Barbara, I had surmised, was the de facto head of the household. My impression was that she was the dominant force in the family, when not under the thrall of her mother's presence, and that Richard on the whole acquiesced in her desires. Richard doted on Barbara, calling her "my bride" and "my little bird," even as she effusively refused his affections. But this time, Richard had laid claim to his presence and power, and Barbara was obviously flustered. She was undoubtedly going to have hell to pay for what had happened and I feared, in my insecurity, that Barbara silently—or perhaps not so silently—would hold me responsible.

An engagement brunch was scheduled for the following morning at Margaret's house, a party I refused to attend without an apology; Andrew was likewise reluctant. Barbara all but begged me to go. Unhappy but not wanting to cause additional strife, I relinquished by midmorning. I was tired and a little anxious as we drove out to Margaret's suburban brick colonial, still feeling the effects of the late-night port and cigars that Richard and the boys and I had enjoyed after the last of the guests had departed the night before.

Margaret greeted us with Virginia charm, smiling and chatting as though nothing at all had happened the night before. Barbara and Richard went in first, and then I stepped in the front door. Andrew kept his arm firmly around me and we stood in front of Margaret, waiting. Margaret stood smiling, looking straight at me.

"I was just havin' fun with you, but you wouldn't play!" she blurted out in her heavy southern drawl.

I looked her steadily in the eyes and measured my words carefully. "I accept your apology, Margaret."

She stood there with a peculiar look on her face; she clearly had not anticipated such a response. I had not anticipated it either; it simply emerged from my lips. Andrew and I walked through the living room and into the dining room where Margaret's large, African-American maid was finishing laying out the buffet. His arm squeezed my waist.

Despite this drama, our engagement put Andrew back on the family map. He felt normal and accepted and delighted in being celebrated. I could see that he was happy. His entire family, with the possible exception of Margaret, was happy for us and extraordinarily welcoming of me; his brother Stephan, the maverick of the family, privately applauded my courage in standing up for myself.

One year later to the day—April 20, 1996—Andrew and I were married in an opulent, elegant, white tie evening ceremony in San Francisco, a gift from his parents. Casablanca lilies the size of dinner plates and sprays of gardenias spilled over the ornate, gold altar of Trinity Episcopal Church where the imposingly large Father Robert Royal delivered the service in an enormous, booming voice. After the ceremony, we were driven in a white Bentley to the hilltop vista where we first kissed, and we kissed again as husband and wife in the breezy dusk of the bay as passersby honked their horns and waved, the intoxication of love contagious.

We joined our guests at the Old Federal Reserve Building, stopping at the top of the marble staircase to take in the overwhelming beauty. We were both euphoric and giggling with delight as we peeked around the corner to take in the spectacle. We made our entrance, descending the curving staircase to applause and the music of a seventeen-piece jazz orchestra. Flowers and giant palms filled the magnificent, marble room, an edifice to money and grandeur of the Golden Age. We danced our first dance to Frank Sinatra's *Fly Me to the Moon*, and finished the evening with Barbara admonishing us to "go get pregnant!" as we cut our stunning cake.

The following morning, we were driven by private car to the airport—me in white suit and corsage, Andrew in a new jacket and boutonnière—where we caught a plane to New York, staying for two days at the St. Regis Hotel before flying to Florence, Italy, where we celebrated my thirty-second birthday. Despairing of the cool, rainy weather in Tuscany, we returned early to San Francisco, telling no one, staying just long enough to tear into the stacks of wedding presents piled up in our living room and to make more travel arrangements. Two days later, we boarded a plane to Maui, where we reveled in the warm, tropical beauty for another ten days.

In less than three years, my life had changed one hundred and eighty degrees. I was ebullient, filled with a joy and contentment and a sense of belonging that I had never known. My life felt perfect, but it was not.

Returning home from Hawaii to our dark little flat in the city, the honeymoon abruptly ended. A quiet heaviness immediately descended over Andrew. He became withdrawn and our usual easy, playful communication disappeared. Tangibly distant, he did not want to make love. When I asked what was bothering him, he said only that he was anxious to open his flight school and settle down into a career.

Now that we were married, he seemed eager to create a more mature life, to be responsible and let go of his dilettantish ways, ironically just when I was ready to embrace them. I wanted to travel, and enjoy our time and money and love. Andrew had done all that already. He was searching for something. He was clearly depressed but said he would be better once we moved. In my heart, I knew better than to think a move would be the answer to this or any other problem, but there was little for me to do but hope. I tried to turn my thoughts to moving and to the excitement of buying a first house. I hoped against hope that this mood would pass as suddenly as it arrived.

# 9

Two weeks after Andrew's thirtieth birthday, on a cold and windy day in August, we left San Francisco and returned to the place where I was raised. Jacksonville, Oregon (population 1,973), was an historic Gold Rush town located just over the California border—a quaint, conservative oasis set in a beautiful valley known mostly for pear orchards and, more recently, vineyards. We chose it in part to be closer to my mother who, having lost her second husband and my step-father of twenty years a month before our wedding, was alone and very lonely. Jacksonville was an easy, charming place and a fairly short drive to San Francisco; most importantly, however, it was a perfect place to open a flight school; the weather and terrain and lack of competition made it ideal.

Andrew got to work immediately, buying an aerobatic plane and setting up the details of a business. Within a week, he was out at the airport all day every day, leaving me in our rental house with Beau, confined by the triple-digit heat and the absence of work and friends that might serve to distract or sustain me. The post-nuptial letdown and Andrew's demeanor left me deflated, and I began to feel physically unwell and mentally agitated. I was at once deeply empty, tired, restless, and worried. At a loss with my overabundance of time and ruminations about Andrew, I delved into the tedious paperwork required to complete my psychology licensing application.

The busywork helped only marginally. As the days and weeks passed, Andrew's mood did not improve. He had become distress-ingly quiet, like a ghost in our own house, disappearing into his office for long intervals upon arriving home. Our usual banter and teasing went missing. This turn of events, coming out of what by all mea-sures had been such a remarkable, romantic love story, was deeply disconcerting. Our blissful bubble had burst, leaving me in a quiet, little house with a quiet, distant husband. Nothing I said or did made the slightest bit of difference. I felt infinitely sad, profoundly scared, and very, very lonely.

⌒⌒

In the midst of this unspoken estrangement, Andrew and I attended a summer art fair on the grounds of the beautiful 1870s brick courthouse. Tarot readings were being offered in a tent under the large, old maple trees on the front lawn. I'd never had a card reading before and I was intrigued, secretly searching for some insight into our situation.

We sat down on two stools at a makeshift table draped with a scarf. The card reader was a very normal-looking, middle-aged woman named Carol. Her conventional appearance surprised me; I had an image of these sorts of people being gypsy-like—or at least witch material. The woman in front of us could just as easily have been standing on our porch in polyester pants, holding a tuna casserole.

She asked us what we wanted to know. I couldn't really ask what I wanted to know, which was, "What the hell is going on?" Instead, we told her that we had just moved and weren't sure if this was a good place for us—a slight divagation from the whole truth.

Carol suggested that we phrase our query to "What will happen if we stay here?" and we agreed that it was a fair translation. I drew a card.

It read, "Ruin."

The card haunted me. There was no way to put a positive spin on it or squeeze around it; "ruin" is a fairly definitive sort of word. But what were we to do with it? We had just moved a few weeks ago. Were we to move again? And, if so, where? More saliently, how could a move change what was happening between us other than to shift the focus for a few weeks?

To the outside eye looking in, our marriage looked ideal, even charmed. No one suspected or imagined the undertow that was swelling below the surface of our lives. I felt it, but I just kept treading water, trying to keep calm, keep positive.

As a partial antidote to my increasing anxiety and loneliness, I went to the animal shelter and perused the pens of sad-looking, homeless animals, promptly deciding on a rejected Rottweiler with an injured leg, whom I named Bella. Bella and I shared an immediate affection: we were both sad, abandoned creatures.

A week later, as I ran Beau and Bella in the field across from our house in the early morning before the heat became too intense, I found myself thinking about a dinner party that Andrew and I had attended some months prior, back in San Francisco. We were seated around a long, narrow table in a beautiful, postage stamp-sized backyard. It was dark and the candles were flickering when I caught a piece of conversation taking place to my left.

"You know what they say," a man said; "The first marriage is for love, the second is for money, and the third is for friendship."

I'd never heard that saying before, and it bothered me. It bothered me at the time and it was bothering me now. I had the inexplicably strong sense that this was a message directed at me from some invisible entity: an omen. It had stayed with me all this time; it was with me now, standing with me in the field, staring at me.

*Well?* it seemed to say, waiting for a response. *Well?*

Love. Money. Friendship. I considered my recent past. It was true that my first marriage had been for love, albeit a disastrous, deformed sort of love. It was also true that Andrew had money, or his family did. He and I lived a very simple life, splitting our small rent and all of our bills down the middle. I was thrilled to move into our current house, to have a garage and a dishwasher, even at the exorbitant rent of $900 a month. But the point was that I loved Andrew. I loved him before I knew he had money; I didn't even know how much money he had until long after we were engaged.

I stood in the field across from our house, arguing in my head with the invisible oracle. *Shut up!* I wanted to say. *Be quiet!* I didn't want to be thinking these thoughts, did not want to hear what I was hearing or see what I was seeing. It might as well have been whispering, *You will be visited by three ghosts.* Three marriages? *No,* I thought, *I don't want this!* I wanted my marriage: not for the money—for Andrew. I just wanted all of this turmoil to disappear.

The oracle just hung in the air, waiting, its message ominous and insistent. A third marriage implied the end of this one, and this marriage was not going well.

We were in trouble.

The degree of our trouble became clear enough a few days later. Andrew and I had tickets to see Bonnie Raitt at the summer music festival in town. Keith was joining us, and he had just arrived at our house and was waiting for us in his black Toyota Supra in the driveway. I grabbed my sweater and called for Andrew, who came to the door of his office.

"I don't think I want to go. I think I'll just stay home," he said in a quiet, off-the-cuff sort of tone. "You two go."

I knew that he was not telling me something. He wasn't talking to me much at all now, certainly nothing beyond perfunctory pleasantries. Andrew knew my history with Keith, knew the intense sexual nature of our past and that I had carried a torch for Keith for years before Andrew and I had met. Now I felt him pushing me toward Keith, encouraging us.

"Are you sure?" I asked. "I really want you to come."

"No, you go."

I turned and walked uncomfortably to the car and got in. Keith sat silently, looking at me expectantly, waiting for me to speak.

"Andrew's not coming," I said.

Keith looked as confused and surprised as I felt. I knew him well, knew his mind was racing like mine to make meaning of this, knew what he was probably thinking. I sat silently staring out the window, wondering what to say, how much to reveal. This was a man to whom I had revealed a great deal over the years, but this time it was too tender, too intimate. I was a newlywed and very much in love; how could I sit and divulge all my fear and longing? How could I tell him about Andrew and what I suspected was happening? Maybe it wasn't happening. Maybe I was wrong. I didn't think I was wrong, but I wanted to be. I felt pawned off and distraught, caught in an unspoken, silent secret.

We sat in silence in the driveway for some minutes, the air conditioning blowing strong and cold. The irony was that for once, after years of longing and an unrelenting desire, I did not want Keith. I wanted my husband, and I wanted my husband to want me, but he did not. We were falling apart, just four months after we had come together in our glorious, springtime wedding.

"Let's go," I said.

By the end of September, Bella and Beau had become my main source of love and comfort. I felt utterly frustrated with the lack of affection and absence of intimacy. Andrew and I had not made love since July; we hardly even felt like friends anymore, and the double loss was breaking my heart. I longed for our talks over coffee, longed to hear his silly puns and to see his wry smile, longed to laugh together. I wanted desperately to feel his affection, to feel wanted, to hear him say, "You look beautiful," the way lovers do, but he didn't.

In my sad desperation at this turn of events, I tried to convince myself that I could make things better if I tried really hard. If I were more cheerful, if I dressed better, perhaps the tension would evaporate. Maybe it was something about *me*. I knew it wasn't, but I wanted it to be. If it were me, I could fix it.

I tried everything I knew. I made his favorite dinners. I dressed up. I walked naked though the living room, but he never even raised his head, never even noticed I was there. I arranged a weekend back in San Francisco, where we stayed in a nice hotel and shopped for furniture. I went to see my friend Nate, a hairstylist, who cut my long, blonde hair short and colored it dark. But nothing changed. All he seemed to want was to disappear into the back bedroom office or the solitude of the sky. I saw him every day, but he wasn't there. He was gone, and try as I might, I could not bring him back.

I was in love and trapped in a relationship I did not completely understand and did not know how to fix. I oscillated between thinking it all would pass and that everything would be okay to a desire to run away. Internally, I screamed, *I don't like this! I don't deserve this!* The persistent pain of my daily reality was so oppressive that I began to fantasize about being alone, about moving to Santa Barbara and being a single student again. I wondered if he would miss me if I left, if it would startle him back into the Andrew I used to know.

I desperately did not want to believe what I knew was happening. I'd been too scared to think about it, but I knew. What Andrew and I both had hoped for and wanted—maybe even believed—was that our love, our relationship, would be the antidote to the persistent pull of his inner demons, and for a while it was. But when the confetti settled and the celebration was over, reality had crept back in.

I was desperate for it not to be what it obviously was. I would have preferred it if he had an issue with me, or if he was caught up in the details of a new business venture, or anything—*anything*—but this, because this I could do nothing about. He had told me that he was finished with his gender struggle and I believed him, but it was not finished with him. The truth encircled us now, wafting like a heavy miasma, taking him away to a place of deep discomfort, of profound unhappiness and pain. And because I loved him so much, it had the same effect on me. I knew that he loved me, but it wasn't enough—not enough to save us.

On a cool day in early fall I went to collect the mail from our post office box in town. I took the pile of bills and letters and went to sit down on a bench outside to leaf through them. In the stack was a letter from Trinity Episcopal Church in San Francisco, the church where we married. I opened it and began to read. As I read down the letter, I caught my breath and my chest grew tight. The priest from our wedding, Father Royal—a towering, larger-than-life gay man with a ponytail and a voice that shook the rafters—had died suddenly of a brain tumor.

I loved Father Royal from the moment I met him. He was a character out of a southern novel transposed into the liberal culture of San Francisco. He was utterly joyful and deceptively committed to his calling. When he spoke the liturgy—standing in the aisle of the church in full regalia, reading glasses perched low on his nose—his voice thundered and echoed and shook everyone present. With his amiable nature, thick Virginia accent and imposing size, he distinctly reminded me of the cartoon character Foghorn Leghorn.

When, after our wedding, I told him that my veil had fallen off as I began my walk down the aisle, he had boomed in his southern accent, "Why, that's good luck!" and I believed him. When he whispered to us as we stood on the altar taking pictures, "Now bring me some babies to baptize!" I wanted to. He was life incarnate, and now he was dead.

I sat on the bench in front of the post office in the autumnal afternoon light, head in hands, and wept. *There's nothing binding us together anymore*, I thought. I knew that was illogical, that Father Royal was not the glue that held us together, but with his departure I felt that somehow our ties were loosed. First, the three-marriages warning; then, the tarot reading; and now, this. It felt like the third omen. *You will be visited by three ghosts.*

I began seriously planning some time away by myself, to clear my head and with the vain hope that my absence might provoke Andrew back to a conversation. I told him of my thoughts. He had already, and without consulting me, booked a trip to New Hampshire, with the thought that perhaps we should move there, and he asked me to go with him. I vacillated, debating whether it would be better to go away by myself, or go with him. I knew that his undergraduate years at Dartmouth had been some of his happier ones, and I knew that he was yearning to recapture the spirit and ease of that time, but this Hail Mary plan he had of moving there was ridiculous: it was simply forestalling the inevitable. Still, I wanted any chance we might have to reconnect so, somewhat reluctantly, I agreed.

The trip provided a slightly relieving diversion. With our minds temporarily turned to other matters, we resumed much of our former ease and comfort, a fact that cheered me greatly. His spirits seemed to lift as we looked at houses for sale. Still, this was not a place I could imagine living, and it was plain to me that this was a desperate move born of fear and avoidance. He wanted to return to his collegiate days, to happier times, and that was never going to happen. I told him as much over breakfast at the local diner.

"You can't go back, you know," I said over a plate of pancakes and eggs on our second morning there. "It wouldn't be the same. You'd be working, and married, not a student. It wouldn't be anything like it was." Andrew looked at me with those sad, brown eyes of his. "You'd be on the outside looking in," I said carefully.

Andrew looked down at the Formica table, considering what I was saying. "You're right," he replied.

We stopped over in San Francisco on our return and had dinner with Ainslie at Firefly, a favorite spot in Noe Valley. It was Halloween and revelers paraded by the tiny corner restaurant where the three of us sat by a plate-glass window, watching the festivities. I was relieved and happy to be back in San Francisco and with Ainslie; for a few hours, it felt just as it always had. We laughed a lot and told stories, and Ainslie's presence kept our conversation light and buoyed. But when we arrived back home in Jacksonville the next day, our polite estrangement resumed and with it my anxiety.

Alone one evening after dinner, with Andrew again secluded in his office, I walked outside onto the front porch and stood in the dark, wrapping the cold night around me.

*I might as well be alone*, I thought. *It would be better to be alone and lonely than married and lonely.* I stood quietly, feeling the agitation in my body, watching the vapors of my breath rising and disappearing into the darkness. Another thought arose: *I wouldn't even feel sad if he died.*

My anger was a hot blanket, covering a heart that was still deeply in love but seriously wounded. I saw no viable, happy solution. This wasn't about me and it wasn't even about us, yet here I was in the middle of it, trapped in an unworkable relationship and in an image the world held of our relationship. *If they only knew.*

There was no good answer, no easy exit. This marriage, in its current incarnation, was not what I wanted, but divorce was not what I wanted either. What I wanted was everything I'd had, everything we were, up until five months ago. My frustration was compounded by the secrecy surrounding our reality; there was no one to talk to. Whom could I tell? Whom could I trust with this? Who would understand? How was it possible that just a few months ago we were fox-trotting around the grand marble foyer of the Old Federal Reserve, delirious with joy, celebrating our marriage, and now we were in a sexless, conversation-less, passionless *what?* What was this? How did this happen? Pain, confusion, and impotence overwhelmed me, and I slipped under a depressive shroud.

# 10

On Thanksgiving, we traveled to the eastern shore of Maryland, a trip planned some months prior. Years ago, Barbara and Richard had rescued a three-hundred-year-old house they found somewhere in Virginia and had transplanted it to the country, where they plopped it on one hundred plus acres of quiet and solitude on the Chesapeake Bay. It was a small, weathered house with a walk-in fireplace, which proved invaluable in the gray, damp winter that blew across the flat tidal land. There was no television or radio to disturb the silence; in the evenings, we played games or talked or read in front of the fire. When it was time for bed, we climbed a frighteningly narrow, steep stairwell to a diminutive bedroom, a room that made me feel ike Alice in the too-small room in Wonderland.

There were two, tiny single beds in the attic room that Andrew and I shared. They were extra small, as if they were designed for little people. It was dark and snug in there, all wrapped up in quilts and listening to the wind howling around corners, rattling windows and making strange, poltergeist-like whistles.

The night was primed for the possibility of romance. I crawled out of my bed and insinuated myself under Andrew's blanket, but Andrew was not receptive. He quickly and silently turned his back to me, wrapping the quilts tightly around his body, rebuffing my advances. The empty feeling that rushed in to fill the void between us felt like a gust of cold air being sucked through a door that was left swinging open. What a beautiful life I had, and how very sad.

A week later, back home in Oregon, I had a dream: I was climbing an incredibly tall, narrow ladder. It felt unsteady, and I worried what would happen if it toppled. As I stepped onto the penultimate rung, the ladder began a slow motion, never-ending fall. It took me for a frightening, surreal roller-coaster ride, up and down, back and forth, never hitting bottom.

In the dream, I thought, *Oh my God, my worst fear has come to pass.*

Two weeks after my dream, Andrew and I lay sprawled on the old futon in the spare bedroom on a Friday night, watching a movie. The entire time I was thinking about us, my stomach aching with anxiety. I wanted desperately to find the thread of our friendship, to follow it back to our love. I would not accept being stonewalled any longer. I just couldn't stand it; the silence was killing me. I wanted to get it all out, to fight; at least then there would be some communication, some passion.

I was no longer angry; I was scared—desperately scared. I loved him, and I wanted him to love me, to be as enthralled with me as he had been just a few goddamned weeks ago. I wanted to be married. I wanted us, and I wanted the extraordinary, charmed life that the rest of the world imagined we had. I had no cards to play, so I lied.

"If you don't talk to me, if we don't do something about this, I'm going to have to file for a divorce," I announced, breaking the ice with a dramatic blow.

I didn't mean it, of course; I had no such intention. Andrew remained silent, not speaking at all, just sitting on the edge of the futon, looking at me. His dark eyes were beautiful, but they bore a look of tired resignation. It was a look that said there was simply nothing he could do, nothing he could say. He looked at me silently, showing no evidence of shock or surprise. He registered no reaction to my pronouncement.

Tears rolled down my cheeks. I had expected, or maybe wished, that such a statement would startle him, that he would look up at me and say, "No, Kate—please!" But he didn't. And, in that moment, I knew exactly what was happening. Deep inside, I finally allowed the truth, which I'd been tenaciously barricading from my mind with a tremendous force of will and limp denial, to descend upon me full force. He did not articulate it, but I knew.

The feelings had returned—the ones that made him overwhelmingly unhappy in his own skin. The desire to have a different body, a female body, had resurfaced. The engagement, the wedding, the honeymoon, and the trips had occupied his mind and heart for a while. He had been welcomed back into the WASP family fold; he was exultant. But once the excitement passed, once our life settled back into its routine, the reality that nothing had really changed became achingly apparent to him—and to me.

Sitting there, looking at him, I understood everything without question, without argument. He had not spoken a single word, but I was overwhelmed with information. I knew that he truly loved me; that was never in question. That was not the problem. The problem was that he did not love himself. He couldn't. He was caught in a torturous double bind. No matter which path he chose—male or female—he would not find peace. This was not a simple, run-of-the-mill couple's therapy sort of problem, nor was it about cross-dressing; it was far bigger and far more complex than that. This was not a story that could have a happy ending.

I stood up, devastated, and left the room. Andrew remained, motionless, on the edge of the futon. I walked across the darkened hallway to our bedroom, climbed into bed, and lay staring at the dark. I covered my eyes with my hand and sobbed.

*Oh my God*, I thought. *Oh my God*.

Tears rolled down my cheeks and into my ears where they pooled up and turned cold. My worst fear *had* come to pass. The thing I wanted to be behind us, the thing that I could do nothing about, the thing that I hoped I was wrong about, was here. What would happen to us now? If we stayed together, it would be a faux marriage, miserable for us both. If we divorced, all the flying monkeys would be loosed from their closet and come screaming out for the world to see; it would be a messy, embarrassing, lurid sideshow—the stuff of Jerry Springer.

This was nothing short of a nightmare. *How*, I wondered, *could something so beautiful and so perfect become such a horrendous mess?* Questions I had previously not allowed to enter my consciousness rushed in—a flash flood of gnawing thoughts: *Had I been blind? Had I made a mistake? But I loved him; how could that be a mistake? He had told me that he was done with all this. Had he lied to me? Or did he really believe that he could overcome this, that he could be happy as a regular guy in a regular marriage?*

I rolled onto my side and Bella set her nose on the bed next to me, propping her large, square head on the mattress. She knew that

I was upset; she could never know how much. This was not the way the fairy tale was supposed to end. Cinderella is supposed to wind up a great success story. She waltzes off to the castle and has beautiful babies and lives happily ever after. Everything about Andrew and Kate looked so lovely from the outside, but it was all a sham. It was a bizarre, sad, impossible situation. The monkeys were howling and screaming inside my head, threatening my entire existence, threatening to tear my world to shreds.

Andrew came to bed some time later. The room was dark, and I could not see his face. I heard him kiss Beau and tell him goodnight and I lashed out, hurt and envious of our dog.

"You can kiss the dog goodnight but you can't even say goodnight to me?"

Andrew said nothing. I turned back and lay on my side, facing away from him, unable to sleep, my pillow wet, my stomach roiling.

The following morning, I woke up early and got ready to leave for my second therapy appointment with Nicole. I had begun seeing her in the hope that some objective insight could help me figure out what to do with a life that was disintegrating and falling through my fingers. I vacillated about even saying good-bye to Andrew, who was still in bed. I was exhausted from my anguished night. At the last minute, I stopped, keys in hand, at the bedroom door.

"I'm going to my session," I said quietly, and then turned to leave.

"Can I meet you for lunch after?" he asked.

I hesitated for a moment at the door, thinking. Then I turned around and looked at him soberly.

"Okay," I said finally, and I left the house.

I did not reveal to Nicole all that was going on during my session—certainly not the sexual part, not yet. My relationship with Nicole was still very new, and I wasn't comfortable spilling it all right out of the gate. I told her that we weren't talking much and that things had changed since the wedding. I filled in some basic information, like what we did for a living (not much) and why we moved here. At the end of the hour, Nicole spoke soothingly, telling me not to worry, that Andrew and I were "just resting." I wasn't sure what that meant exactly, but in my desperation I grabbed onto it like a life preserver in an open sea.

The idea that we were "just resting" allowed me to entertain the fantasy, however briefly, that our situation was perhaps not as dire as I knew it was. Maybe this was a bump in the road. Maybe I made it all up in my head. After all, he hadn't openly confirmed any of my fears. Perhaps, in time, we would figure it all out. It felt more comfortable, more hopeful, to grab hold of the shred of denial still floating in this sea of despair than to release myself to the waves of fear and grief that were lapping around me.

It was a dull, gray December afternoon and snow was on the ground. Andrew was waiting in his car in front of Nicole's apartment when I came out from my session. I got in, shivering. Andrew was bundled in all his North Face gear, ready to give a lesson. We drove to the grocery store and bought turkey sandwiches and Scottish shortbreads and ate them in the car. Nicole's admonishment that we needn't do anything right now had relieved a little pressure. I knew it was just temporary, but I needed the respite. I was tired.

As we sat together in the quiet of the car, Andrew looked down, his long, dark lashes lying in sharp contrast against his white skin. Then he turned to me.

"I'm sorry about last night."

"It's okay. Everything's going to be okay," I said. "We're going to go to Santa Fe and we're going to have a great Christmas."

Andrew was clearly relieved and happy to hear this.

"I love you," he said.

"I love you, too." I looked at him and smiled.

We changed subjects and Andrew began to talk about his students. It was relieving and hopeful to have a real conversation.

"I have a strange feeling about this lesson today," he said.

This caught my attention and it surprised me; he had never said anything like this before. Andrew was a supremely confident, commanding pilot. Flying was his forte, the one place he was bold and assertive. He told me that the other instructors had warned him about this particular student; they said he was cocky, that he thought he knew more than he did. I encouraged Andrew to be the in-charge pilot that I knew him to be, and we finished our lunch. He drove me back to my car and we kissed good-bye. He waved as he drove off and I waved back, watching his white Saab disappear around the corner.

I drove back toward home from Ashland, stopping at Kinko's to make the final, perfect copy of my application for my psychology license—a process that had taken three months of tedious paperwork and assembly, a process that had helped me fill the void that Andrew's physical and emotional absence had created. Afterward, I stopped at my mother's house and helped her outside with some chores. In the process of retrieving a garden hose, my wedding ring—a diamond eternity band—cut into my ring finger, causing it to bleed.

"That's strange," I said, as I looked at the wound. "I don't know how it did that."

It was 3:20 in the afternoon. I left for home, sucking on my finger, and parked in the driveway. I carefully carried the two-inch-thick, paper-wrapped application inside and set it on the entry table. It was sitting there three hours later when the deputy came to our door.

PART TWO

THE DISSOLUTION *or* HOLY SHIT

*Inside the chrysalis, much of the body breaks itself down into imaginal cells, which are undifferentiated; like stem cells, they can become any type of cell. The imaginal cells put themselves back together into a new shape. A few parts of the body, such as the legs, are more or less unchanged during this process. The amount of time required to transform completely varies from one species to another. For species that survive the winter by staying in the chrysalis, it can take months.*

# 11

My mother and I sat in the first row of the Boeing 737, waiting to depart to San Francisco: two black widows in 1A and 1B. It was Christmas Eve, ten days after Andrew's accident, and we were headed to my brother's house for the holiday. I stared blankly out the window. Inside me, everything was still and hollow.

I wondered why it seemed that everyone had to die in the winter: my father, my stepbrother, my aunt, my stepfather, my husband. It was no mystery to me why I always dreaded the arrival of this season, why Christmas was not the manic, joyous, all-consuming event that it seemed to be for everyone else.

I thought how, just a few days ago, I had stood on the front porch, seething and thinking that I wouldn't be sad if Andrew died; I couldn't have been more wrong. I felt guilty for having even thought it; it had been a thought born of supreme frustration. Now, everything that had threatened to tear us apart had, strangely, been resolved in the only way it could to leave everything neat and clean, but I was broken. Our problem was solved, but not in the way I would have ever wanted or dreamed possible. It was like emotional chemotherapy: the treatment killing the cancer but almost killing you along with it.

That night, I lay next to my mother on the too-small hideaway bed in the spare room, restless and uncomfortable. I appreciated Chris and Linda's efforts to create a sense of unity and family this Christmas, but there wasn't anything that could penetrate my sorrow. I fell into a fitful sleep, awakening every few hours, the shock returning and overwhelming me with each reawakening. Every time my eyes opened, the reality of the loss and my aloneness wrapped tightly around me, suffocating me. My heart ached. When I closed my eyes, I saw the plane spinning, nose down, hurtling toward Earth. I imagined—even as I tried not to imagine—Andrew's body hitting the ground. There was no place to hide from my thoughts or from the pain consuming my body.

The next day, I put on a black skirt and top that Andrew had given me; I hadn't eaten much since the accident and the skirt was loose, resting on my hip bones. I wandered into the living room while my sister-in-law and my mother bustled around in the kitchen, and sat on the sofa by the fire. I bent over, head in my lap, and cried.

"What's wrong, honey?" my brother asked, as he walked into the room.

*What's wrong? Was he kidding?*

I turned my head slightly to the left, glanced at him through my tears and, without speaking, put my head back down on my legs. He was in a completely different universe, a different reality. Between the pot he had just smoked and the beautiful wife standing in the kitchen, he didn't get it; he couldn't get it.

We sat down for a cheerless Christmas dinner, mostly out a sense of tradition; certainly no one was very hungry. The artifice of it, the dolefulness, recollected our Christmas dinner following my father's death. I asked Linda for a place to be set beside me along with an empty chair. I was trying to create some sort of ritual, some recognition of this reality that felt entirely unreal. I needed Andrew's companionship, his imagined presence there beside me. With him, I had found a new part of myself, and I desperately wanted to cling to that part, that connection that made me feel loved and understood and appreciated in a way I never quite felt before I met him.

Preparing to leave for the airport a couple of days later, Chris asked me if I wanted to see the autopsy report that, as temporary executor of the estate, he had just received. We were parked in the driveway in front of his house, and I was seated in the back, waiting to go. He handed it back to me and I unfolded it with nervous anticipation. I was hungry for information, but not prepared for what I was about to read.

Autopsy reports are painfully clinical; I'd read many of them in my tenure as a paralegal, and they could be difficult to stomach. To this point I had, in my shock-induced stupor, only taken in the heavily edited description of injuries that my brother had carefully doled out to me: a broken wrist, a blow to the head. I had accepted this sanitized recounting at face value because it was what I could handle. Now, I held the violent reality of my husband's death in my hands. Here, in graphic medical detail, was the reality of what transpires when a human body drops head first from the sky from a thousand feet in the air, nothing between the rocky ground and the head but a thin sheath of fabric.

I wasn't prepared for the explicit, matter-of-fact detail of the official report; I would never have been prepared for it, no matter when or how it was delivered. I scanned down to the bottom: "Cause of death: Massive craniofacial, neck, thoracic, abdominal, and bilateral upper and lower extremity injuries ..."

He had been broken everywhere, every organ traumatized, his head smashed by the 150-mile-per-hour impact. I imagined the blood that previously had not been part of my imagining. The carnage the report elicited in my mind's eye was horrific. I felt an enormous wave of sickness wash over me. I inhaled sharply, and then exploded in anguish. My beautiful husband—my best friend—dying like this; I couldn't bear it. I had chosen not to see his body at the morgue, but this seemed equally traumatic. I now had a vivid, all-too-real image etched in my mind of the plane and Andrew's body hitting the frozen earth, both smashed beyond recognition and covered in blood, a life and a passion extinguished in a span of a few, cold seconds.

My grief now expanded to encompass Andrew's experience, or what I imagined his experience might have been. Did he realize, as they hurtled toward Earth, that he was going to die? Was it too fast to think? Or was he just trying to manage the plane? Was he afraid? Did he feel the impact, or did he leave his body before it happened? What were his last thoughts? And did any of these things matter?

All the fear and anger and frustration of the months preceding his death now gave way to a tremendous deluge of grief. The initial shock was lifting, being replaced by a slow inundation of a very ugly reality. The event of his death was so surreal, so totally unbelievable, that my mind had recoiled and said simply, *"No, this just cannot be possible. No, this cannot be happening."*

Shock and denial exist to protect a person from death or insanity until they can begin to think about things, at which point they may well wish that they *had* died or gone insane to avoid the inescapable hell that is mourning. The immediate, instinctual shutdown lent by my own shock and denial had formed a cocoon that had cushioned me from the potentially fatal impact such news is wont to cause.

With these protective friends now leaving me, I was overwhelmed by feelings, too many feelings: anger, hurt, fear, loneliness, abandonment, grief, confusion. They came at me randomly, constantly, swimming around like a school of great white sharks, threatening and relentless. The barrage was overwhelming, almost unbearable. I envied Andrew for being where he was now, wherever that might be. No matter if or where he was, it was better than where I now found myself. Sad wasn't even the word for it.

*"I didn't want him dead,"* I whispered to myself, to him, to God. *"I just wanted to be free of the pain."*

A few days after the accident, I had sat on the futon in our TV room and spontaneously thanked Andrew for freeing me, thanked him that we did not have to go through all the *Sturm und Drang* of what was inevitably awaiting us. His death left everything neat and clean, at least on the surface of things. There would be no messy divorce, no "open relationship" negotiations.

This clarity and gratitude were lucid moments in what was otherwise a murky, black pit of isolation and pain. It was impossible to remain in this state of spiritual enlightenment for any extended period, impossible to maintain an expanded perspective; emotions obscured the larger picture, and the brief moments of illumination fell prey to the long, gray, quotidian slog of simply getting through the days.

It was incredibly frustrating to know that there was meaning and purpose in this pain and still cry all the time, still lie awake at night, scared and lonely. Balancing the spiritual and the mundane would prove to be no easy trick. I struggled to hold the tension of these seeming polarities of grace and grief.

# 12

The New Year arrived a few days later, quietly and without fanfare. It began with an inundation of rain, a biblical forty days sort of rain: an incessant and heavy record downpour. It flowed through the streets, washing out all the debris and dead wood, leaving stores with three feet of mud inside and dispossessing many people of their homes. The landscape reflected my inner destruction and dispossession. Out went my former life; in came the heavy, wet mud of grief and pain. My life as I'd known it washed away, leaving clogged debris in its wake.

My world became incredibly small. I got up, dressed, brushed my teeth. This could take many hours. I went to therapy three or four days a week where I sat on the couch and cried a lot. I walked the dogs. I received precious few phone calls, and the ones I did get were often unwelcome, like my mother's sixty-something Spanish friend, who persistently called to ask me out on a date despite the newness of my widowing and our thirty-year age difference. I listened to Frank Sinatra, to the Irving Berlin song Andrew used to sing: *"What'll I do when you are far away and I am blue, what'll I do ... What'll I do with just a photograph to tell my troubles to ...."* There was a strange bit of prophecy.

There was nothing to fill the time, nothing and no one that could fill my internal cavernous void. Even books—my longtime companions—were out of reach; my concentration was annihilated. Whenever I tried looking at the words, I wound up reading and rereading the same sentence twenty times, unable to remember what I'd just read.

The one thing I could do easily was watch movies. Most every day, I would go to the local grocery store and stare numbly at the small shelf of VHS titles, just to see if there was one I hadn't seen yet or perhaps would see again. The two hours of escape into another reality was welcome respite from the monotony of days.

I easily and quickly slipped—or perhaps retreated—to my habitual haunt of melancholy and depression. I thought about all the death and loss that had already come into my life: my father, grand-parents, uncle, brother, friends. In the past ten months alone, I had added my stepbrother, stepfather, aunt, and husband to my list. It seemed like an inordinate number of deaths for someone thirty-two years old.

I turned to my journal as a way of doing something with all the turmoil and pain inside of me. It was an outlet, not a catharsis—that implies some relief—but a way to release the horrific pressure that built up anew each day. At midnight on January 2, sleepless and wracked with overwhelming sadness, I turned on the light next to the bed, picked up my pen, and began to write, crying as I scrawled out the words.

*I am desperate without him. The deep ache sinks lower and deeper and farther than any feeling I have ever encountered. I miss him beyond words. I long for his presence: to see his face, to kiss his forehead and stroke his hair, to have him pull me inside his arm, lay my head on his chest, intertwine my legs with his; to feel his warmth and comfort and ever-present love.*

*I cannot imagine that he is gone forever, that this can possibly be real. I cannot express the torture I feel each night—the longing, the grief, the fears. I feel lost in a netherworld. I am no longer HERE. I am most painfully not THERE. I am nowhere. I am nothing. I am lost.*

The year felt a like a loss before it had even begun. I didn't want it to come, did not wish to eke and ache my way through each inter-minable, identical day. I awoke frequently in the middle of the night; immediately upon each awakening, my brain kicked into high gear, my stomach filled with acidic anxiety, and I lay thinking how much better, how much easier it would be to die.

Everything I thought I believed was called into question. My Christian faith, albeit marginal, failed to provide any comfort whatsoever. I cursed God in a bout of tremendous self-pity and absolute impotence. *Where was God in all of this? Why did He allow this happen?* Try as I might, I could see no meaning, no salvation, no direction. If it was, as some people offered, "his time," did that mean I should just graciously accept such an ugly abortion of a life, of a love?

I had to find some meaning or I would lose my mind. *What had happened up there that afternoon and why? Why did he have to die and why did I have to be widowed?* Beyond my own selfish pain, what was the reason for all the seemingly senseless suffering one hears about every day: gang rapes; children dying in Africa; people murdered for being the wrong color or the wrong religion or simply being in the wrong place at the wrong time?

I had been catapulted into a great existential philosophizing, wrapped in a thick layer of grief and tied with a ribbon of self-pity. *What the hell was it all about, this life?* Nothing made enough sense to me or satisfied my longing.

I ran through possible options: If such a tragedy was the result of bad karma, what did Andrew or I do to deserve this? What did those babies in Africa do? If this were Satan's doing, set loose on Earth and allowed to enact terrible evils, why would God sit back and watch such a cruel experiment? To test our faith? That didn't seem like a very benevolent God to me, certainly not one with whom I wanted to be on speaking terms.

If Andrew's life and death were somehow for my personal growth (I didn't really believe this but merely threw it out for the sake of argument), then that would imply that he was merely a pawn in my life's game. I could not accept this; it seemed blasphemous even to speculate about such a possibility, not to mention illogical. Andrew was a whole and beautiful person in his own right, not a bit player in my little life.

So maybe the atheists were right. Maybe life was meaningless: a capricious tossed salad of atoms and energy. If that were so, then nothing had any meaning whatsoever and it was all just absolute insanity: a horrid nightmare of pain, confusion, and wandering, punctuated by flashes of happiness. If this life is it, and there's nothing to follow, no particular purpose or plan, then this random death and my suffering was all just shit, and I might as well hole up and die. *What did it matter? Why suffer? For what?*

Nothing seemed to make sense. Nothing comforted or guided me to greater understanding. Mentally spent, I gave up. I had no answers to any of it. A flood of all my past Eeyore-ish, nihilistic beliefs came gushing back, filling the empty cavity in my soul. Like the sad, gray donkey in *Winnie-the Pooh*, I was not a person who got to be happy. I was doomed to a heavy life of introspection, of dull, chronic solitude and pain. I tried to fight my self-pity and negativity, but there was considerable circumstantial evidence to support it.

*To hell with everything*, I thought morosely. *To hell with God. To hell with struggle.* I believed in God, I just didn't want to talk to Him anymore, couldn't quite conjure any prayers. For the moment, I was holding God directly responsible for Andrew's death. I needed to blame someone, so I blamed Him.

I also privately blamed Andrew's student, Curtis, who I was certain had done something untoward and caused this tragedy and who would never confess to such a mistake. The fact that he refused my calls only buttressed my suspicions. He never even offered any condolences, even when my husband had, by Curtis' own testimony to the Federal Aviation Administration, saved his life.

Sleep was my only respite. Each day, I awoke to two black noses resting beside my pillow, and I would happily reach over and stroke their heads, glad for their presence. But much too quickly, a gradually increasing feeling of sickness crept in with consciousness, and I became a small, scared, orphaned child all alone in an empty house. I tried to fathom how other people got through this sort of thing, what kept them going and trying and living. People need a reason to live—a job or a child or a passion of some sort—and I didn't have one anymore, not really.

☙❧

Exactly four weeks after the accident, Brian drove me out to the site for the first time. I sat in his old truck, anxious and silent, as he tried to make conversation and gently prepared me for what I would see. I had a hard time listening. A dozen red roses lay beside me on the seat—an offering of love for the altar of earth that was the crash site. We drove for half an hour, passing through rolling hills and ranch land, crossing numerous small tributaries, and finally turning onto a dirt road that climbed a hill.

We parked at the side of the road that bordered private cattle land and climbed over a wire fence under a large oak tree. It was cold and the fog swirled around us, making it difficult to discern what I was seeing. Cows stared at us through the mist. I felt slightly ill. I couldn't stop thinking how like the Scottish moors it was here— so foggy and cold—and how Andrew would have made the same comparison.

We walked for ten minutes across a rocky field. Large, leafless oaks and scrub brush dotted the pasture and hawks flew and circled above, even in the foul weather. Finally, Brian pointed straight ahead, just across another wire fence. He held back, letting me approach the site alone.

There was a blackened fire pit to the right where the sheriff's deputies and rescue team had camped overnight before the plane was removed. The fence was still disassembled, and I could see where the wreckage had been dragged out and away, the tire tracks still evident in the wet earth. I turned and looked at Brian, who was slowing walking many yards away, allowing me to have my time and my thoughts.

I walked through the opening left by the rolled-back fence. The shape of the plane was clearly visible in the earth and brush, as though an invisible hand had reached down and made an imprint in soft clay. The dirt was churned up where the propeller had dug in, and there were small pieces of metal and shards of glass and flecks of paint everywhere. I took some deep breaths and poked around, stooping to pick up each little shard, wondering where it had come from on the plane, slowly taking in the extent of the massive destruction that had occurred when the plane made its impact.

I stood up, looked to my left, and let out a quick gasp. There, hanging on a branch of a broken bush, hung Andrew's headphones, his initials "A.A." painted in white-out on the side. I could only assume they had been forgotten, but it felt like they had been left there for me. I took them with me, along with some pieces of glass and a round rock, which I put in my coat pocket. Squatting down, I touched the ground, trying to ascertain exactly where his body had been. When I found what I imagined to be the precise location of the pilot's seat, I lay the roses there and sat down on a granite stone.

My reaction to being there was not what I had imagined. It actually helped me to see the site, to touch it, to have a tangible, concrete image of the place and the event. It made it more real but surprisingly not harder. I had a very welcome and unexpected feeling of peace.

It was not to last.

My mother came over the next day. In the first days following the accident, my mother had been an exceptionally good parent: extremely supportive, strong, and comforting. Soon enough, though, we reverted to our habitual roles—she as child, me as parent—except now I was not willing or able to assume my usual mantle of emotional caretaking; I was too depleted, too consumed by my own barrage of feelings. So when my mother materialized at my bedroom door late one morning after having let herself in, I was in no shape to deal with her.

In her youth, my mother had been a great beauty, and an actress; at least that's what she always said, how she'd been a great actress in college and how she had missed her chance for Hollywood. She needed an audience to feel loved and validated, and for many years, when she and I had been alone together after my father's death, I had served that function.

The problem, from my perspective, was that my mother could not be an audience for me; there was nothing shared that was not translated, through some invisible mechanism, into her personal experience. If I had a cold, she had the flu. If I were hurt, she was devastated. When I received admiration for a theater performance, she expressed wonderment at how I should be receiving praise when it was she who had studied to be an actress (clearly, she mused aloud, I must have inherited her genes). My feelings, my experiences, were never mirrored back; they were lost in the abyss of her hungry, unmet heart.

This self-referential habit was the result of deep wounds that she carried from her own unloved childhood; she was starved for attention and acceptance. The fallout from this was that my independent existence, or that of her listener at any given time, was barely acknowledged. Over the years, I had learned not to share anything personal or vulnerable with her to avoid having it hijacked. It hurt too much to be trampled under; I was always left feeling violated, regretful of having shared at all.

My mother was now clinging to the doorway of my bedroom, very dramatically holding herself up. She began to make crying sounds. My mother never actually cried; there were no tears, just a sort of forced series of "uh-huhs" to convey the impression of crying. I ignored her, and continued putting my clothes away in the dresser drawer. I felt something coming, so I closed my eyes and waited.

"I don't know what I'm going to *do!*" she cried out. "You don't *know* what it's like to see your child suffer."

It occurred to me that this was a highly inappropriate thought to be voicing to me at this particular moment. She reached over and grabbed my arms with both hands, clinging to me.

"I just can't *handle* this! I've lost *everybody,* and now I've lost Andrew!"

I pried her grasping hands off my sweater. *She* lost Andrew? He was now *her* loss? *Were we talking about the same Andrew*, I wondered, *the one she barely knew?*

"*You* lost Andrew?" I said, indignant and instantly fed up. "He was *my* husband. He was a son-in-law you hardly knew. And those husbands you lost? They were also my fathers. I lost Daddy, I lost David, and now I've lost my husband. So if we're going to count up our losses to see who wins, it's me. I win."

I wasn't sure, exactly, what that meant; but it felt necessary to assert sovereignty over my grief, and not have it swallowed up by the black hole of her neediness. I turned and walked into the bathroom and shut the door. My mother had stood quietly as I exploded, with no surprise or reaction of any sort, which was not unusual. She tended to go over these sorts of things after the fact, coming back later—sometimes years later—to ask why I'd said such a thing, or she might go the martyr route, which she often did when confronted by her bad behavior.

"I'm *always* wrong with you," she'd say, avoiding the central topic altogether. "I should just shoot myself."

I heard my mother leave. I came out of the bathroom and sat on my bed, feeling angry and more alone than ever. I desperately needed and wanted a shoulder I could cry on, someone to support me, someone who saw and understood me. Andrew had been that; he had been my shield, my refuge from family, my best friend. We saw the world with the same eyes. He commiserated with me about my mother and made me laugh. With him, I no longer felt mean or wrong or "too sensitive."

Now, I was back in the pit with no buffer or protection. My mother was an albatross that threatened to strangle me. If I pulled her off, I felt guilty; if I capitulated to her histrionics, I feared that I would lose myself entirely. It was a lose-lose situation. Anger seemed to be a positive alternative. It had arisen unbidden and it surprised me; I'd never expressed anger to her before. I didn't know which feeling was stronger: relief or regret.

That same week, Nate, a friend from San Francisco, flew up on his own volition to spend a few days with me. He had called and announced that he was coming, and I was delighted. The timing couldn't have been better; I had an excuse not to see my mother for most of the week and I would have some company.

I awoke before daybreak the morning of Nate's arrival, unable to go back to sleep. I listened to the rain dripping from the downspout outside my bedroom window, like a woodpecker pecking away incessantly. I lay under the warm sheets and reflected on friendships—or the lack thereof. Tragedies seem to produce the most unexpected friends, even as they highlight the shallowness of friendships you thought were so strong. All my formerly close friends were busy with their lives elsewhere; they did not call very often, much less visit or write. And yet here was Nate, my hairstylist, calling and asking to come and be with me.

Nate's visit was extraordinarily salutary. He stayed four days, much of which we spent in pajamas, drinking tea in the morning and wine at night. It felt so good to have a friend in the house, someone to talk to and cry and laugh with. He brought with him a natural flow of ease and generosity, giving freely of his time and his love. His presence was life affirming.

He snuggled with Bella, who did not like most men but who adored Nate, and we took both dogs on long walks together. We fed the ducks in the park—my first pure, happy moment since losing Andrew. We raised eyebrows by sitting in the Bella Union Bar, snuggled up together in a booth, having drinks and dinner, and then played pool at the J'Ville Tavern, where only beer is served and a handwritten sign on the door read "Ladies Welcome."

Nate looked like no one who lived around Jacksonville. He was gay, small and slight of form, with a mop of curly brown hair that smelled deliciously of expensive hair products. He was completely conspicuous. The regulars at the bar had no idea what to make of him.

My mother called on the third day of Nate's visit.

"Hi, Ma," I said, as I smiled broadly at Nate, who smiled back knowingly.

"Kate, I have Andrew's ashes."

My smile evaporated. "You *what?*"

"I went and got Andrew's ashes at the mortuary."

"Why would you do that?" I asked, incredulous and over-whelmed by the shock of her announcement.

"I couldn't stand the idea of him being there all cold and alone," she replied.

My body flushed hot, and I felt tense all over. I had not asked her to get the ashes nor had she asked me if she could. She had uni-laterally decided, on some inexplicable whim, to do this herself. She was unapologetic and seemed completely unaware that such a move might generate an adverse reaction in the widow—*me*.

I hung up the phone, scarcely able to speak.

"Oh my fucking God. She took the ashes. She took Andrew's ashes without my permission." Nate looked at me, his eyes big and round. "I have to go get them. I can't leave them there," I said, as I paced through the living room. "I wasn't ready to do this, and now I have to, goddamn it!"

Maybe Andrew wasn't exactly spinning in his grave, but I imagined him doing the equivalent, whatever that might be. The last place on Earth that Andrew would want to be—or that I would want him to be—was sitting on my mother's lap. *Could anyone just walk into a mortuary and take the dearly departed,* I wondered? That was a frightening thought. *How dare those people hand over the remains! How dare she take them!* I closed my eyes tightly, trying to think clearly.

My mother had been nurturing a fantasy since Andrew's death that he had loved her deeply and that they had been very close. I wasn't going to be the one to disabuse her of that little fiction, but this was just too much. She had gone too far.

I grabbed my keys and we got in the car. My mother lived just a five-minute drive from my house. I was angry but also anxious: I was not emotionally or psychologically ready to hold the box containing Andrew's remains. I had been in charge of getting my stepfather's remains, so I knew what to expect, and I didn't think I could handle it. But I could not, would not, leave them with my mother.

We pulled into the driveway. I turned off the engine and looked at Nate.

"I have a favor to ask," I said.

Nate looked at me silently.

"Would you hold the box for me?"

His eyebrows went up slowly. He was obviously not expecting this. He thought for just a moment.

"Sure," he replied quietly.

I felt bad to ask him; I felt even worse not to hold the ashes myself, but I just couldn't. There was something about the weight and the sound of it that I was not able to handle. Ashes are not just ashes; there are bone fragments in cremated remains that make sounds when the container is jostled. It's disconcerting.

My mother met us at the door.

"Give me the box," I said. She went into the house and came back, holding it. She stood in the doorway appearing utterly unaffected. "You had no right to do this. I wasn't ready for this."

She handed Nate the box. We turned and walked back to the car. Nate got in and held the box on his lap as we drove back to my house.

"I've never felt this before," he said. "I've never held someone's remains."

I glanced over at his lap, and then I looked at the road.

"Thank you," I said quietly.

When we got home, Nate helped me wrap the box in a bright African cloth that Andrew got in Botswana, and we placed it—as reverentially as possible, given the fact that the temporary resting place was a cleared-off space in the linen closet—on the shelf and closed the door. I looked at Nate and he looked at me.

"Let's have a drink," he said.

# 13

At the end of January I went to New York to be with Andrew's family for the first time since the funeral. As fate would have it, my seatmate on the flight had lost his young wife in an accident thirteen years before. He still seemed deeply affected by it, and I had the sense that he hadn't quite come to terms with the loss. He spoke at length about trying to find a new wife and a new life. He was excessively solicitous and there was a palpable air of pathos about him; it made me sad. Our commonalities depressed me more than they comforted. Was this me in twelve years? Would I still be alone and desperate?

I bid him best wishes as we arrived in San Francisco and then sat in the main hub of the terminal. I looked at all the people milling about; they seemed so unattractive, so preoccupied, so ... married. I'd had it so good; I couldn't imagine finding all that again. I thought about my seatmate and how he had barely any criteria for a new spouse: just someone to love him. It seemed so sad.

*Then again*, I thought, *maybe that was all anyone could hope for.*

My journey to New York proved an emotional odyssey of unexpected proportions. It began at Pierce and Brooke's place, upstate. Being back here with Andrew's family but without Andrew drove home the reality of his permanent absence like a stake in my heart. It took everything I had to hold in my desire to scream, "I HATE THIS!" I hated that he was dead, hated discussing the burial of his ashes, hated that he was not there with me.

There was the tire swing he pushed me on last Thanksgiving. There was the spot where we held each other. There was the place where we walked and I took his picture. There we were at the table. We were everywhere and we were never to be again. I tried to sleep at night but could not stop thinking about him. I wanted to hear him call me from the other room. I longed to talk with him.

Although I adored his family, it was hard for us to relate to one another; we approached our grief so differently. They told me what they thought I ought to do (keep busy, work); they didn't seem to understand my sitting and thinking, my not working, my way of mourning.

Brooke joined me the second evening for a few precious, private hours of real talk. I poured out my grief and fear in great, unstoppable torrents as we sat alone on the floor of her bedroom. All my anguish came rushing to the surface, breaking forth in choked gasps of horror and hurt. She was exceedingly compassionate. When my torrential tide of emotion calmed, we sat, talking and drinking wine. We talked about Andrew and we talked about my irritation with people, well intentioned as they might be, who tried to tell me what I ought to be doing with my life. We talked about the family and her marriage and our respective emptiness.

Brooke seemed resigned to the belief that she was not destined to have anything come easy or to be very happy. It hurt me to see such a beautiful, talented, and potentially vibrant woman so beaten at forty-two. Brooke was wounded. She reminded me of Bella when I first found her, lying with a small and withered hind leg in her kennel, a creature that had all but given up hope.

*This woman is hurting,* I thought. *She needs rest and therapy. She needs love.*

She was me.

The drive back to New York City was nearly unbearable. Barbara was backseat driving the entire way, mercilessly criticizing Richard until I thought the only option was to shoot her or shoot myself; the latter sounded appealing. I stared out at the endless winter, wishing I were dead.

The next day, we took a private tour of the Metropolitan Museum of Art before it opened, courtesy of Richard's cousin, who was a docent. Barbara talked the entire time; there was not a moment of unfilled silence. There was commentary about every painting, every sculpture. She made no eye contact as she spoke, giving me the sense that I was receiving a lecture rather than strolling through a museum with family. This feeling was accentuated by her lack of patience for or interest in anything I interjected. When I did manage to squeeze in a comment, it was as if I had said nothing at all and had succeeded only in irritating her, like a gnat flying too close to her face that she waved away. She mostly ignored my comments. I supposed that this was her way of being, of coping, but it made me want to scream.

I walked along with Richard, silently searching for a way to understand both her behavior and my reaction to it. Insensitivity came to mind, but it was more than that: it was defensive armoring. This was her way of overriding her pain, of containing it—the proverbial stiff upper lip. This ability, this propensity, was so completely alien to me that I had no way to metabolize it. I wished to hell that we could just sob in each other's arms.

As we left and walked outside, past the Plaza Hotel, I looked up and saw the St. Regis appear unexpectedly in my peripheral vision. Andrew and I had begun our honeymoon there just ten months prior. I was shocked to see it and, despite myself, I began to cry.

Richard held my shoulder firmly with his left hand, silent, tears in his eyes; Barbara, without missing a beat, took my left elbow and said firmly, "Let's get a drink."

She guided me around the corner to the iconic 21 Club. We went into the mostly empty, dark watering hole and scooped into the booth favored—according to the brass plate on the table—by Humphrey Bogart. Barbara promptly ordered me a Manhattan; this was an expression of care and concern, and I knew it. I knew she cared about my feelings, but I also knew she cared that her feelings not be tapped, particularly on the corner of 53$^{rd}$ Street and Fifth Avenue.

I excused myself to the ladies room to check my make-up and organize my emotions after my outburst on the sidewalk. I walked in and was greeted by a middle-aged woman in a burgundy vest whose name, a smallish pin announced, was Doris. She was the washroom attendant—apparently they still existed—and her presence inside the bathroom took me off guard. I had hoped to have a few moments alone.

Doris immediately approached me with a tissue, a look of deep compassion on her face. I thanked her and immediately gushed out an unsolicited explanation of my tears. Everything came out, everything that I had been holding in the past few days. I showed her a picture of Andrew. Her eyes welled. She said kind things about taking my time and how he looked like a movie star and how young I was. And for those brief, secret moments, Doris—my middle-aged angel in the john—took care of me. I wondered at how, in the most unexpected places and with the most unexpected people, love could be found.

Our pre-luncheon cocktails consumed, we exited into the bright, gray light of a late New York winter morning. Feeling slightly medicated and more composed, we walked across the street and I briefly went into Christian Dior while Barbara and Richard waited outside. The boutique was connected to the St. Regis Hotel by a large, glass door. I looked through the glass into the hotel lobby, the lobby where we sat as newlyweds not a year ago. As I stood, lost in thought, looking through the panes of glass into my past, I became aware of Barbra Streisand's voice singing *The Way We Were* inside the store.

*No one would fucking believe this*, I thought. My life was like a scene from a movie, a well-choreographed tragic romance.

As I left the building, I saw Barbara and Richard standing in the cold. I could see that they were scanning my face for another breakdown. Assured that I was in tact, we continued on to the offices of their financial advisor. We took an old, beautiful elevator up to the 14th floor. The advisor, a family friend, met us in the reception area and escorted us to his wood-paneled office. A large, plate glass window offered an impressive view of Fifth Avenue and much of Manhattan proper. The advisor motioned for me to sit on an expensive sofa against the back wall, while Barbara and Richard sat in armchairs near his desk. He seated himself behind an enormous, mahogany desk, adjusting his dark blue, pinstriped suit as he sat. The entire scene looked like an elaborate film set, all meticulously designed and costumed.

I felt intensely awkward being there. Money was not something the family discussed openly, and certainly not in front of an ex-daughter-in-law. I really had no need or business being there, but there I was.

Richard led the discussion, which was centered on the disposition of certain of Andrew's financial assets. Legally, as the surviving spouse, all of Andrew's financial holdings passed directly to me, but the nature of the assets was such that his parents could make a case for their return to the family holdings. I tried not to listen. The whole money business made me incredibly uncomfortable.

"She has the life insurance," Barbara said. "That's enough." She said this loudly, declaratively, as if I were not present; in fact, she sounded downright angry, as if I had killed Andrew or were taking needed income from her hands. Richard, uncharacteristically and unexpectedly, turned on Barbara.

"I'll take care of this," he snapped loudly. "You be quiet."

Barbara abruptly stood and walked over to the wall of windows. Her lips were drawn pencil thin and taught. Even in her tweedy suit and flat Ferragamos, I could easily imagine snakes sprouting from her head. She stared out and away. I stared down at my lap and arranged a thread on my skirt, wishing I were anywhere else and wondering why they had included me in this meeting. I wished that I could sneak back to the 21 Club and hang out with Doris.

After the financial dealings were done and Richard decided that Andrew's inheritance would be transferred to me, their advisor took us to a diminutive, upscale restaurant for lunch where my awkwardness and discomfort continued over crab cakes and chardonnay. We sat, wedged cheek by jowl, with the tony Wall Street set, privy to a multitude of conversations. There was little I could or wanted to say in such surroundings. I ate my salad in slow forkfuls and wondered why people lived in New York.

After the lovely, lonely lunch, we took a cab back to the cousins' apartment where I spent the afternoon trying to be inconspicuous. I looked around the enormous, labyrinthine apartment, which was bigger than most houses I had seen, and gazed out the windows that overlooked 5ᵗʰ Avenue and Central Park. The cousins, who were in their sixties, knew me only by association and seemed at a loss for conversation, which was fine by me; I had no idea what to say anyway.

I found it bitterly ironic, sitting around a large, circular table that night with the extended New York contingent at Café des Artistes, to be here with these people, in this place, partaking in such an elitist life, all the while thinking that, in reality, I had no life whatsoever. It felt hollow and strange and uncomfortable—although alcohol helped; it made the social register crap a bit more bearable.

It was no wonder that these people all drank so prodigiously; the conversations were intensely boring. Who you knew, where your homes were, who was marrying whom, who was giving birth, who just visited, where you're going next, where you just went—as if anyone really cared. *Who gives a damn,* I mused, sipping heavily at my chardonnay. No one talked about anything *real.* No one spoke of Andrew, or of their feelings about his death, or about anything, really, beyond surface pleasantries.

I called Nicole the next morning, sequestered on my tiny bed in the closet that passed for the housekeeper's room.

"Hi, it's me," I whispered, not wishing to be overheard.

"Where are you, honey?"

"I'm in the broom closet," I replied.

She laughed her hoarse, smoker's laugh. "How are you," she asked quite seriously. "Are you breathing?"

"No. I'm drinking."

Nicole laughed again. I was relieved to hear her voice, to feel connected to a person and place that felt more mine. Being here was a drought of the heart: I was parched by the lack of emotional expression. I already wished that I were back home, which, though painful, was the lesser of two terribles.

Richard, Barbara, and I drove to Boston the next day to stay with Richard's sister Julia and to take in the Museum of Fine Art with more running commentary from Barbara. I knew that Julia had also been widowed young, but our unfortunate shared experience was not proving helpful to me.

"The first year is a write-off," she proclaimed, as we drove together to the store in her Ford Expedition. "The second year is just about as bad," she mused, more out loud to herself than to me.

Then, completely unexpectedly, Julia erupted as though newly widowed, spitting out her vituperation at her husband—a doctor—who had drowned in a diving accident, leaving her alone with three small children to raise. That had been some ten years ago. She grabbed the steering wheel tightly, eyes welling up, and then began beating on it with the palms of her hands.

"Bad Julia, bad, bad, bad!"

I watched wordlessly, captivated by her self-recrimination for having been caught *in flagrante delicto*, expressing long-pent-up emotion.

I sat quietly, observing the outburst, lost in my own thoughts. I was doing the math in my head. *Two more years? I'm going to feel like this for two more years?* I couldn't handle that. I didn't want to. It was unimaginable. I felt like shit, and there was no hope on my horizon. Hell, Julia was still angry and still grieving after more than a decade. I was doomed.

I decided that evening to go home early. I was exhausted by the events of the trip, by being with Andrew's family and out of my emotional comfort zone. There was too much going, drinking, remembering, and not saying what needed to be said. I couldn't sleep well in unfamiliar beds with memories of Andrew choking my every breath. I just couldn't do three more days of it. I called the airline from the privacy of Julia's den and changed my ticket.

That night I confessed to Barbara, in a rare moment of relaxed time together, how I'd wanted a baby that looked just like Andrew. She said she'd wanted the same thing, and then we sat silent. That had been a big venturing out on both our parts to reveal such intimacies. Neither of us knew quite what to say or do after that, but it helped me to know that she thought about such things.

The next morning, as we sat together at the breakfast table in Julia's kitchen, Barbara was uncharacteristically open and personal.

"I'm sorry you're going," she said, looking down at her coffee. "You're welcome any time; you can come without notice and stay as long as you like."

I was genuinely surprised, both that she felt such things and that she would say them out loud to me. We began a much needed, unexpected conversation about the unspeakable: the anger we felt developing around Andrew's death, the long process of mourning, the weariness of seeing all the relatives and feeling all the emotions. It was a brief dialogue, but it was genuine and very, very welcome.

I felt bad for all my harsh thoughts and for all my nervous anxiety; there was clearly more to Barbara than met the eye. It was both confusing and relieving to see this other side of her. It was hard to reconcile the diametrically opposed aspects of my mother-in-law: a woman who could look right through me; a woman who never asked me anything about myself; a woman who openly argued against my receiving any financial remuneration; a woman who, albeit in the third person, questioned my actions and argued with my statements, and then could come down for croissants and tell me, obliquely, how she cared for me.

I felt sad to leave now, but I knew I needed to, and it was good to leave on this note. It was likely that she could only have made such open admonitions at the edge of my departure, when any awkward follow-up would not be required. That was fine with me. She had given me a little gift, and I was grateful. The sudden cloudburst of honest expression seemed to settle the dust of a multitude of raw emotions.

Richard drove me to Logan International in his white, dog-dirty minivan, entertaining me en route with stories about his family: the forebear who was governor of Virginia; the great-grandfather who drove the family into poverty with his "absentmindedness"; the grandfather who was determined to be rich and who hit it big with a little investment in a certain startup pharmaceutical; the father who was "sharp in every way"; the cousin who was Andrew Carnegie's financial advisor. I heard about secret abortions of would-be siblings and great childhood loneliness, and I began to understand just how and why Richard was so penetratingly sweet and loving: He was hungry for love and happiness and tried to create it everywhere he went.

It was difficult to say good-bye. I held him as long as I could, and then forced a smile.

"I love you," I said, even though it felt a little vulnerable to say it out loud.

"Thank you," he said, and then added, "Much love," in his characteristically lilting, soft, high voice—a bit awkwardly, but the feeling was palpable.

On the long flight home, I sat musing about everything as I stared out at the sky at thirty-three thousand feet. Descending over the San Francisco Bay Area, I looked for the sight markers that Andrew had used during my flying lessons in an attempt to get me to fly straight and level, which I never could. In my mind I questioned, for the hundredth time, what had happened up there that day, what went wrong, and why.

I turned my body toward the window to hide my tears from my seatmate, drying them as we skimmed the bay and touched down on the tarmac beside the water. It always felt good to be back here, back where the hills looked familiar and where I could imagine, even enclosed inside the airport, the smell of eucalyptus trees and fresh ocean air.

I walked into the center of the United Airlines terminal and sat in a café, watching the waves of people pass by and wondering about them: where they were going, where they'd been, what they were thinking about. I found myself looking long and hard at an attractive man and, for a few seconds, I left my widowhood. For a brief moment, libido overcame my grief. I had no real desire to be with anyone, couldn't imagine it happening, yet here I was, staring at some handsome stranger, feeling young and alive again.

Almost immediately a sense of shame swept over me. I hoped that no one had seen me staring. What would they think? What did I think? I'd caught myself looking, lusting, and I felt like a traitor. How could I do this? It was very confusing and contradictory behavior. Not an hour before I was thinking suicidal thoughts and contemplating years of solitude, and now I was tripping over my own lust?

The widow betrayed by the woman: apparently, hormones did not die along with the heart. This unconscious, surreptitious desire demonstrated the tenacity of life's longing for itself, life that persists through death, like a new phoenix arising from the ashes of its immolated predecessor. It pointed to something beyond me, something bigger. It surprised me, and I wasn't quite ready for it. Still, it had arrived, unbidden and very much alive; I supposed it was a positive sign, my chagrin notwithstanding. I took my confused and still-blushing self to my gate.

I was happy to be back home, back with my dogs and my bed and my familiar surroundings, but I was also back in my aloneness and sorrow. Not back, really: I had never left them. I could not escape them. I awakened multiple times each night, my mind racing through an internal photographic montage of memories, thinking a million thoughts. I felt Andrew beginning to slip away from me. I tried, as I lay in the dark, to see if I could remember his voice, if I could still hear, inside myself, the sound of his laughter, his words. I tried to imagine what we'd be talking about if he were here.

The waking and wondering accentuated my aloneness. I turned on the light and opened my journal to write out my thoughts, even though it was enervating to be going through this process of death and to be writing about it, too; it felt redundant and excessively taxing. But there was nowhere else for me to release the horrendous pressure that built up inside me every day. Writing in my journal, as hard as it was, had become very necessary. Nicole told me it would become the basis for something one day. I doubted that.

Andrew's brother James drove up from Stanford in late January to visit for a day and to take Beau back with him to California. My rental company would not agree to two dogs and I had decided, after tremendous agonizing, that it would be best to keep Bella and let Beau go to my brother-in-law, who wanted him. Beau needed more than I could give him, and I knew it was the best decision given the circumstances, but it pained me nonetheless.

James took some of Andrew's skis and bikes and then, when we could delay the inevitable no longer, he loaded a willing but confused Beau into the back of his Saab, hugged me stiffly, and drove away. I stood looking at our puppy, who stared at me through the rear window, wondering what was happening. As James made a U-turn and drove away, I watched Beau's brown eyes watching me, and my throat filled with an enormous ball of sorrow. I wondered what he was thinking as he moved farther and farther away from me and his home and everything he knew. I wondered if he was scared or confused or sad.

I was all three.

# 14

Seven weeks after Andrew's death, I began to unravel. I awoke at 5:30 early one February morning in tears and scared—*really* scared—about something unseen, unknown. I felt desperate, unsure what to do, how to handle the panic. I counted the minutes to call Nicole, picked up the phone and put it back down, debating. Finally, I dialed Nicole's number and let it ring. It was now six o'clock. She answered.

"You told me to call any time of day or night, so I'm taking you at your word," I said.

"Let me get my coffee," she replied. I heard her set the receiver down on the counter and I waited, lying in my bed, for her to return to the phone. At last she picked it up and said, "What's happening?"

I imagined her in her nightgown, leaning on the kitchen counter, as she drank her black coffee and smoked a cigarette. I talked for an hour straight about my fear, my anger, my sadness, the dreams I was having, the increasing horror, the mystery and the goddamned unknowableness of it all.

As usually happened when I talked with her, I emerged from that particular pit of emotional quicksand feeling better and more stable—at least competent enough to take a shower. By evening, however, I fell apart again, slumping onto the kitchen floor and crying out my agony and despair to Andrew and to no one.

"I don't want this!" I screamed into the silence. "I don't want him to be dead! I don't want my kitchen appliances and my house and my life all alone. I want my marriage! I want Andrew! I want my life back, the life I had before everything went to hell!"

I sat crying on the floor, acutely aware of the silence that met my outcry. The silence made me sadder and angrier, emphasizing, as it did, the reality of an imposed solitude. It mocked me. *Who are you crying to? You're all alone and no one is here. Nothing's going to change that.*

My sense of impotent frustration morphed into palpable fear. I did not want this to be real—any of it. I never imagined anything could possibly hurt so much; my body ached and my head hurt. A choking sensation welled inside my throat until I couldn't breathe. It came from way deep down and it felt unstoppable and all-consuming. It arose and then passed like a summer thundershower.

Bella came over and leaned against me, licking my face. I held her strong body next to me, appreciating her aliveness. I got up from the floor, wiped my eyes, and went to our bedroom, where I undressed and lay in our enormous bed, made all the larger for the absence of a second body. I fell asleep and dreamed of bears stalking me and children torturing me inside a locked house. I startled awake, began thinking, and decided to write it down in order to try to understand what was happening:

> *All these philosophies about life: it's fated; it's destiny; it's all accidental; it's free will; it's all known but not managed. If this was God's will, then God was a sadist—"the Vivisector," C.S. Lewis called him.*

I wrote in a torrential stream of consciousness:

> *Who the hell cares? It doesn't matter what I believe or wish to be true. I haven't the dimmest clue what's true or where Andrew is or why this happened or what it means. All I know is that my husband, my beautiful, thirty-year-old handsome pilot, heart of my heart, is gone, and there are no fucking answers. None. Nada.*

As I ranted, it became apparent just how removed Andrew was from my torment. Certainly *he* was not crying and mourning, dying daily deaths as I was: quite the contrary. According to a dream my friend Marcia had about him, Andrew was just fine and strolling around with his grandfather somewhere in the ethers, laughing about how Grandpa left him all this money and what did he do with it but buy a plane and smash it into the ground, *ha ha ha*. She said that in her dream, they actually laughed about the crash. That really sent me.

It occurred to me that Andrew didn't give a good goddamn what I did or didn't do down here: whether I visited the crash site every week or every month or never; whether I slept with every guy I met or sat and mourned my life away in black, like Queen Victoria.

I wanted to imagine that, on some level, Andrew cared whether I was in agony or happy, but maybe he was simply unaware of life down here, being otherwise occupied doing whatever incorporeal energy does. After all, spirit is spirit; by definition, it is not subject to Earthly cares. This heavy, trapped little carcass I was hauling around might house a spirit, but it was pretty well mired down in feeling damned sorry for itself. I was lost and angry and tired—very, very tired.

I began to sleep for extended periods: eleven or twelve hours of drugged-like sleep followed by a two-hour nap. I liked to sleep; it felt infinitely better than being awake, even with the nightmares, and most of the time the dreams were astounding, like the one that followed my kitchen collapse.

In the dream, I was in a space that looked like the Metropolitan Museum. I was trying to leave to meet Andrew. I couldn't find my way out, and I was very frustrated. I took an elevator with many people but, instead of stopping on the ground floor, it turned on its side and shot along into the bowels of the place. In the dream I thought, *Oh, shit. Oh great, another glitch.* I felt impatient and frustrated that so much time was being lost. Then I found myself on some enormous marble stairway, and I could breathe again. Keith was with me, holding a huge, thick green snake, many yards long. The snake was writhing and trying to get at me. I saw the head lunge toward me repeatedly. I tried to grab it behind the head to hold it still, but it bit me, its fangs sinking into my flesh between the thumb and finger. I looked up and saw the exit right in front of me, and I thought, *it's been there all along.*

I knew the dream was important, but the snake image was disconcerting. After I woke up, I looked up the snake in my book of symbols. The book said that the snake was a symbol of transmutation—of turning a toxin into a pathway for divine revelation.

Valentine's Day was coming. I hated the thought of it. I hated that my birthday was coming, and our anniversary. I hated every day without Andrew. It was getting worse. Harder. More agonizing. I hurt all the time. I did not smile. I looked at myself in the rearview mirror of the car one day and saw the knitted brow of a preoccupied, unhappy woman. Every time I thought about my future and what lay ahead, I came undone. Not only was everything that I had with Andrew gone, but I faced years of aloneness and then rebuilding—if I were lucky—with someone else; the thought of that made me sick to my stomach. I wished that I could go to sleep and never wake up, or else wake to him holding me, comforting me, kissing me and telling me "Shhh, it's okay. I'm here. I will never leave you."

That's what he used to say.

# 15

On Valentine's Day, I awoke from a wonderful dream: Andrew was lying on top of me in a passionate embrace. My back arched up in pleasure; we were completely lost in one another, sweaty in our lovemaking ... then Bella barked and woke me. I cursed her but couldn't hold a grudge. She was too loving, her eyes too soulful for me to be angry. Besides, it was the first lovely, loving dream I'd had about Andrew and on Valentine's—it was a gift.

I'd decided to spend the afternoon at the crash site; I felt close to him there. I bought some roses and drove out to the site where I parked under the oak trees. It was a clear, sunny day. I walked down and across the undulating hills to the site, where I found a large rock next to the plane's imprint and sat down. I set the roses on the ground, and then stared into the thin, blue sky, watching the Red-tailed Hawks circling and crying overhead. I sat for a long time, quiet and warm in the sun. I felt peaceful.

At home, I felt very different. At home, I wanted to die, to go to sleep and never wake up. I cared about nothing. I had no appetite. All I wanted to do was sleep. Even then, every time I lay down to rest, unbidden images filled my mind: always the little red, white, and blue plane, spiraling, spinning down to the ground; always Andrew trying to correct it; always our last good-bye.

Clinically I knew what was happening. I opened up my *Diagnostic and Statistical Manual of Mental Disorders, Volume III, Revised* and read the symptoms of Major Depressive Disorder, Single Episode: "depressed mood; diminished interest in activities; weight loss; hypersomnia; fatigue; feelings of worthlessness; inability to concentrate; recurrent thoughts of death." I had them all, but I couldn't care less. I felt unable and unwilling to hazard leaving such a consuming, demoralizing state: too much work—and for what? I could envision no future for myself.

This territory of depression was not unfamiliar; I'd traveled in its outlying areas for many years. But what I was experiencing now was heavier and darker than what I had known to this point. I was embarking upon a full-blown depressive journey, layered on top of my normal, chronic, low-grade depression, which I knew simply as "my life."

Depression is a departure; it is a metaphorical and visceral abduction into a lifeless world. It can be, despite its painful nature, a normal experience. A short visit to this dark country is often a necessary and valuable thing; it's taking up residency there gets you in trouble. Getting trapped in the very bleak country of Major Clinical Depression without a visa is a real problem. It's not safe. You don't eat or sleep well. You have no friends, no one to help you escape. The only information you receive is deceitful propaganda sent by the depressive state: "You are worthless. No one would care if you died. There's nothing to live for." Depression is the North Korea of mental disorders: if it doesn't kill you, you wish that it would.

The depression snuck up on me before I realized it. It was easy to miss, since grief and mourning are pretty depressive experiences all on their own. I expected to feel lousy. I expected to be down. My life before Andrew had acclimated me to this cold climate; I was conditioned to an outlook of expectant sadness. My mantra before Andrew had been, "I don't get to be happy in this life." Marrying Andrew had begun to loosen such negativity, but his death, so early in our life together, served to buttress these entrenched beliefs. Like Eeyore, I slowly walked back into my house of sticks, flopped down, and glumly accepted my fate.

Intervention into my gloom came in the form of antidepressants, at the insistence of Nicole, who threatened hospitalization if I did not cooperate. The thought of being sent to 3-North—the psychiatric wing of our hospital—was a fate worse than either death or depression. Imagining myself in a sterile white bed, surrounded by schizophrenics, an IV stuck in my hand, I capitulated to medication, secretly a little pleased that someone appeared to actually give a damn.

And so, late Valentine's afternoon, after I returned home from the crash site, I dug out Andrew's bottle of Paxil from our medicine cabinet. I looked for a long time at his name on the label. Staring at it, I remembered how he had resisted going on medication, how it made him feel as though he were weak and a failure. I remembered how depressed he had become that summer before our wedding, how I had come home to find him lying coiled into a fetal position on the sofa, dishes piled in the sink and blinds drawn. Thinking back with my current clarity, the signs and symptoms of his repressed pain seemed painfully clear. But the medication brought him back and he seemed better—at least for a while.

I wasn't really sure why I should take an antidepressant, except to avoid the cuckoo's nest of 3-North; I was not entirely uncomfortable in my gloom. The upside to my depression—and there was one—was that, suspended in the netherworld of being neither alive nor dead, I was absolved of having to deal with anyone or anything. I was miserable, but I was also freed from having to do anything that I did not wish to do, and I did not wish to do anything except sleep and pray that I might cease to exist.

What did it matter if I wanted to hole up and disappear? No one else had to schlep along in the quicksand of my dark mood. No one depended on me for anything, except perhaps Bella; certainly someone else could care for her, I reasoned. My mother and my siblings—well, my brother anyway—might be sad if I died, but they'd get over it. Hardly anyone would really notice my absence. This, too, was depressing.

Weighing my options as I stood at the bathroom sink, I opened the bottle and popped one of the little white pills into my mouth. It didn't feel like much of an intervention: just a little pill, swallowed with some water—very undramatic. *Well*, I thought, *I could always swallow the whole bottle if need be; that would be an easy and convenient way out.*

I spent my days and weeks alternately retreating into my melancholy and racing in manic desperation to fill the terrible void that loomed just inches away. Both alternatives left me tired and unsatisfied. When I would, in moments, peek out of my gray gloom, I would immediately fill with turmoil. There were so many uncomfortable questions, so many unresolved issues, so much internal mess that needed to be tended and addressed, sorted and cleaned and organized.

I stood at the edge of this bed of hot coals, vacillating, fearful of being burned yet not completely committed to giving up. I would tentatively reach my toe toward that burning path, wanting to cross back into life, only to pull back to the familiar protection of a cold, isolated sadness. I tried on new activities, new identities, even brief flirtations; when they fell flat, as they always did, I felt singed by the attempt and despaired all over again at what I had lost.

The death of my previous identity left me feeling vulnerable and disoriented. I was neither caterpillar nor butterfly, just an amorphous black blob of goo in a protective, hard cocoon, neither dead nor animated. I'd gone from wife to widow, poor to rich, happy to miserable, productively employed to an early retirement—all in eight months. Multiple adjustments were all happening simultaneously. It was an invisible, inescapable mess of dissolution and rearrangement, a massively uncomfortable limbo. I had two choices: I could try to bear the pain and hope for reemergence, or I could give up and—either literally or metaphorically—disappear.

My greatest and most secret fear was that I was fated to be sad and unhappy for the rest of my life. I feared moving back into life only to discover that there wasn't any lasting joy or happiness waiting for me. Until I met Andrew, I was, by and large, a lonely and vaguely depressed person, a person to whom the vicissitudes of life felt particularly poignant and weighty. That had changed when I met Andrew; his kindness, his love, and the life we shared together had created a blue and optimistic horizon. Now, though, I was back in my familiar, almost unbearable existence, terrified that I would be alone and lonely for the rest of my life; that I was destined, like Job, to suffer without understanding and without purpose.

Something in me was not surprised to be back in Gloomsville. The real surprise had been the lovely detour into a brief interlude of happiness and joy and dreams-come-true that was the first three years of my life with Andrew. The beautiful vision that had been, the unfolding of love and a beautiful future, now began to seem like something I had dreamed one night. If not for the wedding pictures,

I might have begun to doubt the reality of any of it, it was over so quickly. Eeyore was waiting for me when it all came crashing down.

"It figures," he said. "It was too good to last."

I grappled day after day with the barrage of emotions. I was not inclined to write, although I did for lack of any other outlet. I didn't want to be with people, and yet I desperately wished that I had a close girlfriend who would sit with me or drag me out for a movie or a walk. The feeling of being so deeply, penetratingly alone was incredible: incredible, as in hard to believe.

*February 16*
*A deepening pain is filling my heart and body. I have shooting pains that run down my left arm. It's a heart attack of sorts— not a real heart attack, but a symbolic one. I stop breathing, feel a constriction in my chest, and realize that I have forgotten to breathe. My breathing is shallow and restricted to the top inch of my chest, like someone in constant panic, and I am. I'm driving today, thinking, "What's wrong? Something's wrong. My chest hurts. Oh, I need to breathe. Take a breath." And with some difficulty, I force myself to inhale.*

*I chew on my lip and bite the inside of my mouth constantly. I clench my jaw until it hurts. I watch banal TV to dull my senses. I sleep all the time. I sleep thirteen hours a night and nap in the day and am still so tired that my eyes can't focus.*

*I hide in my womb-bed to shut out my life. Sleep is my sole refuge, my one solace. Waking, however, is another thing: it's a raw kind of horrible. The rush of reality hits me over and over, repeatedly, like a rough and rolling sea, waves pummeling me as I regain consciousness on the shore where I have washed up, the sole survivor of an unseen disaster.*

Only Bella, with her sweet face, provided the love I so needed. She was there when I awakened each morning: her big, black head resting quietly near my pillow; her sad, dark eyes looking right into mine. She stayed constant and close, leaning against my legs, head on my lap. She became a touchstone for my sanity, for my sheer existence; without her, I feared that I might disappear into some underworld, drowning in a despair that had no words.

The Paxil proved disturbingly effective. I awakened on the morning of the fourth day of taking it and realized that I felt different: I was no longer pondering my own suicide. I was still miserable but not suicidal. I wasn't sure that it was much of an improvement. Not feeling like ending it all actually bothered me a little. I tried to get back to that feeling, to the Eeyore in me who could so easily disappear into the dark world of perpetual hopelessness and gloom, but I couldn't quite touch bottom. The drug created a sort of psychic life preserver that prevented me from drowning, all my best efforts notwithstanding. It lifted me enough to avoid drowning but not so much that I couldn't still feel the emotional sharks circling: Loneliness, Heartache, Sadness, Fear, Anger—even the Depression—were all still there, taking little chomps out of me as they passed. I had hoped that the medication would take away all the suffering; instead, it just forced me to deal with it.

This was a mixed blessing. I was grateful not to feel so weighed down and consumed by darkness and sorrow, but being pulled back from the abyss meant having to deal with the mess that still spread out into eternity in front of me. I could no longer simply float away on my sea of sadness, never to be heard from again. Medication took me out of my North Korean exile and back to a more normal, less life-threatening depression: the DMZ, as it were. It still wasn't pretty or pleasant there, not colorful or vibrant. The most I could say was that the tiny, white tablets kept me alive, but I was not sure for what purpose.

*FEBRUARY 17*
*I am lonely beyond description: a deep down lonely with a restless lonely in the middle and a scared lonely layered on top of that. The house is heavy in its stillness. The hallway is dark and I always feel spooked, as though I might see Andrew's ghost sitting at the computer in his room. I am incredibly lost and alone without my partner. It's as though we were traveling together on*

*some path through the woods when, all of a sudden, he vanished. I don't know where I am. I can't go back. I'm frightened to move ahead, and no helper has yet appeared.*

*Everyone asks if I am eating (yes), exercising (no)—not the point whatsoever. I am most certainly not all dead, yet I am definitely not completely alive either. I am half-dead. Dead inside. On the outside, I am walking around, raking leaves, drinking lattes. Inside, though, I am gone, and I don't know where I went, or when or if I'll be back, or how to get back if I even wanted to.*

I did not want to face the piercing pain and undeniable aware-ness that the person who was my life and my future was no longer here. I did not want to do the work that was going to be required to come to terms with this dreadful, new reality. But the rest of the world was continuing on, with or without me, and if I were not going to permanently absent myself from this forward impulse, then I had to face it head on. I had to cry and mourn, but I also had to fashion some sort of new life for myself—one that I could not envision; one that I wasn't sure I wanted to envision.

I began taking walks in the historic cemetery, up on the hill. I took Bella to roam in the quiet and to place myself in the midst of death; since it haunted me anyway, I decided that I might as well look it in the face. I walked slowly, reading the inscriptions on the old stones, most of which dated back to the late 1800s.

During one of these walks, I stopped at a particularly old and beautiful plot, and carefully studied the dates and names that were slowly fading into the granite. Five of the couple's children had died before they reached the age of six; they lost one child every year, some-times two. *How did that mother, that woman, survive such pain?* I won-dered. But she did survive, well beyond the deaths of her five children.

As I stood reading the names and dates, I slipped into reverie, seeing the women as they stood in this selfsame spot, watching them lay their children in the ground. I tried to imagine what went through their hearts and minds. People say that losing a child is the worst loss there is; I doubted this, based on what I was feeling, but of course I couldn't say for certain, not being a parent; just looking at the size of the tiny graves made me want to weep.

My mother continued to insist that Andrew's death was wrong, that he was too young to die, that it was "not his time." Standing there in the graveyard on the hill, watching deer pick their way silently among the headstones, I realized that it was a common thing, this dying young, and I was, in a sense, in good company. I was not alone, although it felt that way.

From a more distanced, objective point of view, perhaps even a more spiritual perspective, someone dying young is really no different from someone who is old and infirm dropping off the twig; less expected, perhaps, and harder to accept. But left to its own devices, death, like birth, comes when it's good and ready.

There are no guarantees on our shelf life. We make up dates in our heads. We imagine that a person will live for a certain span of time, but it's all just an imagined number that we turn into a promise in our minds. We convince ourselves that a person ought to live for eighty years. Not so. We just made it up, because it's damned hard (and this, the understatement of a lifetime) to lose someone you love before you expect to.

I did not believe that Andrew's death was wrong or untimely; it apparently *was* his time, even if the rest of us could not make sense of that. But believing this did not make my process any easier. Understanding that a person's time is up is one thing; mourning that person's departure is another thing altogether.

I walked back down the hill and into town. I stopped at the post office to pick up my mail and then went across the street to the Good Bean, where we always had our coffee together, and ordered my double hazelnut latte. As I stood waiting at the counter, I opened an official-looking envelope. A slip of paper fell out and drifted to the worn, wide-planked floor. I picked it up and turned it over: it was a check. My eyes quickly scanned the paper: it was the life insurance money. I had never seen so much money, never held so much in my hand. For any other reason, seeing this would have made my heart leap. A lump began to form in my throat as a wave of thoughts and feelings rushed through me.

My husband was gone—forever. I would never, ever see him again, never hear his voice or smell his cologne or touch his hair. My friend, my companion, my husband, was smashed to pieces and this is what I got in compensation: a little slip of paper. It was as if his whole self had been reduced to this one, small, thin sheet and handed back to me, two dimensional and lifeless. A visceral, grotesque feeling came over me, as though I were experiencing the transubstantiation turned upside down: the body and blood of my beloved had become only this. This was all I could have of him now: something abstract and flat and cold.

Objectively, I supposed that I should feel a bit happy—or at least relieved—but I was not objective. No matter how many figures were on that piece of paper, nothing could compensate me for my loss or fill the crater formed by his absence. It was repulsive, this surreal experience of my husband, of Andrew, flattened and falling out of an envelope. It made me ill.

# 16

*FEBRUARY 22*
*NOON – FILLMORE STREET*
*I am in San Francisco to see friends. It is an astoundingly beauti-*
*ful day. It's the kind of day that urges me to live here forever: a*
*sunny, warm Saturday with streams of people passing by the café*
*where I sit at a small, sidewalk table, watching it all.*

*I am half gone. I sit and feel myself breathe. I go over a thousand*
*things in my mind, a thousand images of us, a thousand thoughts*
*of love. Everything inside my skin feels shattered into a million*
*pieces. I've never imagined such complete, internal devastation. I*
*feel like a shredded flag, flapping in the wind, tatters of what I*
*was. I am invisible. I am nobody. I am nothing.*

*I see a white Saab drive by and my heart lifts for a fragment of a*
*moment, but Andrew is gone, and someone else is driving his car,*
*and someone else has our dog, and someone else has taken my soul*
*out of my body, and this sad shell just sits and breathes.*

There was a push-pull to being back in San Francisco: on the one hand, it felt comforting, familiar, and full of happy reminders; on the other hand, those happy reminders simultaneously stage-whispered to me: *It's all gone.* I thought about moving back, but the busyness of the place, the energy of it, combined with my multitudinous memories, made it overwhelming. I couldn't imagine being here alone, without Andrew.

So at the end of my trip—after the walks on the beach with girl-friends and warm, balmy weather, the special gathering at the clinic with all of my colleagues, sleep, Chinese food, and hugs—I returned home, leaving the warmth and love for my slow, safe, solitary cocoon.

The FAA report arrived on February 27. It ruled the crash "pilot error." If they can't find an obvious mechanical failure in the wreckage, it's ruled "pilot error" by default. This doesn't mean that something couldn't have gone wrong mid-flight, or that the student didn't do something stupid and then lie about it, but there was no way of knowing. Well, there was one way, but it was hardly the sort of information that the FAA would take into consideration; I don't think that dreams are factored into their rulings.

I had recently dreamt that Andrew was standing with me as I was getting ready in the bathroom. I was overjoyed to see him. I asked him what had happened and told him the FAA said that the accident was due to pilot error. He rolled his eyes and looked hugely frustrated. I knew that he was angry about the ruling, and angry that he had no opportunity to defend himself, and tell the truth about the accident.

Then he said, "The firecrackers wouldn't fire," which I understood immediately to mean that the engine would not reengage.

I told him that I had to go to an appointment and asked if he would still be here when I returned. He shook his head no. I told him that I loved him.

The FAA report detailed the testimony that Andrew's student Curtis, who was in the plane that day, gave about the minutes preceding the crash. I read his words carefully, hungry for information, for clues. According to Curtis, Andrew had asked for help with the rudder. Curtis had depressed one of the pedals and Andrew had barked at him.

"NO! Not *that* rudder!"

What did that mean? Did his student inadvertently seal their fate by hitting the wrong rudder? I had so many questions.

Mostly, however, I just wanted to hear Andrew's final words, to hear about my husband straight from the only witness, but the detail in the report was frustratingly unsatisfying. God knows what Curtis had edited out when he spoke to the FAA. He could have said anything, made up some story or conveniently left out something, and no one would be the wiser. The guy had been in three major aircraft incidents—wasn't that just the least little bit odd? Suspicious? Why wouldn't he speak to me? He never even sent a note.

It infuriated me to think that I would never know what happened, that I would always have suspicions. I didn't want to punish his student; I wasn't looking to blame anyone. Well, for a while I blamed him, but I couldn't for long. Everything happens for a reason; I believed that. Still, I couldn't stand not knowing the truth.

Although it was tempting to see Andrew's death as a suicide (for me because of Andrew's unhappiness, and for the insurance people because of the brief amount of time that elapsed between the purchase of life insurance and the accident), I knew it wasn't. If he'd wanted to commit suicide, it would have been easy enough to go up and crash by himself; he flew every day. But he did not do that. His moral and ethical nature would never have allowed him to put someone else at risk. No, I concluded, if it was a suicide, it was an unconscious one.

# 17

The arrival of spring brought the reemergence of my hormones along with the pansies: hormonal prodding that confused me and made life messy. I started tango lessons with Keith, which I liked. We made out one night in his car following class. I felt fine about it when it happened; I had no guilt. I could hardly sleep after rolling in at one o'clock in the morning, and I was up at 6:45. It was wonderful to kiss someone, to be engulfed by that feeling, to be touched and spoken to in that way, to be desired. I realized how I much I had missed that and for how long.

The encounter left me momentarily flushed with life. The following evening, as I sat listening to music in front of a fire, drinking an Old Fashioned, I had the odd sense of enjoying being single. For a brief moment, I was lifted out of my gloom and resurfaced into life. It was an enormous relief.

I had no idea, of course, that this sort of interlude is completely normal, that the intrusion of desire in the midst of death is part of the manic-depressive nature of mourning. There is a misconception that nothing penetrates mourning, but that is not true. Mourning is a meander: an undulating, confusing panoply of emotions. It's all your cells gone wild in a dramatic reconfiguration. The brief flare of passion is a sort of quickening, letting you know that there is life yet inside of you, just not quite fully formed, not completely ready to survive out in the world.

I called Keith in the flush of bourbon and desire, and asked him to come over. He questioned the wisdom of this, but I insisted. For mostly the wrong reasons, albeit understandable ones, I wanted to make love, to be in someone's arms. It had been almost a year since I'd made love or been held, and I missed that feeling. At this moment, the woman encased in the widow had needs: she wanted Keith.

There was also some measure of retaliation in my actions. Andrew's private forays into various and unusual on-line sexual explorations—forays I discovered when subscriptions for pornographic sites came up for renewal in our email—felt like a breach of faith; it hurt and angered me and it strengthened my sense of self-righteousness. If Andrew had been doing *that*, I rationalized, then I could do *this*. As if anybody cared.

Earlier that day, I had purchased a black chemise and a new bra at Victoria's Secret, and then I bought some flowers. I'd changed the sheets and shaved my legs. Throughout these preparations, I was both subject and observer. I watched this woman—me—doing these things as if she were not me, as though I were having an out-of-body experience. I was preparing myself for this liaison while simultaneously denying that I was preparing myself.

By the time Keith finally appeared it was late and I had already given up and gone to bed. It all felt a little contrived and after the fact, but I asked him in anyway. He looked tired and ruddy; likely he had just come from some bar or maybe some other bedroom; he was just Don Juanish enough to do that. We went into the bedroom and sat down on the bed. It felt stilted, like teenage virgins sneaking in a quickie when the parents are gone.

The tryst was not what I had hoped it would be. I cried, quietly, throughout: cried for it not being Andrew; cried for the realization that, in making love to another man, I was officially acknowledging that I was alone. I cried because it did not make me feel loved. Even though it had been many months since I'd had sex, it was not what I needed or even really wanted. Afterward, I wasn't exactly sure why I had done it. It felt a bit like having to operate on myself without benefit of an anesthetic.

For days afterward, I analyzed the whole experience. It was odd to make love with someone new, even when that someone was an old lover. On a very banal level, it was eye opening to have sex with someone else. I didn't realize how different and, in this case, better it could be: longer, more intense, and more satisfying.

I'd felt self-conscious having a different nakedness beside me— my friend, not my husband. It felt adulterous. Back when I met Keith, I was just out of college and as naïve about love as any twenty-two-year-old. Our affair was ardent and adulterous; it had ended his second marriage just months after he'd wed. Nine months after I met him, I moved to San Francisco, knowing that my life lay elsewhere. But our sexually charged friendship persisted.

Now, finally both truly single and available, it still felt adulterous. It was strange to be without Andrew, strange to be with Keith, strange to be doing this, three months after the loss. I wondered if it would feel much different if it had been a year later. Was it really about the first time after Andrew or something else?

I had once thought that I would wait to make love until I was in love again; now I was thinking that I wanted to stay single for a while and have a lover, or lovers. Making love without being in love was a different kind of experience than marital love; it wasn't bad, just detached. It was fun in a way, more powerful and less spiritual. But I missed being married, the sureness and comfort of it. I only wished that Andrew and I had been able to keep the passion, too. This was certainly part of my mourning: not just for the person I'd lost, but also for the love affair that died before he was killed.

The act of making love also forced the question of Andrew's gender confusion to the forefront of my thoughts. I began having dreams that clearly raised the gender identity question that was lingering in my mind, perhaps because now it was safer to look at it. Did Andrew's death, in some ironic way, save me from losing us? Did it save us from torment? I was hesitant to examine this thorny issue, fearful that, if I looked at it, all my happy memories would be stripped away, leaving only disillusionment and hurt, but I couldn't avoid it.

To the rest of the world, ours was a tragic story with a clear throughline, but not for me. There were all sorts of twists and turns, and things that didn't make complete sense, things that I needed to straighten out. I needed to see if I could absolve Andrew of any ulterior motives in marrying me, and absolve myself for any denial I may have harbored in loving and marrying him. I had to work through it all to find a conclusion for myself, to know what was true, so I could return to simply being the grieving widow that the rest of the world saw.

I went through a protracted, internal, mental trial, putting myself through rigorous cross-examination:

*Did he really love me?* Yes, Andrew loved me. I felt his love. It was palpable.

*Did I really love him?* Yes, that much I knew without question.

*Did he use me?* No, he was not that kind of person.

*Why did I marry him knowing that he had sexual identity issues?* He said that he was over the gender muddle, and I chose to believe him, and why wouldn't I? Why would I say "no" to love because of a "what if," as in, "What if he's not telling me the truth? What if he still wants to cross-dress or become a woman?" He told me that he was done. He told me that he loved me. He *showed* me that he loved me. We had everything going for us. Why wouldn't I hold fast to that which was real and in my hands? Do you choose not to be with someone you love out of fear of what *might* happen?

It was all so confusing and hard, this questioning. Only he could answer so many unanswerable questions, and he was gone. It was painful to be reminded that our life together was not idyllic. I had forgotten, in these initial months, how upset I was with our relationship, how estranged we'd become. It wasn't that I'd been in denial; it's just that the mind and the heart like to remember the joy and the love, not the problems. The problems end with death—at least some of them—but the love goes on.

I began watching a television show called *Touched by an Angel*, whose premise is that three angels (the first an Irish female; the second a big, black Della Reese; the third a long-haired white guy) are sent by God to help some poor, conflicted soul, and to let them know that God loves them. Watching it was a guilty pleasure: I would have been mortified had anyone known. It was contrived and squeaky clean and saccharine. Initially I liked it because it made me feel good, but soon I became obsessed with the Angel of Death. I found him sexy and compassionate: a potent combination. I watched every week, just to cry and see the hot angel, whose name—I discovered when I sat down to write him a fan letter—was John Dye.

# 18

*Brother Hawk circles*
*Red feathers on a blue sky*
*Waits for me to know*

This haiku came to me early one April morning as I walked Bella home and saw him again, making large spirals high above me. Hawks were always near me now, following me, circling. As soon as I came out of the house, they would appear above me. When I told Nicole about it, she laughed, but I knew. Watching the hawk that crystalline April morning, I finally understood that Andrew had kept his promise never to leave me. His body had certainly left, and I missed it, but he was still there, wherever "there" was. I just wished that I could talk to him.

I knew that the Paxil was helping me to think more clearly, to cope with the depression, but those benefits came with side-effects: I was all flattened out. My passion was quenched, and I felt like a zombie. This was disconcerting, to be without my usual, deep feelings—feelings that seemed to have gone away or hidden themselves somewhere. I couldn't even conjure them up with effort. There was no deep sadness, no overwhelming despair, no wrenching fear, hardly anything. This frustrated me. It's one thing not to feel like killing oneself, that's all well and good (maybe); it's quite another thing not to feel at all.

And so, eight weeks into my Paxil journey, I decided to go off the medication. I didn't feel unusually or dangerously depressed, I didn't like the way I was feeling—or not feeling—and I didn't much like the thought that I *needed* medication. So I stopped taking it and, two weeks later, I crashed in a big way. When you're on antidepressants, it's easy to forget how depressed you are underneath them; discouraged, I resumed taking it.

Ainslie and I were planning a trip to Mexico for late April, for what would have been my first wedding anniversary. Ainslie was palpably excited, but I was ambivalent, oscillating between the thought that it was a bad idea and the vague hope that it might be a good distraction.

I confessed my ambivalence to Nicole, who immediately castigated me for "focusing so much on the negative." I thought her frustration with me was absurdly unfair. Why on Earth would I be cheerful? Besides, I didn't think that the entire world was black; I was aware of beauty and love, but I still felt lonely, angry, sad, and scared despite these things. That's just the way it was.

Her seeming impatience with my mourning, my suffering, mirrored the rest of the world; everyone wants you to "get over it" and "move on" two weeks after your world has imploded. No one seems to have the understanding or the emotional maturity to wait for you as you journey through loss; it's get on with it or adios. Nicole's criticism made me feel bad for feeling bad—a double dose of depressing.

I stood one evening in the kitchen listening to Enya, wishing I were waiting for Andrew to come home from work. I wanted to make cookies but had no one to bake them for. The sadness was as penetrating and subtle as the cold that I constantly felt, except when I was in bed, warm under our comforters. Unfortunately, a well-developed tension headache was squeezing out any chance for incubation. I was in pain and restless, wanting to do something, not knowing what that something was.

I thought about my brother and his beautiful wife. I envied them. I thought how they probably didn't truly appreciate their good fortune in having each other. No one does until they lose someone, not really. I thought of all the things people worry about and spend their time doing, when none of it really matters. The only thing that matters is love. That's all there is. It is all so precious, this life, and so ephemeral. I'd spent too much of my life living for the future. I wished that I had lived more in the present—not this present, though; the *past* present. I didn't want this present at all.

I took Bella out for our morning walk after a fitful night's sleep. It was the only thing I did that felt a little good; walking with her made me feel vaguely normal, and I liked being out in nature. We walked into town and up the hill to the Britt gardens, where it was quiet and we could walk on the trails and see the wildflowers that were starting to sprout up.

On this particular morning, a wisteria vine, not yet in leaf, caught my attention. I stopped to examine it and noticed two, thin tendrils, entwined, coiled around each other, swaying in the April air. The image was entrancing. I looked more closely and saw that one of the tendrils was dead, broken off down low, but the living one was still clinging, wrapped around its dead partner. When I carefully unraveled them, the live one retained the shape it had when it had been curled around its former lover. It seemed sad yet somehow reassuring in its shape.

Despite the symbolic beauty and messages I was receiving from hawks and wisteria vines, I was devastatingly lonely. I'd been alone now for a million years, four months and four days. The phone rarely rang. Every time I passed through the living room on the way to the kitchen, I glanced toward the answering machine, as if a secret, silent message might have been left while I was in the other room.

I was on a forced march through grief: no stops, no detours, no phone calls, no companionship—just me and my cloven heart and thoughts and words and phrases that came with the cadence of my solitary cortege.

*Perhaps*, I mused, *the thoughts and feelings wouldn't come, couldn't come, if I were otherwise occupied by fun, joy, titillation, or an embrace*— all the things I desired and was denied by God or by circumstance. *Perhaps*, I told myself, *something good would come of all this aloneness.*

In her condolence letter, my clinical supervisor had said, "I hope you will wrestle with this angel until it blesses you."

Maybe that's what was happening. Maybe God was forcing this isolation on me to keep me wrestling with the angel. *What a beautiful phrase for such a hellish ordeal*, I mused. I kept pointing a finger heavenward. "This had better be good," I'd say, looking heavenward to where people imagine that something dwells, moving the pieces around. There was no answer. I wanted to believe that something positive awaited me in this nightmare, but I secretly worried that I was creating a fantasy to rationalize my loneliness.

I knew that I should try to cultivate some friendships or go to a support group, but the thought of listening to other peoples' stories of loss sounded particularly dreadful. I didn't want to hear their stories, didn't want the comparisons. My grief was my own; I didn't want to be around more sadness, sitting on some sofa while everyone looked miserable and cried into Kleenex, each of us silently believing that we had it worse.

No thanks. Knowing that other people were suffering did not soothe me; it just made me sadder. So instead, I would go to a nursery to look at flowers, or to the drugstore to meander a while. During one of these sojourns, I found myself standing in Rite Aid in front of a huge display of Hallmark greeting cards. I picked one from the condolence section and read, "When one door closes, another opens." I shoved the card back into its slot and began to seethe. Then I began to talk back to the card rack.

"Maybe the door just closes," I said sarcastically. "Maybe there *isn't* another door. Or maybe the doors were all open until God slammed them shut, one by one."

I looked around but saw no one quietly calling 911 to have me removed and evaluated.

All these platitudes, all the trite condolences, had some truth to them, but that didn't prevent them from rubbing me very wrong; reading or hearing them felt like someone slapping my sunburned back. It had been a major miracle for me to get to the stupid store in the first place. The very last thing I needed, the last thing any person in grief needs, is a fucking platitude.

My grandmother was infamous for her unhelpful platitudes. One of her favorites was: "Just tie another knot in your rope and hang on."

*Oh gosh*, I always wanted to say, *is that all I need to do? I feel so much better now. That really did the trick!*

As I emerged from my emotional fugue on the drive home, I began to wonder what, exactly, I was so mad about. Almost immediately I realized that the cards were the stand-in for my displaced anger toward all the well-meaning but inept people who tried to smooth it all out and make it okay, instead of just listening, just acknowledging the pain. My anger had nowhere to go, so the inanimate well wishes smiling out at me from the card rack in the middle of Rite Aid became the target.

As if to emphasize my frustration and try my patience, or lack thereof, that same evening I ran into two of Andrew's colleagues, a couple, at the Bella Union Bar. It was the first time that I'd seen them since the memorial. As we talked about Andrew and his death, which I did not want to be doing as I went out to avoid such things, Mary inadvertently stepped right into the molten core of my anger.

"Well," she said, "maybe God needed him."

I stood quietly, incredulous that an intelligent adult could say something so patently ridiculous. An omnipotent God, by definition, lacks nothing; *ipso facto*, God did not *need* Andrew. It would have been laughable except that I was not in a laughing mood.

I wanted to say, "That's just plain bullshit, Mary." Instead, I said, "I have a hard time believing that."

"Well," she demurred, "my Christian faith ..."

"I have my faith," I interrupted, although it was riddled with doubt at this point, "and I have a hard time accepting that."

Mary looked uncomfortable, glancing quickly at her blond-haired husband, Tim, who was listening wordlessly next to her.

"Well," she said, "if I lost my husband, I guess ..."

I stopped listening, having decided that there was nothing more she could say that I would possibly be interested in hearing. What I wanted to do was get right up in her face and tell her exactly what I thought. I'd never felt that strong an urge before.

It was offensive when someone didn't get it, when they didn't understand the depth and breadth of my loss. Not that it was their fault; it wasn't. Innocence and naiveté are not faults, but they are intensely maddening and frustrating to someone who is in the midst of terrible suffering. The innocent comments, although meant to console, serve only to irritate. Platitudes, religious and otherwise, come across as simple-minded arrogance. I tuned back in just in time to hear Mary validate these beliefs.

"Really," she was saying, "you should be happy."

I stared at her hard and long, incredulous. I could not fucking believe this woman. I should be happy? Happy for what, exactly? I *was* happy that Andrew did not to have to struggle and suffer with his gender issues—something she, of course, knew nothing about. This woman, who knew nothing about Andrew, or about me, or about what it was like to have your heart mangled, chose to bypass empathy and go straight to sermonizing. "God needed him. You should be happy." What shit.

People were incredibly uncomfortable around me after my father died, and again when I was widowed. On one end of the spectrum there were those who avoided the obvious like the plague. They pretended that they didn't see me. They fumbled for words or decided not to mention my loss at all, thinking, perhaps, that it would be best not to bring it up. *Death is just so darned awkward and unpleasant. Let's talk about something else.* This avoidance exacerbated my grief, the lack of ritual and common courtesy underscoring my loneliness.

Then there were people like Mary, who said all kinds of wrong and stupid things in their attempts to be helpful, such as, "I lost a friend," or—and this is the God's honest truth—"I lost a sheep once, so I know how it is," or the ever popular, "He's in a better place now." I wished that people would just say, "I'm so sorry for your loss," instead of trying to make it okay with their insipid remarks, their compassion trumped by their personal discomfort with death.

I wanted to educate people, to give them some guidelines, as much for myself as for them; dealing with total ineptitude on almost a daily basis was wearing me out. I wanted to tell people to say *something,* but for the love of God, *don't* offer lukewarm platitudes. Just ask, "How are you?" or say that you're at a loss for words; that's far kinder and more welcome than silence or, worse still, "It was God's will" or "You'll marry again" or "I know how you feel," because it wasn't, that's not the point, and no you don't.

I was dismayed to discover that there is no longer any collective etiquette for dealing with loss in our culture. Sometime around the turn of the last century we abandoned the God of Death. Perhaps nuclear warfare made the scale of death too large and overwhelming.

Perhaps Christianity, with its emphasis on heaven, bypassed death entirely en route to eternal life. Perhaps, as an immigrant nation, we left our rituals behind when we arrived in the New World, focused on the future. Whatever the reasons, we seem to have discarded death, and we go to great lengths to skirt the whole messy, loathsome business of suffering.

Because our culture has done everything in its power to deny death, we have lost the ritual wisdom of how to cope with it when it arrives—which, strangely, it always does. Neglecting the fact that the endless cycle of life includes loss, and a long lamentation for that loss, leaves us unprepared and disoriented when death comes.

There is a peculiar proclivity in this country that wants everything connected to death to go away and be cleaned up quickly. In its zeal, it attempts to make a recovery before anyone has had the chance to grieve or mourn. A hurricane sweeps a city off the map, or a bomber destroys hundreds of lives, or some sociopath guns down a group of innocents and two days later there is talk of "letting the healing begin." It's not normal.

Being a widow at thirty-two was like becoming The Ghost of Christmas Future. When people looked at me, they couldn't help but face the brutal reality that terrible things happen to people—things you'd like to think cannot, will not, happen to you; but they can and they do and I was living proof. My very presence raised the specter of death, and they couldn't make me go away. My presence haunted them with a reality that they did not want and could not clean up.

I did not like being the ghost; I didn't ask for this.

⌒⌒

I was living on a diet consisting almost entirely of Raisin Bran, bagels, artichokes, and lattes: The Death Diet, I called it. As with The Divorce Diet, it was proving exceptionally effective at shedding unwanted pounds—except I didn't have any unwanted pounds to lose. I was becoming slightly skeletal. Food had become uniformly uninteresting: an annoying necessity.

I'd always possessed an unquiet mind, and that was more true now than ever, diligent efforts at yoga notwithstanding. Toweling off after my shower one morning, I noticed the early budding of what looked like a mole or some sort of odd growth on my chest, and my first thought was, *Oh, God. I'm really, truly growing old.*

This was not a new thought. Andrew used to laugh at me and tell me something to make me laugh when I said such things. Besides, we were going to grow old together, so what the hell? I wasn't laughing now. I was thinking about my body, how old I felt, and how one day, unless I wanted to spend the next number of decades alone, someone else was going to look at my naked body. At some point, I'd be obligated to enter the dating pool, exposing my literal and metaphorical warts and all.

That thought was nauseating. I'd just been fortunate enough to leave that overcrowded public pool. I sighed. I looked at myself in the mirror. Who would find me attractive, let alone beautiful? I looked pale and tired and flat. I was about as hot and sexy as a potato. I even had a growth like a potato eye, sticking out on my chest.

I couldn't tell anyone this stuff because they'd laugh at me; they'd tell me I was ridiculous, that I was young, that these things didn't matter. But they *did* matter. On the level of the cosmos? No. Compared to losing Andrew? No. But as a female on the planet? You bet they mattered.

How could I admit to anyone that I was worried about dating, about finding a man, about having sex? I was embarrassed and uncomfortable even thinking such thoughts. It was hard to be negotiating this terrain of half-widow, half-woman. Half of me was in death, in another world, but the fact was that I was still here, still alive, still in a body—as unhappy as I may have felt about that particular fact— and as long I was here, I was obligated to navigate certain annoying, mundane realities, like aging and dating.

In the meantime, however, I was alone and I was lonely. Loneliness, it was now clear to me, was the worst of all feelings to endure, and one I'd experienced way too much in my short existence, but that was clearly what I had to do: endure it. Knowing this made it no more palatable, but I was hopeful that it would make it somehow easier to suffer. Resistance, as they say, is futile.

So I tried not to resist. I allowed myself to feel frightened and sad that I could no longer hear the sound of Andrew's voice in my memory. I could hear certain words and phrases, but his daily parlance had slipped away from me. I'd lost his sound and his smell and his touch. I could still see him, in pictures and in dreams and in my mind's eye, but that was small consolation.

# 19

APRIL 15, PUERTA VALLARTA
*I am in Puerto Vallarta at the old El Camino Real Hotel. Ainslie
and I arrived yesterday to overcast skies and heavy humidity. It
was a very long day of travel and waiting. I felt good until we
got here, but being here is very hard. The sound of the surf makes
me extremely sad. The shoreline and beach take me back to Maui
and our honeymoon, and the sweetness of those days that were only
a year ago. I almost can't stand it.*

*All the things that one could imagine would be painful are, like
the couples holding hands or the parents with the new baby, playing together in the sand. Everything, even the unexpected things,
hurt: the air, the pool, the candlelight, the swim-up bar, the loneliness, the aloneness, the not being loved, the brevity, the snatched-
away quality of it. Everything reminds me of something else. I
feel as though I am watching a movie in which I am the lead: a
witness to my own pain. I feel like hell and I look like hell. I feel
like hiding.*

*I don't want to travel anymore; it's just too painful. The expec-
tation is that it will be a relief, a distraction, but it's just the
opposite. It forces thoughts and memories to surface. I've spent a lot
of money to be so unhappy. I love being with Ainslie; she's funny
and easy and so loving and patient with my heartache. It's not
her, it's here: anywhere away from home.*

Puerto Vallarta was a strange place, cobbled together and ram-
shackle, dissected by rambling, narrow streets and alleyways that
led to unexpected plazas and hidden places. It felt empty in many ways.
I couldn't find a good drink or a vegetable to save my life. I couldn't

find anything interesting or especially beautiful because I couldn't get out of myself.

I bought a Cuban cigar and stood alone on the beach one night, watching a comet slide across the black sky and thinking of Andrew. I smoked the cigar because it made me think of him, but it wasn't good. I wanted *him* to be smoking it. Nothing was good without him. Nothing satisfied me, nothing tasted good, no place felt good. I stood there in the dark, ankle deep in the ocean, brooding. I wanted the plurals back: "ours," "we," "us." I was half of "us," even if I were a whole "me," which I doubted.

*There's a good riddle*, I thought. *What is whole and half at the same time?*

*Me.*

After my walk I returned to the room, where Ainslie lay sprawled on her bed writing in her journal. I sat down next to her and she read me a beautiful passage in which she likened me to a walnut shell devoid of its meat. I didn't feel that hard on the outside, but I did feel as though my insides had been ripped out—not removed; ripped. I lay with her and cried for a while. It helped to cry, at least temporarily.

I closed my eyes, purposely trying to escape into a better, sweeter time. I felt Andrew's neck with my lips. I saw him fill out his blue polo shirt and his loafers and the wedding ring on his finger. He had once told me that if I ever doubted his love, I should look at my beautiful engagement ring and be reminded of how much I was loved, and always would be. I could feel him holding my hand in his and hear him telling me, so seriously and lovingly, those reassuring words, and I wondered if they were still true. I prayed and clung tightly to the hope that they were. I needed him to love me still. Forget therapy, forget emotional and political correctness; I was half a person without him. I was incomplete. Were that not true, I would not hurt so much.

The sun finally emerged on the third day of our Mexican meander and Ainslie disappeared to the beach, where she plopped herself in her boy shorts and bikini top onto a chaise lounge, determined to get a tan as she lay drinking banana daiquiris, brought by the beach boy. Being blonde, blue-eyed and sun-challenged, I preferred the shade. This required frequent rearranging of furniture and umbrellas in order to be protected from the Mexican sun and still be able to chat.

Ainslie made fun of me, in my hat and long-sleeved, white linen shirt, but she accepted my disability—disabilities, to be precise. This widow role was a major disability: no ability to relax, to truly enjoy, to feel deep happiness or peace. Not much fun for a friend who needed a raucous vacation.

I lay staring out at the surf. All I could think was that I didn't want to be there, and I didn't know why. It was quiet, it was beautiful, it was new—and I desperately wanted to go home. This was not going the way that I hoped it would. I couldn't lighten up. In fact, the opposite was happening: I was getting heavier and heavier. When I awoke each morning, I wished that I hadn't; I wished that I could sleep the whole day away. This trip was making me very anxious about going to Cape Cod later in the summer to bury Andrew's ashes. I was afraid to go anywhere, scared that it would feel like this, or worse.

Ainslie's sun worship, coupled with a bad lobster, left her completely incapacitated and bedridden the following day. Her entire body was a hot, bright, vermilion red against the white sheets of her bed; she was unable to move or roll over for fear that her crisped skin might crackle and break off. The only time she did move was to painfully throw herself up and into the bathroom, a few feet away, where the lobster made its final appearance; then she resumed moaning and sleeping. My white-shirted practicality vindicated, I stared out of the floor-to-ceiling windows in our room, looking at the dull, overcast sky and listening to the relentless surf. This sucked—*all of it.*

I left Ainslie to sleep off her multiple maladies and went for a walk. As I meandered aimlessly, I cursed Andrew in my head. I told him that I hated him for leaving me so alone, so bereft, and then I apologized. Then I cursed him again. I walked, oblivious to my surroundings, lost and wallowing in my pain, unable to extricate myself from the torment.

I was a ghost; I didn't fit anywhere or with anyone. I didn't belong. My future stretched out in front of me, horrible and eternal, like Velveeta cheese. There was no one who saw me or knew me deeply or fully any longer, no one who could tease me and make me smile. I had felt safe and seen and loved with Andrew; now I felt erased, invisible. We all feel alive in relationship to another; when that other is gone, where do we go? Are we still alive, still visible?

I wondered why I felt so utterly annihilated when the truth was that Andrew and I were facing a serious impasse, at least at the end. But the truth was that ninety-five percent of what Andrew and I had in the years we were together—not what was coming or what might have been, but the majority of what we actually shared—was wonderful. How glad could I be for a fictitious future that was spared?

I had never stopped loving Andrew, even with the emergence of our troubles. When he died, our troubles died with him, but at the cost of losing my partner and my best friend, a person whom I adored and with whom I had spent four years of my life. I didn't just lose Andrew; I lost myself and my future and my dreams. The Kate I was with Andrew, the Kate I used to be, was burned up as surely as Ainslie's freckled skin—worse. It was blackened, disintegrated, and I did not know how to rise from those ashes. I would have preferred to lie down in them and die.

Ainslie and I decided to return home early. Our trip, on the whole, had been a flop, ruined by sunburn, parasites, and grief. Ainslie twisted and tilted awkwardly to lay her head on my lap, fidgeting uncomfortably in our cramped coach seats during the flight back to San Francisco; all I could think about was how desperately I wanted to escape from the heavy weight of her head dropping repeatedly on my legs. We'd had no real fun, no escape from our quotidian lives. I felt stupid for having thought that I could escape myself, and guilty for using up Ainslie's vacation time.

When we landed, Ainslie plopped into a waiting wheelchair, and I pushed her slumped form down to baggage claim, relieved that the trip was over. By the time we stuffed ourselves into her friend Thomas's Triumph, Ainslie had made a remarkable recovery. She and Thomas laughed and shrieked at private jokes, Ainslie hitting him on the arm in mocked amazement at the gossip he shared.

I sat crumpled in a ball in the back, annoyed at their loudness, their joy, and Ainslie's sudden wellness. *What had happened to me?* I wondered, silently. *How did I end up like so much baggage, stuffed in the back of a stranger's car? Where was my fine and beautiful life?*

I spent that night on Ainslie's couch, quiet and grumpy, watching her dance with Thomas around her living room, still shrieking and shaking the Native American rattle that I had made for her as a sacred and special offering of friendship and love. I was hurt and irritated that she was mocking it, abusing the gift that I had so laboriously created. I wanted it back.

I wanted everything back.

⌒⌒

I lay in bed, listening to the April rain spattering against the bedroom windows. It was a warm rain and a spring-moist scent filled the air. I was relieved to be quiet, to be lying in my own bed, to be where I could comfortably (a relative term) be myself. It was the only place I sort of belonged. Big Dave had stopped me on the sidewalk outside the J'Ville Tavern earlier in the day and offered me some fresh asparagus and a birthday ride in his "cowdelac"—an early seventies, pale yellow Cadillac with the roof sawed off and longhorns attached to the front.

Now it was almost midnight, and I sat propped up, writing in my journal. I glanced at the clock. One year ago at this time, our rehearsal dinner was just coming to a wonderful, happy close in preparation for the day to come. We'd had such fun. The clouds broke up just as the dinner had ended, giving way to a glorious pink-and-orange sunset, fifty stories above San Francisco. Richard had played guitar and sung a calypso song he wrote just for the occasion. Everyone had toasted and fêted us. The three-dimensional biplane from the groom's cake, with its wombat pilot, was still in our freezer, carried all the way up Interstate 5 when we moved from San Francisco, lovingly cradled on ice against the August heat.

I remembered how, on the morning of our wedding, I had awakened at six a.m., too excited to sleep. I went out on our hotel balcony, in the middle of the Financial District, completely naked, and watched the sun come up over the bay. I was standing above the street where I had worked as a paralegal three years prior. Everything in my life had changed one hundred eighty degrees in a surreal, storybook fashion. I'd stood there with the cool air wrapping around my bare skin, watching the sun break over the eastern horizon, its rays touching the skyscrapers one by one, bringing to light the perfect day, the perfect life.

I awoke a few hours later, the morning of our first anniversary, not in a hotel but in my little town, looking at a sparkling azure sky outside my bedroom window. The temperature had dropped to below freezing the night before, and the pear trees in the orchard across the street had been watered by overhead sprinklers in order to freeze and protect their flowers. The trees, with their millions of white blossoms looking like cotton balls that had fallen from the sky, were dripping and shimmering in the sunlight, festooned with thousands of icicles. This blue-and-white effervescence, sparkling in the morning light, made me catch my breath. The analogy was not lost on me: A freeze protects the blossom; the fertile potential is there, safely hidden inside its cold cocoon.

I had missed much of the winter, being so frozen myself. It seemed that now, all of a sudden, it was spring, and blossoms were everywhere: first the plums, then the daffodils, followed by forsythia, apple and pear blossoms by the millions, quince and tulips and lilac. Everything was green and lush and wet. It had been pouring for days, with breaks of blue sky cradling big, white clouds. Tiny calves dotted the swaths of newly greened fields that bordered the route between my house and Nicole's apartment twenty miles south.

The lush rebirth did not include me, however. I did not feel at all spring-like, not new or fresh; I felt like a molting chicken: deformed, raggedy, miserable, and slightly pathetic, wanting to hide and protect myself. But, if I followed the analogy to its logical conclusion, I ought to come into full, glorious feather again one day. It was difficult to imagine, but that was the idea.

My thirty-third birthday arrived five days later, dawning clear and warm. In the days just before, I'd tried to think of what I wanted to do to mark the occasion, and had plopped a bottle of champagne in the fridge out of habit. Normally a good start, I had no desire to drink it by myself, and no idea what to do with it—or what to do in general. A high school friend sent an email, congratulating me on hitting thirty-three, the age at which, she reminded me, Jesus was crucified and Mozart died in poverty.

I wished that I were at the Park Hyatt, where Andrew and I were supposed to be. We would have come back from La Casa Que Canta in Zihuatinejo, Mexico, and overnighted in San Francisco to celebrate my birthday. We would have lain in bed with the city below us, ordered room service, sipped drinks on the balcony. He would have surprised me with a small but stupendous gift. I would have been in my heaven; instead, I was here.

I rolled out of bed, put on my robe, lit a candle and some sage, and went out into the backyard. I glanced around to see that no neighbors were out, untied my robe, and let it fall to the ground. Naked, I smudged myself with the sage smoke, trying to rid myself of negativity, sent some blessings to Andrew and some prayers to the future, and then smudged Bella, who stared at me dolefully, for good measure. I put my robe back on and went inside to open my gifts from Brooke and Barbara and Richard. Birthday festivities were over by eight a.m.

Later that evening, I sat outside at the Bella Union. The bar there had become my personal kitchen, the place I went when I needed not to be alone. I could have some dinner and remind myself that there was still life "out there." The waitress always talked with me, looking at me with compassion devoid of pity. Tonight, my manicurist and her coworkers came over to join me, ostensibly to celebrate my birthday but mostly to shake off their workweek. The volume and banality of their banter was rising in direct proportion to the number of drinks consumed.

I pushed myself into the corner of the booth and mentally disappeared, as I often did, escaping into thoughts of my past: my life in other, more pleasurable, more gratifying times. These thoughts were quickly punctured, however, by the inevitable, razor-sharp awareness of Andrew's absence and my perverse existence here, in this place, in this ridiculous setting where I didn't want to be. I didn't want to be in this bar, in this town, with these people on my birthday; I wanted to be somewhere wonderful and special with a wonderful and special someone. I wanted to feel loved again.

Being here with Andrew had felt serene and simple, but now it just felt tight and small. I felt abandoned in a familiar yet terrible place, trapped, unsure where to go or how to get away. Subsumed under the crushing weight of unhappiness and self-pity, I jostled my way out of the booth and, pleading tiredness, departed abruptly for home, back to my solitude and my journal, where I excoriated everyone and everything.

I looked at Andrew's picture, which sat on my side table, taken on his twenty-ninth birthday. A year before, on this day, we were in Florence, Italy, on our honeymoon. We'd taken a long walk and Andrew had bought me a dozen red roses. I remembered the pleasure of sitting together on a stone wall in a piazza, eating gelato, married all of five days. I belonged somewhere else. I belonged to another life, now gone, and to another life not yet arrived—which was to say that I belonged nowhere.

I lay in my stream of consciousness, letting it rush by me. As I mulled, some not-so-pleasant memories drifted by. Our life certainly hadn't been without its bumps; I was beginning to recollect these now, along with the happier memories. Andrew could be incredibly passive-aggressive, rebelling against others' attempts at control, or what he perceived to be control—like me nagging him to do the dishes—by simply shutting down and ignoring or "forgetting" to do them. We went round and round on that one. He'd let those damned dishes pile up for a week, let the dirty clothes basket grow into Mt. Fuji on the floor. I sighed, remembering the stupid fights. Those were gone, too.

This habit of retreating into memory was sometimes unbidden, but often it was purposeful. Memory was far preferable to my current life, particularly when I was in uncomfortable social situations. I could silently, invisibly withdraw to another time, another place, and be the person I used to be with the love I used to feel. In my memories, I was whole again. This retreat into the past helped me escape my present. Focusing on the beautiful parts, the joy, was a welcome break; it was like going to the movies in my mind, escaping my difficult reality.

The following day, I decided to begin to record my memories of Andrew so I didn't forget them, which I supposed in time I would. Since the recollections dogged me at every turn, I thought it might tame them to commit them to paper; besides which, it provided a happy diversion to an otherwise desolate day. I lay on my stomach on the bed, allowed myself to slip easily into the images, and wrote them all down with as much detail as I could recall.

I wrote about that hot summer day in Napa when we stopped at a secluded creek. It was canopied with cool trees, leaves coated with the dry summer dust. The water there was so cold, so clear. Beau loved it, tromping through it gleefully in a way that made us happy just to watch him. We waded and floated sticks, racing them. It was a hot, slow day, alone together in the summertime heat. We loved Napa, loved the smell of the vines and the earth. We loved escaping the city and spending a long, languid, unplanned day of wine tasting, stopping at Domaine Chandon for a glass of champagne at a little table overlooking the rolling landscape.

I wrote about watching Andrew walking in Golden Gate Park with Beau, going to the "dog party" as I was driving off to work. I always hated to leave them, often running late because I would stop to kiss him one more time.

I remembered watching him take off in the plane and the surging pride I felt every time I watched him fly. Although I wasn't a fan of aerobatics, I loved being able to fly places together. I recalled the look on Beau's face the first time we took him with us in the plane to Oregon, his eyes bugging out and tongue lolling sideways in his anxiety at seeing the ground disappear from under him. I remembered the time we flew up to Healdsburg, where an old man, who was just hanging around the airport, gave us a ride into town and then picked us up later that afternoon—just out of spontaneous kindness. I wrote about when my stepfather died and we'd flown up to Oregon, six weeks before our wedding, almost dying ourselves when the wings iced over and we lost electrical power.

One of the saddest aspects of being widowed was the accompanying loss of these shared memories. The loss of a corporeal being is huge; the loss of love enormous; the loss of a unique individual, irreplaceable. But what is also lost in a spousal death is the one and only person who knew you intimately, who understood your references to things and events, who laughed with you. No one else shared these experiences with you, shared your body, shared your idiosyncrasies and private jokes, and no one is left to share the stories. To be the only one who remembers something, a something nobody else cares about, is a profound sort of aloneness. Let's be honest: No one wants to hear your stories about this person, not really.

Not only are these years of shared memory packed away, interesting and important to no one save you, but—should you be so lucky—you will have to start all over with someone new, creating new shared experiences, collecting memories and jokes and private intimacies. Maybe that prospect sounds good to someone young and never married, but for me as a widow, it just sounded sad and depressing. It made me tired to think about it. It was like being sent back to "Go" with all of my Monopoly money gone, just when I was winning the game. It sucked.

This, I was discovering, was a great, unspoken side effect of being widowed. After the initial physical grief came this quiet, ongoing mourning for the loss of a shared memory, the loss of laughter and connection. You don't think about how much laughter and shared memory means until it's gone. I was afraid that this particular loss was going to have a long half-life.

∾ ∾

Andrew had been dead for five months, and while I was not adjusted to the loneliness, I was becoming used to being alone. It was strange to observe how quickly my mind adapted to my new reality. When Andrew first moved in with me, when I went from being single to being part of a couple, the transition had been natural and seamless. And while this transition back to being single was anything but natural or smooth, I was—emotional roller coaster notwithstanding—adjusting to being a "me" and not a "we."

I still thought of him constantly, and part of me remained incredulous that any of it had happened at all. But then I'd look at his wedding ring or his hairbrush, and they were still there: tangible proof that he existed, that the whole beautiful, dreadful story was real. Had these objects not been there, had I not seen them every day, I would have supposed myself crazy. I would have believed that I had made up the entire love affair, the death, everything.

In my desire to remain tethered both to reality and to Andrew, I left all of his shirts and pants hanging in our closet; I had no desire to move them out. Before entering the ranks of the widowed, it used to make me slightly uncomfortable when widows talked about keeping their husband's clothes. I didn't understand why my mother kept my father's clothes, why she liked to look at them and touch them; it seemed morbid. Back then, back in my happy state of ignorance, I had not understood. Now I did.

It was neither morbid nor unduly saddening to have the clothes there. Every morning when I awoke, I could see them hanging in the closet across from the bed. They were the vestments, the existing reminder of the beautiful body that once filled them. They touched him, and I could touch them. There was a way in which he seemed more alive when I looked at his clothes. When I moved them, put them away, gave them away, I knew that he would be further removed from me, and I would be entering a new and unfamiliar chapter of my life.

# 20

In early May, I flew to Louisville, Kentucky. Richard's ex-brother-in-law, Tom, was on the board of directors of the Kentucky Derby and had promised Andrew and me a trip to Kentucky one day. He kept his promise.

It had been arranged for me to stay in the home of a gracious Louisville couple who were friends of a person who knew my (former) uncle-in-law and, with three or four degrees of separation, took me, a complete stranger, into their house for the Kentucky Derby. This was true southern hospitality. It was odd to be staying with strangers, especially under these circumstances and without Barbara and Richard staying with me, but they were so kind and gracious that I felt completely at ease.

Barbara and Richard picked me up the morning of the Derby, and we began our day at the Louisville Country Club, a place that was, in every way, exactly what I might have imagined a country club in the Deep South to be, had I occasion to think about it: beautiful, spacious, classically elegant rooms; enormous sprays of flowers adorning the tables; clusters of white people in big hats and plaid pants picking at plates of hors d'oeuvres; black people in long, white aprons bringing trays of frosted silver cups filled with Mint Juleps and Ramos Fizzes.

For someone born and raised in the very middle of the middle class of the rural west coast, this was an alien, storybook sort of experience. In my graduating class of 667 people, there was precisely one person of color, and no one I knew drove a BMW or played tennis at a country club. My upbringing was remote and rural enough to be more akin to life in the fifties. Our big thrill was cruising on Friday night in a '66 Ford Mustang up and down the main drag in town. Yet here I was, a west coast widow, sipping on a Mint Julep brought to me by a black waiter in a private club on a hill in Kentucky. It boggled the imagination.

After brunch, we drove to an unremarkable, muddy parking lot by a nondescript stadium. The sky was a steely gray color, threatening more rain. I wished that I had brought a coat. I picked my way in heels through the horse trailers and mud as we walked together to the paddocks and then to our box, which was front and center on the finish line.

I had a difficult time getting into the spirit of things, not just because of my recent widowing, but also because it was an unusually cold and rainy weekend for the normally warm Derby. I had worn my going-away suit, the one I wore garnished with a corsage all the way to New York the day after our wedding. I had to cover my little suit with a rain jacket supplied by Richard and a large knit stole lent by Barbara, who was wisely layered and wearing sensible shoes. My feet were numb, making it difficult and painful to walk around.

We couldn't sit in our box due to the rain, so we stood for hours. One of the things you don't think about when you watch races on television is the enormous expanse of time between the start of the festivities and the actual race, which lasts for just under two minutes. I wondered, as I shivered, why the board of directors didn't have a skybox. Even alcohol was no help: Mint Juleps—a personal favorite and icon of the Derby—lose much of their appeal when consumed in a steady, cold rain.

As we stood waiting for the various introductory races, Barbara, to my surprise and horror, began pointing out good-looking men. This took me completely off-guard. I appreciated her awareness and unusual openness to the topic of romance, particularly considering that it was her son from whom I would be moving on, but five months is hardly the point at which one is ready to leap into a new love affair. It made me uncomfortable. My fling with Keith had been just that: a fling with someone I had known for ages. A completely new nice-to-meet-you-my-name-is-Kate sort of *real* relationship was a whole other thing. Flummoxed by both her uncharacteristic behavior and the topic in general, I demurred a lot, saying things like, "Oh, I don't think so," and a string of neutral and innocuous, "I don't knows."

I went to Kentucky because I was invited and because I wanted to remain connected to Andrew's family. I went because it was a rare opportunity, one I likely would never get again. I went to try to escape myself—and I was miserable. I missed Andrew like mad, watching well-heeled couples holding hands and laughing, happy despite the weather. I felt, as I later confessed to Andrew's cousin Eliza, invisible.

It was a mistake to make this confession. Eliza protested fiercely, stunned by my admission. She told me that her father—Andrew's Uncle Tom—was bending over backward to make me feel welcome, that I was being treated as an honored guest. She did not, could not, understand that what I was talking about was an internal state of mind. I tried, futilely, to explain that it was not her father, not my hosts, or my in-laws who looked through me; it was the nature of my condition, an internal disappearance.

It was foolish to try to communicate my inner experience to a non-initiate. It was impossible for someone like Eliza—young, unmarried, inexperienced—to understand the feelings of invisibility and abandonment, the pervasive sadness that attaches itself to you with a gluey tenacity, regardless of where you go or what you do. Depression, like the dark night it imitates, eventually drains all your color, fading you into the shadows. After so recently being exultant, it was particularly unnerving to disappear so violently. It's not good to feel dead when you are, in fact, not.

The day after the race, the weather returned to its normal, southern sunshine and humidity and Richard, Barbara, and I drove from Louisville to Lexington. I stared out at the horses and the endless line of white fences that lined a limitless carpet of green grass regularly punctuated by large, brick homes. It was good to be warm, good to be done with the Derby and its requisite formalities—good, even, to be alone with my in-laws.

Then Barbara began to talk—to no one in particular, but I knew, or at least feared, that she was talking to me.

"I just don't understand," she said, "how Bif (one of Will's many second-cousins) can do nothing. Not work, not do anything."

The allusion was transparent. I squirmed in the backseat.

I was already painfully aware that Barbara neither understood nor approved of my "doing nothing." Although I tried not to be unduly paranoid, all of my neurotic fears kicked into high gear. I couldn't help but imagine that she was angry that I was living on their money; the little scene on Wall Street back in January had made that pretty clear. But maybe, I thought, she was truly baffled by my inactivity, or perhaps she was worried about me; I doubted that, but it was a remote possibility.

I stared out the window, saying nothing. The juxtaposition of being an adult—a therapist, no less—and feeling like a child was disconcerting. Richard said nothing. The car fell quiet. I tried to stem my hemorrhaging anxiety by talking to myself in my head. *"You don't know what she truly thinks, Kate, and it hardly matters anymore anyway."*

Barbara resumed her third-person musings as we toured the Lexington Horse Museum, this time wondering aloud whether it wasn't better to be busy, better not to be thinking and feeling too much.

"How," she asked, "does one find a middle ground between feeling and avoiding feeling?"

It was abundantly clear that I fell into the former camp while she was squarely in the latter. I honestly didn't know if one were better than the other; it was all hard. Of course, I did not say this. I said nothing, assuming that her question was rhetorical; it would have been rather awkward to answer her. She was trying to find her way through this brave new world, just as I was.

At the end of our time in Kentucky, as she and Richard were departing, Barbara admonished me to "come home soon." This left me speechless, stumped by what seemed like conflicting messages of "You're doing this wrong!" and then "Come home soon!" indicating that she felt me to be family. The dual messages likely revealed her great confusion, her ocean of messy, uncomfortable feelings—feelings she usually tried to keep at bay but which recent circumstances had caused to flood over her. I began to see that she was, indeed, probably worried about me, unable to understand my tendency to wallow in grief. When I hugged her good-bye, I told her not to worry about me, just in case.

The trip to Louisville, like the trips preceding it, had shown me again that my sorrow, like an orphaned child, was intent on following me everywhere, on keeping me in sight. Travel accentuated the sadness because it put me out of my comfort zone. It did not provide a respite or a diversion because I always wanted to be sharing the journey with Andrew, not experiencing it alone, or worse, experiencing it alone in the presence of others.

Travel also evoked the discomfort of being bombarded by the endless reminders of Andrew's love of airplanes, his love of flight. I stood in the airport in San Francisco staring out the window at the planes rolling around on the tarmac, waiting for my connecting flight home. Andrew's great love was flying, but what was mine? Who was I? What was *my* calling? Barbara's musings about "doing something" had stirred up an old, lingering question, one I had tucked away with Andrew's death. Underneath the grief and mourning, this question still quietly plagued me. What was I going to do with my life?

I felt an empty hole in place of an identity. The only thing I identified with was being a widow: I had no focus, no occupation, no hobby, no social life. I didn't have the ability or even the desire anymore to practice therapy. Maybe that was okay, but it didn't feel okay. I didn't feel comfortable or secure, particularly when people asked what I did for a living.

I knew that question was just small talk. I knew no one really cared what I did or didn't do, that they were just trying to make conversation, which, God knows, was no easy matter; I wasn't exactly a charming conversationalist lately. After a while, I decided to be honest, and when someone would ask me what I did, I'd say, "I'm healing," which was true enough. That was usually sufficient to end the conversation.

I deplaned in Oregon and walked through the security gate, watching people greet and hug one another and listening to their effusive, joyful reunions. I waited at the baggage claim, feeling conspicuously unaccompanied for what seemed an inordinate amount of time, listening to my fellow travelers catch up with their family and friends. When my bag finally appeared through the chute, I snagged it, relieved, and dragged it out to the long-term parking area.

I drove myself home through lush, green vistas, irritated by the caress of summer's encroaching heat, wanting Andrew to be here in the sensuality and sweet tiredness of coming home. As I drove, my depression settled back on me like volcanic dust, covering me completely, the fallout from the rupture still prodigious. I checked for messages when I got home; there were none.

*MAY 8*
*I am sitting outside under the umbrella, watching the sprinklers water the lawn. It was hot today, and it's just now cooling off. I love how the droplets of water hold on to the blades of grass, just hanging there, glistening and sliding off from time to time to the absorbing earth below. It's a very soothing, summery experience, watching it. I thought how nice it would be if Andrew were in the empty chair beside me, enjoying the coolness, drinking a gin and tonic. But the chair is empty, and I am alone, feverish and miserable, illness exacerbating my melancholy.*

I wondered how I was supposed to get through the weeks and months ahead. I didn't even know how I had negotiated the ones behind me. I didn't know how I'd survived even this long. I thought about a line from *Sleepless in Seattle*, when someone asks Tom Hanks, the grieving widower, what he's going to do.

He said, "I'm just going to keep breathing in and out. And, maybe one day, I won't have to think about breathing in and out anymore."

May brought with it gorgeous days full of emptiness. An early summer blast of ninety-two-degree heat had transformed the field across the street into a thick, tall jungle. Overnight, everything had become lush and full of flowerless foliage. I disliked the intense heat but loved the warmth and expansiveness of the burgeoning season, even as the sensual weight of it pressed upon my heart.

My days consisted largely of deadheading pansies. It was a mindless occupation that satisfied my limited capabilities. As I poked around in the flowers, feelings of stupor continued to wash over me in waves: in and out; now more, now less, but always near. I couldn't get away from it. Every thought I had, every word I wrote, every feeling I experienced was a repeat of the day—or sometimes the hour—before it; the repetitiveness of this process was relentless.

It occurred to me that I was finally realizing, on a profound and permanent level, that Andrew was never coming back. I'd known this intellectually for some time, but this was a very different kind of knowing: an embodied knowing. The realization came to me with great clarity and great sadness, though not fully formed; it was the first glimmer of a dawning awareness—an awareness that I was, like it or not, metabolizing my new reality.

Six months had passed already and life was moving on; strangely, so was I. It was not the kind of "moving on" that people usually mean when they say it—becoming active, reengaging. My moving on felt like I was sitting on a conveyor belt, being carried passively, mindlessly, the scenery behind me changing.

A large part of me wanted to retain my position as a new widow, to keep the understanding of those around me, to be given a reason for not knowing what I was doing with my life. I was beginning to feel that I no longer had the latitude not to work, not to feel good, not to function. People had stopped asking me how I was doing, graduating me out of my grace period of mourning. I was supposed to be moving on and getting better, but the reality was that I was in the same emotional bleakness as I was five months before. I was no longer in shock, but the sadness was carving itself deeper into my soul.

The idea of returning to the world was not only anathema; it put me at a total loss. To what, exactly, would I return? I could not go back to the life I'd had; that was gone. I couldn't move forward with our plans as a couple. I had to create or discover something altogether new. Loving and losing Andrew had altered who I was deep inside; it was remaking me. I didn't know who I was or how to go on. This was both frightening and daunting. I had absolutely no idea what to do.

At nine o'clock in the evening it was seventy-five degrees outside: weirdly warm—earthquake weather, we used to call it. I took Bella down the block to the elementary school football field and there, for the first time in forever, I prayed. It was choked and short and inelegant, but I prayed and I cried. I asked God, or whatever energy was out there, to please help me use my life for some good, to help me find a purpose. I asked for help to see my talents rather than my shortcomings. I expressed gratitude for anything good I could think of: Andrew, the beauty around me, my dog. It felt odd to pray. I was unsure anymore whether I was heard or how this all worked, but I tried to fan the tired little flame of faith that once burned so surely and brightly in me.

I decided, that evening, that a ritual cleansing was in order. After much contemplation and beseeching of Andrew's blessing, I took the stack of photo negatives from the files in his office and carried them to the fireplace. I began to look through them, examining individual frames, but quickly set them down where they were out of focus. I never knew Andrew as "Sonia," never saw him cross-dressed; in my experience and memory he was always and only a roguish, handsome, charming man.

What lay in my hands, though, were images of an Andrew just as real, just as true, as the images in my memory. These images were sacred. They were part of him and a part that he sacrificed—literally—in order to try to have a more acceptable and normal life, to have love. These pictures belonged to him and with him. One by one, I placed each photo sheet into the flames and watched it burn, commending it to his spirit. No one else should be looking at them, gawking and judging—not even me.

# 21

At Nicole's suggestion, I began riding lessons toward the end of the summer as a palliative for my ongoing depression. I embraced her suggestion with a certain ferocity and, within a month's time, I had a horse and a trainer and was spending most of my days riding, if poorly, at a nearby dressage stable.

I'd never ridden a horse before except once on Maui with Andrew. The lack of familiarity and my learning curve demanded a great deal of attention, which itself was therapeutic. I liked the ritual of horsemanship: the grooming and tacking up, even the lessons in which I just couldn't seem to relax and get it right. I loved the breeze that hit my face as I opened the enormous, sliding barn door. I liked the smell of the barn, especially on a hot day, when I walked into the coolness of the big, long aisle that ran between the stalls. I liked the breeches and the boots and the idea of it, so I kept going. And between the half-hour drive each way, the brushing, the tacking up, the lesson, the conversations, and the cleanup afterward, it consumed much of my day, and that was the main thing. It took my mind off the rest of my life.

I was assigned a fourteen-year-old white Arabian horse named Sammy. His real name was Sampari, but everyone called him Sammy. I liked Sammy. He was spunky and small, and he knew everything, which made him easy to ride, and he was very affectionate for a horse. He would push his long, soft head against my body and rest it there as we stood in the soft darkness of the arena, his large, dark eyes and long lashes blinking slowly as I stroked his smooth, white neck.

Sammy's only fatal flaw—or his best defense, depending on one's point of view—was his tendency to bolt like sheer hell when spooked, and I quickly learned that Arabians, a hot-blooded breed, spook every ten seconds. Sammy knew immediately and instinctively that I was a novice. On our first outdoor excursion, he bolted across the length and breadth of the farm, making hairpin turns, jumping over fences, and galloping around obstacles at an alarming speed. Oddly, I was too preoccupied to be scared.

I could hear my trainer screaming at me from the distant barn, "Pull up! Jerk his head!"

Pulling up was not in my repertoire; it was all I could do to hold on. As we screamed across the outdoor rings and grass lawns, I sensed that Sammy was having fun at my expense. When he finally came to a halt by his own volition five, long minutes later, it was just as suddenly as he had taken off. I sat, heart thumping, as Sammy blithely dropped his head and began to munch some grass. His nostrils made loud exhalations. Embarrassment at my total lack of equine skills notwithstanding, I felt a strange sense of personal pride that I had managed to stay in the saddle. I had held on. I was victorious.

Dr. Rothschild was thrilled with my newfound enthusiasm. Rothschild was not her original, given name. She had forsaken both her birth name and her husbands' names in favor of her maternal grandmother's more famous one.

When I asked one day why she had changed it, her answer was simply, "Wouldn't you?"

Nicole's East Coast past was living vicariously in my present and she imagined, or at least hoped, that my recent horsiness would take me places—a hope that she often repeated. How this would work, she never said, but I could see that she had a vision of the kind of life she wanted for me, one not unlike the one she had once enjoyed.

Although she claimed a Ph.D. and had counseled many people, over the course of time I had come to the conclusion that Dr. Rothschild was neither a doctor nor a therapist; I saw no proof of either on paper or in practice. There was nothing the least bit "by the book" in my relationship with Nicole. I knew all about her personal life: her strained relationship with her daughter and her wonderful, talented son; worse still, I knew about all her other clients. I knew who was an alcoholic and who was pregnant and who made how much money. I didn't want to know. I ran into these people all the time, living in a small town, and I always wondered, when their eyes met mine in an uneasy sort of way, exactly what they knew about me.

Nicole and I had lunch together regularly, took walks, and went shopping. I called her at all hours. She tried hooking me up with men she knew, usually clients.

"How about Ben, honey?" she might say. When I expressed my distinct lack of attraction or interest in Ben, she would incredulously retort, "But honey, he's rich!"

She was the Jewish grandmother I didn't know I always wanted: a petite, white-haired woman with a petite, white-haired dog; a woman who said exactly what she thought, whether I liked it or not—and I frequently did not. Once, during a session, she paused to light a cigarette, took a drag, and, after exhaling up and away from me, stared me down.

"You know, honey, Andrew was gay."

That off-the-cuff remark had sent me on a crazed, emotional jag for days.

I saw her four times a week, usually before or after riding. Sometimes she came to the barn and watched me ride. Looking at her, it was easy to imagine the socialite she once had been: bone thin, rich, and coiffed. In some not-so-distant past life, Nicole had enjoyed the privileges of money and status. She showed me her gorgeous gowns and rings, and a newspaper article from Milan with her photograph and a caption that revealed that she was, in fact, the "Countess Elena." She came from money and then married money on top of that; then, through time and marriages, she lost all that money—mostly, I assumed, to a handsome Italian whom she had recently divorced and whom I suspected might be the missing count.

Nicole would often end our sessions, regardless of the time, by saying, "Bianca wants to go for a walk," and we would stroll the blocks of the historic district, arm in arm, as she told me things like, "My rabbi says that I do not have to speak to the man who lives in that house. He's a child molester."

I silently questioned the wisdom of the rabbi and Nicole's smug satisfaction in shunning her brethren, but the way she said these things, I couldn't help but be amused.

After our walk, I would get in my car to leave. As I pulled away, she would wave as she stood on the corner, her diminutive body enveloped in a disfiguring, oversized, blue down coat, cigarette in one hand and Bianca straining on her bejeweled leash in the other. I mused about what the Italian paparazzi would do for a picture of the Countess Elena in a dumpy, twenty-dollar parka.

I never knew how much of Nicole was fact and how much was fiction, but I did know that, for a time, she saved my life—not with good therapy, but with the odd friendship that developed over the days and weeks and months at fifty dollars a visit.

# 22

It was the last day of August. The phone rang and I picked it up to hear my mother's strained voice.

"Turn on the television."

*Oh God,* I thought, *now what?*

I turned on my television and stood back, immediately transfixed. Princess Diana had just been in a car crash in Paris. I sank down onto the futon in shock and horror, staring at the screen. She was still alive, they thought, but something inside me said that she was not going to survive the obscene mess I was witnessing. I sat glued to the television, watching the entire tragedy unfold, my stomach nauseated. I couldn't stop watching.

Diana was as close as I ever came to being obsessed with celebrity. Normally, I had no interest in celebrities whatsoever; they left me unfazed and unimpressed. Diana was different. I read everything I could about her. I cut my hair like hers and often got comments that I resembled her, comments I enjoyed. I identified with her: we were soul sisters, she and I, both of us spit out of tragic, doomed-from-the-start relationships, both of us naïve in our very honest love. I admired her grace and style and the way she stepped onto the world stage to bring attention to those who suffer with AIDS and land mines. She was a tragic heroine: deceived, lonely, trapped, beautiful, struggling, victorious. She was the me that I wanted to be.

I felt her death deeply and personally. Everything in me turned up and over again; I could not absorb it. First my husband and now my idol: both taken so young and so traumatically. The impact of her death was terrific and terrible, just as Andrew's had been. The loss of Diana touched on all of my own losses: loss of a parent, loss of a partner, loss of love, loss of a future.

I mourned for Diana for weeks, unable to describe my feelings to anyone, at a loss to explain why her death meant so much to me; it was something that I could not, and felt that I should not, try to explain. To talk about it was to trivialize it, and it was not trivial to me. I could not begin to describe what she symbolized, what she inspired, what she touched in my own life. No one understood. This, like my mourning for Andrew and the confusion and grief I had about the secrets he harbored, was something I carried alone.

In the midst of this new mourning, I was preparing myself to make the trip to Winslow Cove to bury Andrew's remains, my fifth trip in eight months. My in-laws had graciously allowed me to make the decision about where to bury the ashes. I had thought about scattering them from an airplane—a poetic and appropriate ending—but decided that Barbara and Richard needed some tangible presence of their son. The one place that Andrew truly loved was their summer retreat in Cape Cod, so I decided that that would be the best place for all involved.

I began my journey in line at the airport to check in for the first leg of my flight to Massachusetts. In my carry-on were Andrew's remains, which I held close to my body. Directly in front of me in line stood a man who, from the back, looked precisely and eerily like Andrew. He was wearing a jacket and a baseball cap identical to Andrew's, and he had the same dark hair and build. I could feel my heart begin to beat harder and my breath became short and shallow. I tried desperately to see his face.

There was, in that fraction of a second, a suspension of all logic. For a few moments my mind took off in a furious, excited frenzy, like a Jack Russell Terrier released from its cage. From some place deep in my cellular memory, there came an outpouring of delirious joy and relief: an invisible, interior manic attack.

*He's alive! He's still here! Thank God it was all a nightmare, and I'm awake!*

For a few moments, I thought that Andrew had, perhaps, just disappeared for a while; it seemed within the realm of remote possibility. I followed the man to the boarding area, hoping that it was Andrew, believing that to be possible, even though some part of me knew that it was not—*but it could be.* When the man turned and glanced at me blankly, without recognition and without a smile, my mind churned, confused and off-kilter.

We boarded the plane and I made my way down the narrow aisle, looking for my row, thinking about what had just happened. I glanced up, saw my row number, and then looked at the passenger in the middle seat.

It was the man.

What were the odds? I smiled at him and sat down, feeling strange and off-balance. I knew that it wasn't Andrew, but it was his double. I bent over to place my purse containing the ashes under the seat in front of me. As I did, I glanced over at the book in his lap: a flight manual. He was a pilot, who looked and dressed like Andrew, and whom fate had seated next to me.

Why was this happening? What did it mean? Was it a message? A visitation? It was Andrew sitting next to me, except that he did not know me, did not speak to me, could not have begun to understand what his mere presence in the seat next to me was doing to my body and my heart.

The doppelgänger ignored me during the flight, making it clear after a couple of questions that he had no interest in having a conversation. I didn't blame him—he probably felt my craziness—but I was disappointed. When we deplaned in San Francisco, I watched him walk away and disappear into the crowd; I watched him because he looked like my husband and I liked seeing him again.

The entire experience hurt, and it puzzled me. It was a very unexpected reunion fantasy, something I thought only a child could experience; perhaps it was the childlike part of me that responded. I kept thinking that life was not only difficult, it was goddamned strange.

This bizarre beginning set the surreal tone for the trip across the country to the tiny, private enclave that is Winslow Cove. I stared out the window of the plane, my husband's remains in a box on my lap. The beautiful, corporeal being that I had sat next to on so many flights—holding hands and talking about our lives, Beau in tow somewhere underneath in cargo—was now reduced to bone and ash in a twelve-by-eight-inch box. There was a sense of morbid humor about it: I could now stow my husband as a carry-on under the seat in front of me. I felt like an actor in a movie, as though I were playing a part; it was all so strange.

I stared out at the stars that were beginning to appear in the velvet night sky. I had not seen Andrew's family since December, and I was dreading it. I did not want to be at Winslow Cove without him. It was a special place to be together: a place that we both loved; a place that I had visions of bringing our children in the many summers that spread out in our future.

The day of the burial arrived, cloaked in a hot, heavy humidity. Everyone that morning was subdued and quiet around the breakfast table, where the windows were open to the cries of the herons and osprey and the smell of the marsh. Just before eleven o'clock, I walked up the painted stairs to our bedroom and to the dresser where Andrew's ashes lay. I unfolded the African cloth that wrapped the box, exposing the wood and the metal tag that read, "Andrew C. Alden, 1966–1996."

I carried the box from our bedroom back down the stairs. Brooke met me at the bottom of the steps and put her hand on my arm, looking at me quietly. Tears welled up in my eyes. Whispering, I asked her to cut a lock of my hair, which she did, and I tucked it into the box to be buried with him. Brooke gently took my arm, and we walked out the front door and into the warm, humid Cape Cod afternoon.

Thirty or so members of the immediate and extended family had already assembled at the side of the house and stood quietly talking. As I rounded the corner and saw the sad and pained faces of everyone gathered there, familiar knots of grief began to form in my stomach and my throat. It was utterly silent, except for the birdsong from the marsh and the shout of a child's voice on a sailboat in the distance. Richard's eyes were filled with tears behind his tortoise shell glasses; Barbara's thin, narrow face was tautly somber.

I glanced down at the hole that Richard had dug that morning to receive the remains of his son. I wasn't sure how to proceed. I walked over to Barbara and silently offered her the box containing her first-born child. She had birthed him; she, more than I, should have the dubious honor of burying him. Barbara refused, shaking her head in silence. I looked over at Richard, who stood crushed and strong, and then I walked around the hole in the earth and knelt down at the edge of the small grave.

I sat for some minutes with the box in my hands, resting on my knees. I was painfully aware that this was the last, unfinished piece of the death. It was both a symbolic and a literal letting-go, and I was overcome by the finality of it. I was also peripherally aware that I was the only one crying. Lifting my eyes without raising my head, I could see the legs and feet of all those gathered, waiting and silent. Finally, I laid the wooden container gently in the dirt and began to sob uncontrollably.

"I love you," I whispered, as I looked at the box in the hole, waiting to be covered.

I lifted my head, my face and hair wet with tears, and saw Brooke's cherubic five-year-old son looking at me, watching me, curious. I gazed at him for an elongated moment, seeing his interest, his confusion and uncertainty. In that frozen moment, I knew that I could stand up, wipe away the tears—Alden-like—or I could let it all out, which is what I wanted to do, what I needed to do, despite the self-conscious awkwardness, despite the solitary nature of my outpouring of sorrow. I followed my better instinct, dropped my head, and wept.

*Let little Spud see what the meaning of love is,* I thought. *This is the agony of love.*

After a few minutes, when my lone lamentation exhausted itself, I stood up. Richard took up the shovel that had been resting on the trunk of the old tree, filled it with some of the loose earth, and dropped the soil onto the box. He passed the shovel, eyes wet, to Andrew's aunt, Julia. One after the other, each family member took a turn, placing one shovelful of earth into the grave and passing it on to the next person.

I stood back, alone, watching the ritual. The sound of the dirt hitting the box was the worst sound I had ever heard. I winced at each thud, each raining of the earth, so insistent and real, impressing the finality of a life and a relationship.

The next day, Richard drove me down the long, narrow road that connects Winslow Cove to the mainland. We passed the security guard at the entrance to the compound, and Richard gave him a wave before we entered West Yarmouth proper, driving across the bridge that spanned the entrance to Nantucket Sound. I wondered if I would ever come back here again.

At the airport, Richard held me before I walked out to the small island hopper that would take me to Boston. I wished that he would hold me forever, wished that he would stay in my life forever. Richard had been the bonus prize in the already incredible windfall of marrying Andrew. His generous, earnest spirit assuaged my father-longing. I loved him and needed him, needed to stay close to him, protected by his arms and his love and his care until I found a way back to myself.

Reluctantly I turned to leave, and walked toward the waiting plane, turning back once to wave and seeing the tears in Richard's eyes as he stood, motionless in the low-ceilinged terminal, tears in his eyes that evoked my own. I walked quickly outside and into the humming prop plane. I ducked my head and boarded, sat in the first seat, and peered out the tiny window. Richard stood at the chain-link fence, waving, watching me go.

# PART THREE

## PUDDLING *or* EATING AT BURGER KING

*A newly emerged butterfly gathers its required salt and minerals from urine, dung, and standing water. Such water has absorbed minerals from the soil beneath. This process is called "puddling."*

# 23

I came home and bought a house. Something about the burial had closed the chapter of our life as a couple, and I wanted desperately to move out of our rental, to be in a place without memories and sorrow attached to it. I had already sold the cars and furniture and given Andrew's personal belongings to his siblings. I'd even let go of all of Andrew's clothes, sharing some with my brother and the rest with a local shelter. I was down to just my clothes and the bed and a new car I'd bought in a fit of expansiveness. Divested of most of my material possessions, I was ready to leave this place that held nothing more for me.

I called our realtor and asked if the house that I had fallen in love with last summer was still available. Although a year had passed, it was—to my joy and amazement—still unsold. My first offer was accepted in ten minutes and, on an early October afternoon, I packed my few remaining objects into a small U-Haul trailer and left my life in Jacksonville for Ashland, Oregon, eighteen miles and a world away.

I had loved this Ashland house from the first moment I stepped into it. That first time, last summer, Andrew had dismissed it out of hand; he had wanted something old and dark and more New Englandy, the total antithesis of my aesthetic. We had completely exhausted both our realtor and our possibilities with our inability to find a compromise.

Now my desire was fulfilled. The house was brand new and without history. It sat high on a hill a few blocks above town and close to the barn where I rode. Standing inside, I felt that I could breathe— a rare and welcome experience. There were windows in every room that looked out on the mountains and hills. The kitchen was spacious and white with smooth, hardwood floors. The master bedroom, and the living room directly above it, had fireplaces and large mahogany decks that faced east. I could see the sun rise over Grizzly Peak and watch the fog roll into the upper part of the valley. Deer roamed in a small park a half block away.

I walked across the footbridge to the front door, turned the key in the lock, and walked into my first house. I stood for a moment in the clean, silent emptiness with a stillborn excitement. This was not how it was supposed to be. There was no one to share the celebration, no one to excitedly race around to each room with me, no one to toast a new beginning or carry me across the threshold, no one to make love with on the wide, open floor. Andrew's ghost wasn't even here.

I had not brought Bella with me when I moved: she was too aggressive and too much of a wanderer for my new, unfenced neighborhood up on the hill. I had left her with my mother, in the country. I missed her, and I felt guilty for giving her away, just as I had felt guilty about sending Beau off with James. Now it was just me, empty and enveloped in a big, empty house.

For many months, I did nothing to furnish it. I put my mattress on the floor in front of the fireplace in the bedroom and some weeks later, after weeks of Nicole's incessant nagging, unpacked my kitchen items, stowing them in the endless array of cabinets. I changed all the light fixtures and installed double ovens and a huge refrigerator, even though I barely ate and had no one to cook for. I lived in this hollowness for a number of months until Nicole got fed up and told me in one of my sessions to "get up off the floor."

Although her admonishment was intended as more of a metaphor, I took it literally and hired a designer—a friend of Nicole's—and went to San Francisco where I bought some custom-made sofas, a dining set, a couple of occasional chairs and an antique, Japanese altar. When it all arrived some months later, it didn't come close to fully furnishing a room, let alone a whole house. The result looked like a staged setting, like what realtors do to an empty house to give it a veneer of looking lived in. It was still a hollow shell because I was a hollow shell. And although the house made me feel peaceful and safe, it also accentuated the reality of my new existence.

On Thanksgiving I invited Brian and his wife Janice, my mom, and a couple of other friends to drive out to the crash site, about half an hour away. We caravanned to the dirt road that led up to the pasture where the plane had gone down. Parking alongside the wire fence, we got out and crawled over and through the barbed wire, one by one. We walked in a small group across the field and to the place where the plane had gone down. I had placed a rock engraved with his initials there earlier that spring, and we formed an impromptu circle around it.

I'd brought a bottle of vintage port, one that Andrew and I had been saving for a special occasion. We opened it, only to realize that no one had thought to bring glasses. This fortuitous omission lent itself to the creation of a spontaneous wake: one by one, we shared a memory of Andrew, and then lifted the bottle to our lips and took a long drink before passing it to the next person. After everyone had spoken, we poured the remainder on the earth, for Andrew.

The mood of this gathering was surprisingly joyful. As a light mist began to coat our hair and dampen our coats, we were all smiling, connected through this ritual of remembrance on holy ground. The fact that we shared the bottle only heightened the sense of communion. I knew that Andrew would have loved it.

Widowed life consisted of these sorts of small, sweet moments punctuating the tedium of a long litany of days. This existence wore on me as time went on, morphing into a three-headed Cerberus of loneliness, anxiety, and impatience. I wanted companionship. I wanted to feel loved and to have someone to do things with. I wanted to smile and be playful. I wanted to evade this monster that was sucking up all the oxygen in my cramped, confined world. I didn't want to feel the seemingly endless pain and suffering that this loss had shoveled upon me.

I sat one night in my echoing, empty kitchen, a large appliance box for a dining table, talking with Ainslie in San Francisco. I loved talking with her because we laughed ... a lot. We talked about our respective lonely lives and the lousy dating and relationship choices we'd made out of desperation and isolation.

Hunger for a relationship, I posited aloud, is akin to the hunger you develop on a long car trip. Bored, antsy, uncomfortable, your stomach starting to growl, you tell yourself that a good restaurant should be coming up any minute and you should wait. But when no good restaurant appears, hunger takes over. An ache begins to form in your body and animal instinct replaces logic. The fast-food places you keep passing start to look appealing.

"If you get too hungry," I told Ainslie, "you wind up eating at Burger King."

This made Ainslie laugh.

A relationship forged in a state of desperate hunger gets you someone who might sate the emptiness for a little while, but it doesn't satisfy the deeper need for something nourishing and restorative. Beyond this, it's almost always unhealthy. Yet this is precisely what I did, all my training, all my better wisdom, all my therapy notwithstanding; I did not want to tolerate the hunger of my loneliness any longer, so I attempted to eradicate it by filling the empty space with a Whopper.

It was Nicole who pimped the first warm body my way, right about the time that Princess Diana was killed. She had arranged for "the nice young man" who worked in the office below her apartment to join us for a drink one evening.

Derek was the antithesis of the blue-blooded Andrew. He had long, bleached hair and multiple piercings. He was small in stature, penniless, and a divorced father of three. He was pushing forty, a fact that he detested and tried to hide by dressing like and hanging out with people half his age.

Derek was not without his charms, however. He was quick and clever and a good listener, which I liked. He played the guitar and cello and was a good dancer. He was receptive and compassionate about my loss and my ongoing grief, which, at that moment, was my main requirement of another human being.

Derek took the edge off my hunger. Like Keith and the other men who'd caught my eye over the past year, he was the absolute wrong sort of person for me, which made him, in a strange way, perfect. There was no way such a relationship could amount to anything, and on an unconscious level, I knew it. It made it safe: a practice run, as it were.

I'd been seeing Derek for four months as Christmas and the first anniversary of Andrew's death approached. I decided to go to Georgetown to be with Andrew's family. My mother was hurt and

not-too-quietly peeved that I had not invited her and that I was abandoning her for the holidays, but I couldn't help it. I couldn't imagine
staying home in the place where it all happened. I needed to be with
my other family, and I needed to go by myself.

I arrived at Dulles International Airport in a dark, pouring
rain. Barbara and Richard came to the airport to greet me. I sat in
the backseat of their car, looking out at all the cars driving across
the bridge, lights bright and glistening in the rain. I looked at the
faces of the drivers, trying to imagine who they were, where they
were going, what they were thinking about. I wondered if they were
happy. I wondered what Barbara and Richard might be thinking, the
poignancy of Andrew's absence made all the more acute for my presence there. I couldn't imagine their pain. I watched the rain beading
on the glass and felt a quiet, relaxed sort of sadness.

We stopped at a red light and I glanced over at the car that was
stopped next to us. In the backseat was a very handsome man, about
my age. He was sitting alone behind two people that I assumed were
his parents. I imagined that he, too, had come home for the holidays.
He looked over at me, a faint smile on his lips, a smile I returned. We
recognized our mutual situations, or I imagined that we did, recognized the unique moment we were sharing. It was a long red light,
and we did not break our gaze. As the light turned green, both cars
began to move ahead, but we remained locked in our visual embrace
until his car veered off to the right. He lifted his hand to gesture
good-bye, and I returned the wave.

On Christmas night, I called Derek from the privacy of Andrew's
old bedroom—now Barbara's office—to wish him Merry Christmas.
He voice was distant and his answers to my questions evasive; something was off. Then, as we were talking, an unexpected thing happened: I saw Derek lying naked in bed with a woman. I saw them as if
I were standing at the foot of their bed. It was not my imagination; it
was real. It was a vision. I'd never experienced anything like it before.
I said nothing about it, but after we hung up, the vision stayed with
me.

Derek was not there to meet me at the airport when I arrived
home. It was late, and I was tired and irritated. I thought about my

clairvoyant experience. I knew where he was and whom he was with. I waited for a few more minutes, my unhappiness swelling with the passing moments. I found a pay phone and called his number. He picked up.

"Where are you?" I asked.

"Oh shit," he said. "Are you at the airport?"

"Yes, but you're not."

"I'll be right there."

I went outside, rolling my suitcase behind me, my coat wrapped tightly around my body, and sat down on the long bench that lined the terminal building. There was no one else around. I watched the security guard walk slowly up and down the sidewalk under the streetlights, and smiled briefly when he looked over at me. Thirty minutes later, I saw my black BMW wrap around the curve at high speed and stop in front of me. Derek jumped out and gave me a quick peck on the cheek as he grabbed my suitcase and put it in the trunk. I slid silently into the passenger seat. Derek made a few attempts at small talk, and then disappeared into a nervous quietude.

"Where were you?" I asked.

"At a party," he said.

"Was Angela there?" I ventured.

Angela was a mutual acquaintance and the woman I had seen in the vision. She had been shadowing me for months. She'd sold her car and bought one like mine. She'd taken up dressage at the barn where I rode, cut her hair like mine, bought a black horse when I did. She was at every gathering we attended and flirted openly with Derek. There was a quality about her that said "Poppy-cooker"—something slightly off and disturbing.

"The party was at her house. We were smoking ..."

I looked straight ahead. I already knew everything he was saying and not saying. His quiet responses only served to confirm my imaginings. I had suspected for some time that Derek was using drugs, although he never used them in my presence. When he missed the exit on the freeway, taking us all the way to the California border, the anxiety filling my stomach told me all the truth I had not wanted to hear.

The following day, I walked into his office and stood in front of his desk. He looked up, wordlessly.

"Did you sleep with her?" I asked.

He wavered, ever so briefly, and then quietly replied, "Yes."

I turned and walked out, furious with him, and with them, but mostly disgusted with myself. What had I been thinking? I hadn't been thinking, just feeling scared and lonely. I'd gotten too hungry. That was the problem. It served me right; I'd gotten too hungry and I'd wound up eating at Burger King.

A feeling of shame quickly supplanted the anger. I'd known from the beginning that Derek and I did not belong together, and yet I had allowed myself the guilty pleasure of his companionship. I had, in my vulnerable emptiness, tried to create something from nothing. I had put myself in this situation.

Still, despite the brevity and wrongness of our relationship, the betrayal hurt. It dredged up the terrible, familiar feeling of loss: not the loss of Derek but of loss in general—the horrible, aching, twisting pain of an unhealed heart.

I packed some clothes and went to my mother's house where I stayed in my pajamas for a week, sleeping in my brother's old bedroom that looked almost as it had when he'd moved out some thirty years before. I shuffled around, not eating, crying in the cold, daylight basement bedroom, and unraveling. My ridiculous attempt at filling the hole in my heart had been exposed for what it was: not just poor judgment or bad luck, but a pathetic and inappropriate stab at avoiding what was waiting for me. I had tried to assuage my deep hunger and the emptiness, tried to escape it, but there was no avoiding it.

I lay in bed, staring at the gold glitter on the ceiling. Everything in me ached, and I was filled with remorse for everything but particularly for the relationship with Derek. I was in the midst of a horrific emotional hangover, the result of my strange, four-month-long bender. The binge had felt like an excellent way to find some fun, but it had resulted in this crashing disaster. Now sober, I shut my eyes tightly as the reality of my ill-fated foray came into focus. The shame wasn't Derek's; he was who he was. He hadn't pretended to be anything more. The shame was mine. I had compromised myself, and I had tried to evade the inevitable.

I lay there, feeling the weight of the multiple blankets I'd stacked on top of me, feeling emptied out, flat and deflated, like a balloon that had been released, spitting out all its air as it zigzagged across the sky before it fell to the ground, spent and flaccid. My entire life to this point was calling to me; all the losses, all the pain, all the abandonment, all the isolation beckoned me with bony finger.

"Who the hell *am* I?" I wondered aloud. "I have no idea who I am anymore!"

The back of my hand lay on my forehead, and tears slid quietly down my cheeks to the waiting pillow.

*No,* I thought, *that isn't quite accurate.* The truth was that I hadn't known who I was for a long, long time—not since I was eight years old.

# 24

It was 4 a.m., December 23, 1972, when I awoke in total darkness, hearing noises in the hallway. I sat up in my pink canopy bed, wondering what was happening. Christmas wasn't for two more days, so I didn't know why anyone would be awake at this early hour. The sounds of my mother and older siblings moving hurriedly in the hallway, talking in hushed, urgent tones, made me curious.

I got up and opened my bedroom door. My mother was telling my older sister, Connie, to get some pajamas for my father. My brother Chris was sick with the flu, but my mother was telling him to go to the top of our driveway with a flashlight to direct the ambulance.

"What's going on?" I asked.

"Go back to bed," my mother said. I stood mute. "Then go sit with your father," she said, and disappeared.

I walked carefully to my parents' bedroom door and looked in. I saw my father lying in bed. He looked normal, but I knew from the activity that something was terribly wrong. I felt scared as I crawled up and lay beside him. He turned his head on the pillow and looked at me.

"I'm sorry I spoiled your Christmas, Loadstone," he said. He reached out and took my hand.

"You didn't, Daddy!"

I began to cry. I still had no idea what was happening, but the activity and the tone told me it was bad ... very bad. Whatever it was, my father obviously knew that it was serious.

"I love you," he said, still looking at me.

"I love you too, Daddy," I replied, now very frightened. "You're going to be okay."

My mother rushed in, fully dressed. Then the paramedics were there, putting my father on a stretcher and carrying him clumsily up the stairs and out to the waiting ambulance. Chris and Connie and I followed and stood shivering in our bathrobes on the gravel driveway.

I watched my mother climb into the back of the ambulance with my father and the paramedics, and then watched as they drove away in the early morning darkness, red lights flashing.

We turned and went back inside. My sister, who was twenty-one at the time and home from college for Christmas, went to the kitchen to make us some hot chocolate. We sat silently in the living room, huddled together. I still had no idea what was happening. The orange and blue and green Christmas tree lights looked preternaturally cheerful and slightly obscene.

My brother, who was seventeen, broke the silence. He lifted his mouth slightly from his mug and spoke into his cup.

"He's probably DOA."

"What's DOA?" I asked.

My sister shot him a look. "Shut up, Chris," she said.

Chris looked down at me, sitting on the floor near his feet. "Dead on arrival," he replied.

I burst into tears.

My sister drove us to the hospital around eight o'clock in the morning. We met my mother in the Intensive Care Unit. I watched my siblings and mother talking, clearly communicating something they did not want me to hear. After a minute or two, my mother came over to me.

"Your father's unconscious right now," she said. "The doctor's made a hole in his neck and he has a tube in his throat to help him breathe. I think it would be better if you didn't see him." I stood there, imagining a knife making a hole in someone's neck, its sharp point cutting into skin.

The family disappeared into the ICU, the big, blue, metal door closing heavily behind them. I looked around the empty waiting area, unsure what to do. Few people were around at this hour in the morning. I sat on a chair for a while, swinging my feet.

After a while, I noticed a door that led to a large, concrete balcony. I crossed the waiting area, pushed hard on the large, glass door, and went outside, hearing it click behind me. I rested my arms on the thick, concrete balustrade and stared toward the west hills for a few minutes, trying to figure out where our house was located in the distant hills.

The air was sharp and cold, and I realized I'd left my coat inside. I turned to go back in and pulled on the metal door handle. It did not budge. I pulled harder and realized to my horror that the door had locked behind me. I tried again. I knocked loudly and peered inside; I could see no one. I paced back and forth in the cold, shivering and feeling desperately scared. I wondered if anyone would notice me or if I might die, frozen and forgotten on a hospital balcony. After what felt like half an hour, but was likely closer to ten minutes, a nurse finally saw me and let me in. She must have felt sorry for me, because a few minutes later she reappeared with a pink origami elephant folded from a hospital admittance form and presented it to me.

I took my elephant with his penned-in eye and strangely high eyebrow and walked around the hospital floor until I discovered a tiny, dimly lit chapel. I went in and sat down on one of the six brown benches. The light was yellowish and the small space was carpeted and quiet.

"Please, God," I prayed silently, "Please don't let my Daddy die."

I had every faith in my innocent heart that God heard me, that He understood, and that He would, because of my sincere request, certainly see the lack of reason in taking a father away from an eight-year-old girl. There was no doubt in my mind that such an awful thing was simply not possible. It was inconceivable. The god that Mrs. Langhoff talked about in Good News Club every Wednesday after school didn't work like that.

As I stood to leave the chapel, I spotted Todd Gustufson standing in the middle of the wide, white-tiled hallway. Todd was in my third-grade class. He had what would now be called Attention Deficit Disorder, but in 1972, he was just called "hyper." He had a hard time sitting still and went outside to the van for special reading lessons. He had a particular fondness for the rock group Three Dog Night and would play *Jeremiah Was a Bullfrog* over and over on the eight-track tape player he brought to school.

I had no idea why Todd was at the chapel at that early hour. His father was a doctor at the hospital, so maybe he had been dragged in while his father had rounds. I walked out of the chapel and over to where Todd was standing.

"Hi," I said.

"Why are *you* here?" he asked.

"My father is sick."

Todd looked down and fished around in the pocket of his brown corduroy pants. He pulled out a silver horseshoe medallion with a penny in the center of it from his pocket and handed it to me. I looked at it closely, thinking that this was a perfect good-luck charm. God had no doubt heard my prayer. I was softened by Todd's offering and his kindness, coming as it did from one of the misfits of West Side Elementary School. Maybe I'd misjudged him. Todd was okay.

At eleven o'clock that morning, we left my father at the hospital in a coma and returned home to await further news. The phone was ringing as we walked in the front door. My mother picked up the olive green receiver from its cradle on the wall and I watched her face contort.

"Oh God," she said, and hung up the receiver. She began to cry; I had never seen my mother cry. "He's gone," she sobbed.

My father had died of a massive cerebral hemorrhage, two days before Christmas, at the age of fifty-two.

⌒⌒

My father was not a happy person. He'd survived four years of war in the South Pacific before going to Stanford on the G.I. Bill to study writing and directing. He taught theater briefly at a couple of universities and he and my mother, whom he met in the theater department at Stanford, did summer stock together. But with few theatrical opportunities and money scarce, he'd quickly abandoned his dreams of writing and directing for the more mundane exigency of supporting a family.

His drinking increased proportionally to his level of frustration, which was considerable. "Happy Hour"—a misnomer of gargantuan proportions—was a nightly event. He would sit with his bourbon and cigarette and decry the numerous injustices of life, both personal and political. There was a pervasive and oft-stated belief that life was incredibly, stupidly unfair.

When my father drank to excess, which was regularly, he swore and lashed out vituperatively. Unlike those more fortunate alcoholics, who become funnier or more creative when they drink, my father became angrier and more labile. We were all slightly afraid of my father, held hostage by his explosive anger.

I used to sit on the floor, positioning myself between my mother and father, who sat on orange vinyl-covered chairs at the Formica counter for their nightly ritual. They would drink and he would smoke a cigarette or two while I played quietly. I listened to their conversations and to his rants. I listened to how the Kennedys were killed by a conspiracy—a favorite topic—and I listened to his polemics against blacks and Republicans and others whom he considered less than his equal, which was everyone.

He was forever seeking the mystical, elusive Moment of Truth: the point at which, one could only imagine, the Secret of Life was revealed. Somehow, that moment never arrived. My mother would say that it was time for dinner, and he would sit back, looking heavenward.

"We were just at the Moment of Truth," he would say, exhaling deeply and with palpable disappointment at having come so very close to the Holy Grail, only to have it vanish before his eyes.

Despite all this, my father and I had a uniquely pleasant and loving relationship. He adored me. I was the unquestioned apple of his eye. Born relatively late in his life, I was a happy diversion: precocious and clever and, unlike the rest of his life, so very uncomplicated.

I liked to sit on the bathroom counter as he shaved, watching him soap his face with a badger-hair brush. He would soap my face as well, and I would use my index finger as a razor, cleanly scraping off my imaginary whiskers as he cut his own. Often he would record our intimate conversations on a reel to reel as we shaved, asking me questions and laughing at my answers.

He had a beautiful voice. He told me stories about imaginary friends and things he saw in the South Pacific. He shared his great love of books and reading. He fairly popped with pride as he sat in the audience of the grade school gymnasium, watching me in my first play as the letter "C" in Christmas and presenting me with a nosegay of flowers at the curtain.

I deeply loved my father, even as I feared his anger and hated the way he treated my mother and siblings. This complex emotional experience of my father was, at eight, confusing and guilt provoking. I didn't understand why everyone else received his anger and not me; it tore me in two and divided my loyalties. His death compounded this guilt and confusion, layering it beneath unspeakable sadness and fear.

On Christmas morning, we took the presents intended for my father from under the tree and unwrapped them solemnly, placing them on the coffee table. I had bought him some Old Spice aftershave at the drug store—the same gift I bought him every year, courtesy of my mother.

We sat down later that day for dinner, complete with white tablecloth, cranberry sauce, and a turkey. Mrs. Lumen, my third-grade teacher, came to the door in the middle of our meal to offer her condolences. I stood silently beside my mother as they spoke briefly, my teacher still on the doorstep, the cold air rushing in. I wondered how she knew. I wondered whether she had children of her own whom she had left on Christmas in order to come to our house. Mrs. Lumen was beautiful and kind and I loved her for coming. Her simple act of appearing at our door moved me deeply; it would be the only gesture of compassion that I would receive for the loss of my father.

A few days later my siblings and mother and I buried my father's ashes on our property, near the creek and beneath the tree that he used to help me to climb. It was a serene and lush spot in the spring and summer months and one of my favorite places to hide and play. Enormous blackberry bushes grew there, spreading exuberantly down into the cool water below. A large, well-worn log lay across the creek to the right, perfectly positioned for crossing over to the steep bank on the other side. Deer trails ran across the flat area and Ponderosa pine and madrone and oak formed a canopy overhead.

Now, though, in the last days of December, the sky was gray and overcast. Snow had fallen and the black branches crisscrossed above our heads. The wide parabola that formed the creek bed was stark and sharp. The water ran full and gurgling, cascading down waterfalls and forming icicles where the twigs bent low over it.

My brother dug a hole at the base of the curving tree, just large enough for the small, black metal box containing my father's ashes. We placed the box in the cold dirt, shoveled the earth back in, and covered the spot with a simple, flat-sided granite stone pulled from the creek. We stood in silence, shivering. I felt the sharp, cold edge of my tears as they traced a path down my cheeks. Then, after a few minutes, we turned and walked wordlessly back up the hill to the house.

I returned to school after the New Year. In the two-week interlude since leaving for Christmas vacation, my world—and my childhood—had ended. At recess on the first day back, I stood by myself, leaning against the railing of the wide, concrete breezeway, looking out on the rainy playground. Out of the corner of my right eye, I could see Kelly Mason approaching me tentatively.

I hated Kelly. She was cute and blonde and had a cute nose and cute clothes and she lived in a big house with a swimming pool and rode in a big, blue Cadillac with an opera window in the back. She was mean, and she teased me mercilessly and constantly. She and her pretty-girl posse made my early school life a living hell.

Kelly now stood about five feet away from me, leaning on the heavily painted metal railing of the breezeway.

"I heard your dad died," she said.

"Yes," I responded warily.

"I just want to tell you that I know how you feel."

I stared at her. "No you don't."

"Yes, I do!" she asserted. She was strangely stubborn on this point.

I replied that it was impossible for her to know how I felt because her father was alive. She said she could imagine it. I told her that she could not. Although I really ought to have given her points for making this unusual foray into kindness, I hated her all the more for saying that she knew how I felt; no one knew how I felt. How could they with their alive fathers and their intact lives?

From my first steps back into that cold, windy breezeway of West Side Elementary School that January, I felt different from the girl I had once been and different from my peers. I was privy to a knowledge and a suffering and a loneliness that they could not understand and that I could not articulate. Because I felt so different and out of place, I turned my attention away from socializing with other children and oriented myself instead to my teachers, whom I imagined understood.

Because children often do not display their pain in a manner easily recognized—because they continue to play and eat and go to school—adults often erroneously imagine that they are unscathed by such events. It is a dangerous belief, a wish really, that children do not feel deeply, that they don't really *understand*.

I understood. I understood that my father was gone, and I understood that the other kids could not begin to know what I was going through. My own mother did not know what I was going through; she was too absorbed in her own fear and pain.

That winter, I became my mother's sole companion and caretaker. It was a job that I took extremely seriously because her continued existence was intricately connected to my own. My job, my life for the next four years, involved excelling at school and then hurrying home to be with my mother, whom I feared might expire from loneliness.

It was an innocent but not completely unfounded belief: in her emotional distress, she frequently voiced her wish that she were dead. The obvious implication was terrifying enough, but the underlying subtext was equally disturbing. My existence, it seemed, was not enough to warrant her desire to live. It was as if I were not there in those moments, as if I did not exist. Caught up in a deluge of her own suffering, she seemed ill prepared to notice mine.

But being physically present with my mother and being an easy, good child did provide me with a sense of value and importance. She was, both literally and emotionally, my reason for being. My mother reinforced this every time she told me that God had brought me to her and kept me from certain miscarriage because He knew that she would need me for just this circumstance in her life. As a child, this made me feel special; several years into therapy, it made me feel sick.

Hypervigilence became my *modus operandi*. I declined invitations to play, concerned that my mother would not be able to tolerate her aloneness and would, perhaps, decide that she was done. When gas rationing began later that year and my mother was, unbeknownst to me, stuck sitting in line at a gas station, I sat at the top of our driveway for hours into the evening, waiting for her, crying, certain that I had been orphaned.

My special purpose and destiny was obviated four years later with the arrival of a new man. David was near sixty when he met my mother. He was playing viola for the local classical music festival, held every summer near our home. He was recently widowed and my mother seized upon the opportunity for love and companionship before she even had an idea who he was. She toted me along to every morning rehearsal, every concert and special event. They had an immediate and passionate three-week affair.

I liked David. He was like a grandfather: bald and kind and gentle and sincerely interested in me. But when the summer ended and the affair did not, the equation changed. My mother began visiting him in his home in central California. When she informed me that they were getting married and that we would be moving to San Luis Obispo, I balked. I liked David well enough, but the prospect of a new father and of being uprooted mid-year from junior high and my familiar life and surroundings turned me defiant.

It was not the fact that my mother was remarrying that upset me; what bothered me was being dumped. The much longed for *man* had arrived, filling my mother's deep internal void and giving her back a sense of self. She no longer needed me and I felt disposable and discarded.

When my mother stated—and she stated it often—that she was nothing without a man, she meant it. When David arrived, I watched her inflate back into a vibrant woman. She and David began traveling together frequently, enjoying their second spring as late lovers. They flew to Europe for a month and then to Hawaii, Japan, and cruises in various parts of the world. They were in love and having fun: fun they both richly deserved after difficult first marriages, but fun that did not include a twelve-year-old daughter.

This left me alone, dumped at Mrs. Meyer's, a pale, doughy-faced friend of my mother's whom I did not know well or like very much. Sometimes I got to stay with my sister and her husband who lived a few hours away, which I liked better. But wherever I was sent, it hurt to feel so unwanted where I had, until recently, felt indispensable. I felt rejected and alone.

My mother inhabited a realm of eternal emotional adolescence. A beautiful woman, she had always focused all her energies on her appearance and her relationships to the opposite sex, eschewing feminine companionship in favor of more satisfying, erotic pursuits.

"I don't like women," she liked to say.

The moment a man entered her life, she shaped herself to his proclivities and opinions, giving him dominion over her time, her body, and her activities. Like many woman of her day, my mother found identity only as a wife and a mother. Now, apparently, even the mothering was none too pressing. She was too happy, too relieved to have escaped middle-aged widowhood.

# 25

I could not seem to escape my own widowhood; it shrouded me. I returned to my house in Ashland after a week of moping and thinking at my mother's. I kept myself busy with therapy and Sammy, but I always returned to my quiet, empty house alone.

One by one, all the pieces of my former life had, in strange and not-so-strange ways, disappeared: first David; then my work; then Andrew; then Andrew's belongings; then Beau; all followed by the furniture, the car, the house, and Bella. There was a powerful impulse in me, after Andrew died, to shed everything, to go light. It wasn't, as so many people imagined, the desire to get rid of reminders; that was impossible. Everything is a reminder after someone you love dies; every street you cross, every meal you eat, every story you tell, every picture you see, every song you hear—*everything* elicits a memory. The things themselves don't trigger memories; love does, and the love is imbued in everything.

The first sign of new life arrived, serendipitously and appropriately, the following spring. In mid-March, I suffered a riding accident. Sammy had thrown me and stepped on the small of my back, his hoof crushing a number of nerves. I was taken by ambulance first to the hospital and then to my house, where I had spent ten days lying in bed, stoned out of my mind on a potent cocktail of muscle relaxants and painkillers. By month's end, I began to recover with the help of physical therapy and had begun ambulating again.

I went to see Nicole, who informed me at the end of our session that she had discovered a homeless dog on one of her walks around the historic railroad district. He had been taken in by a group of pot-smoking college students after being found alone on the hiking trails above town. Determined to rescue the creature before he starved to death or suffered irreparable brain damage from the pot fumes, she enlisted me in what amounted to a dognapping.

"I don't want a dog," I had demurred. "The only possible dog that I would take would have to be non-shedding. And small. And white. And preferably a male."

"Of course, a *male*," she quipped, derisively.

I ignored her and continued. "And quiet and loving. A lap dog that doesn't yap."

"You don't have to take it," she said. "I just need someone to help me get him from that house. I'm taking him to the groomer. It's my mitzvah for the month."

I drove with her over to the house after my session and watched her walk up to the front door. She spoke to an invisible entity, and then stood for a minute before a man appeared on the stoop and passed something into her arms. He stood at his screen door, watching Nicole carry the rather largish ball of matted white fur back to the car where she deposited it through the passenger window onto my lap. She got in, laughing her broken, smoker's laugh at her own audacity.

"We just kidnapped a dog, honey!" she croaked. She was delighted with herself. "We saved his life. The pot smoke in there—I almost got high just standing at the door! We rescued him, honey!"

I looked down at my lap. I could see no face, no paws. I pushed back the hair where I imagined a face ought to be and was greeted by two enormous, round, brown eyes staring unblinkingly back at me. The creature was utterly still and calm; he did not pant, or blink, or move a muscle. It was unnerving how un-dog-like he was.

I wanted him.

We drove directly to the groomer to get him cleaned and clipped and when I returned two hours later, the cloud of hair that I first saw had been shaved down to the skin, leaving what now sat before me: he was a Lhasa Apso, but not like any I had seen. He had been shaved down to a shivering, pitiful, bowlegged creature with a puffball face, twice as long as he was high. He looked like a large, naked mole rat with a permed head. I questioned his desirability for just a moment before scooping him up and taking him home.

Even shaved and looking slightly deformed, I knew that I had found the perfect dog. He met every demand on my list; this was no accident. To me, his arrival was nothing short of divine intervention. I was certain that he must be a bodhisattva—an enlightened being who chose to remain on Earth to help me. I named him Bentley.

Two weeks later, the groomer called me.

"I think I found his family," she said. "I'm going to give you their name and number, but it's up to you what you do with it. I haven't told them about you, so if you decide not to call them, I won't say a word about it."

I hung up, closed my eyes, and sighed. I couldn't bear the thought of losing him. I loved him already, but I knew that I couldn't live with myself if I didn't call.

I looked at the number written on the back of an envelope for a couple of days before finally marshaling the courage to call. When the woman answered, I told her only that the groomer had reported to me that her dog was missing. She told me that he had been lost while hiking with her son. I offered very little information, listened to her description of the dog, and finally, against all my wishes and hopes, confirmed that I did indeed have their dog.

Crestfallen, I called to Bentley, put on my coat, and began the short walk to the library, four blocks away, where we had arranged to meet. I talked to Bentley as we walked down the steep hill toward town, telling him how glad I was to have shared this brief time with him and how much I would miss him. He trotted happily beside me, his plumed tail blowing in the breeze.

I sat on the library steps with Bentley beside me, waiting sadly for the family to arrive, steeling myself for the good-bye. I watched a car pull up twenty yards away, and a gaggle of children disgorged, running toward us, shouting.

"Shorty! *Shorty!*"

A boy about seventeen ran across the grass toward us, shouting the name. Bentley looked up and trotted toward him in obvious recognition. Tears were running down his cheeks as he scooped up Bentley and held him close before setting him back down. The younger children all squatted down to greet their dog, petting and cuddling him. Then, Bentley ran back to me, equally happy. The boy saw this and his look of joy turned to one of compassion.

"Thank you for finding him. Thank you for taking care of him," he said, his voice full of gratitude.

"It was my pleasure. It was the happiest two weeks I've had in a long time."

The boy's mother thanked me profusely, and then the family turned to go. The boy stood with Bentley in his arms, and I stroked his soft, gray and white head.

"Would it make any difference if I offered to buy him?" I asked, glancing up at the boy's face.

The boy paused and thought for a second, and said, "Let me talk to my mom."

He walked over to his mother, and they spoke quietly. I watched and waited, focusing on the shape and movement of my breath as it traveled past my lips and into the cold, spring morning. I tried not to think at all.

After three or four minutes, the boy walked with Bentley back to where I stood on the bright, green lawn. "My mom told me your story," he said, "and I feel bad for you, but I just can't give him up."

I nodded in understanding. "I wouldn't give him up either, if I were you."

We stood in silence for a few moments more.

"Would it make any difference if I offered you $500?"

The words had shot out of me without any conscious forethought. It was a last, desperate move. *Why not?* I thought, surprised by myself. *It's worth a try.*

The boy looked up, clearly surprised and shocked. "Can I talk to my mom again?" he asked.

"Of course. Take your time."

This was good. He was considering it. I sat down on the steps of the library while the family reconvened, forming a discussion huddle a few yards away. My offer clearly had intrigued him, despite his obvious love for the dog. They talked for at least ten minutes.

Finally, after what appeared to be a very emotional conference, I saw him walking back, Bentley in his arms, and tears flowing down his face. He sat down next to me on the steps.

"If he means that much to you," he said, "you can have him."

I couldn't believe what was happening, couldn't believe that my desperate offer had made a difference, couldn't believe that this story was going to have a happy ending.

"I'm going to college in a few months," he continued, "and I could really use that money. I'm working at Burger King to earn the tuition, and this would help me a lot. I know that I won't be at home as much."

I had bribed Bentley away from the boy. I was filled with a guilty joy in using money to buy myself love, taking it from someone else's arms. At the same time, I felt true compassion and respect for this kid and the sacrifice he was making—for his future and for me.

I quickly took out my checkbook before he changed his mind and wrote a check for $750. My gratitude and guilt were such that I thought I could at least pay for his first semester at the local university. I handed it to him, and he looked down at it, eyes growing wide. I thought about how hard he worked at Burger King for his five bucks an hour, and how much this sum represented to him, so painfully yet easily won.

He thanked me and I thanked him. I promised that I'd take wonderful care of Shorty. He asked if they could visit, and I said they could any time they wanted to, but I knew they wouldn't. The boy's younger siblings were crying as they left, but I knew they'd be okay. They had other dogs, and they had each other; now I had someone, too.

I couldn't believe my incredible fortune. I hadn't felt this happy in two years. I was ecstatic. I walked briskly back up the hill with Bentley bouncing beside me in his peculiar and charming way, his right front paw making strange little circular loops with each step. I wanted to get home before the spell broke, before the boy changed his mind and grabbed the little naked rat back into his arms. I smiled broadly as I walked, filled with a pure, expansive joy.

Bentley became my constant, quiet companion, accompanying me to the grocery store where he rode in the cart, on rides in the basket on my bike, into shops and massage appointments. He slept at the foot of my bed. He was unlike any animal I'd ever known—not just because he provided me companionship and solace when I most needed it, but also because he was always utterly silent and calmly present. He had the disquieting ability to stare at me without blinking. Bentley looked at me in a way that said he knew everything that needed to be known. He did not pant or bark or seek affection or play. Bentley simply *was*. Bentley was a Buddha in a dog suit.

Now, in the warmth of spring and with my new companion accompanying me every day, I returned to the barn—at first just to brush and talk to Sammy and, in time, to riding. Bentley loved the barn, and I loved his company. He was exceptionally fond of both Sammy and Sammy's dung; Sammy, for his part, was tolerant of the Buddha and kind enough not to crush him as we trotted, the three of us together, around the dressage ring.

⌒⌒

My wedding anniversary and April birthday came and went again. Barbara and Richard called me frequently. Barbara had become noticeably softer and kinder.

During one conversation, she had even said, "We don't want to lose you," which is about as emotional and intimate as she'd ever been with me.

These were, after all, the sort of people who never said, "I love you" to anyone. The closest they came was to say "much love" or "lots of love"—phrases devoid of subject. So when I heard Barbara say so openly, so forthrightly and with real human emotion that they did not wish to lose me, I was deeply moved.

Barbara was now working on her second book, and she and Richard were about to go to Greece where she could do some research and where they would visit Richard's sister and brother-in-law, Jane and Stephanos. She told me this on the phone as I stood at the sink in my antiseptically white kitchen, staring across the street at my neighbor's unfinished house, wishing it weren't there.

Impulsively, I blurted out, "I want to go too!" before I really thought about what I was saying.

Barbara, perhaps equally impulsively, invited me right then to join them and, one month later, I was sitting on a Boeing 747, downing one of Nicole's Restorils with a glass of wine, hoping to sleep most of the way to Athens and wondering, for the first time, what in the hell I was getting myself into.

# 26

Whatever fantasy of closeness Barbara's kind comments had planted in me was quickly uprooted once I arrived in the claustrophobic, stifling city of Athens. I immediately realized, far too late, that Mid-June is not the best time to place oneself in a blisteringly hot climate in geography completely devoid of green vegetation. The temperature was something on a par with Dante's Fifth Circle of Hell. All I could think was how much I wanted to have a drink and some dinner and fall into bed.

Barbara had other plans. She greeted me with a brief hug in the foyer of the hotel and suggested that I have a quick drink, informing me that there was not enough time for me to even go up to my room; the opera was in less than an hour. Richard pressed a gin and tonic into my hand.

I took a long drink from the little black straw. An opera? I desperately hoped that I had misunderstood. Surely they did not intend for me to join them after just making a trip halfway around the globe. Surely they meant that they were going, not I. Then Barbara's hand was on my back, and she was steering me toward a waiting car, my drink only half-consumed. Had I been more on my game, I would have pursued my case for humane treatment and begged off to bed, but that would have entailed a battle of wills.

Barbara was famous—or infamous—for making plans and keeping everyone occupied, whether they wanted to be or not. Sometimes this could be very lovely, as when she purveyed theatre tickets and gave a couple of days' notice; other times, it was a Verdi opera outside in the Grecian heat in an amphitheater designed for people who were, quite obviously, far smaller than 20th century Americans.

Thirty minutes later I found myself, after eighteen hours of travel and half of a gin and tonic in my stomach, in a near-fetal position on a narrow, stone seat in the middle of an ancient, Athenian amphitheater. My knees were pushed into to my chest, and a stranger's legs dug into my back. The discomfort and the exhaustion were overwhelming. The fact that it was a three-hour opera did little to ameliorate this. Opera, even in a private box seat at the Kennedy Center with a cocktail at intermission, was tedious at best; this was outright torture.

I sat, silently giving myself a pep talk: *You are in Greece, sitting in a three-thousand-year-old amphitheater, watching an opera. How amazing is this?* But my feeble attempt at positivity was drowned out by the louder voice that kept insisting, *I can't believe she made me do this.*

The next morning, the cultural death march resumed bright and early. Barbara happily disappeared into the bowels of the Athenian archives to conduct her research for her book while Richard and I boarded a chartered bus for a full-day tour of Delphi.

After a long, winding drive though barren hills, we reached the home of the ancient oracle. I could not imagine making this pilgrimage on foot, as the ancient Greeks had done for centuries, navigating the hot, dry, dangerous terrain only *perhaps* to speak to the oracle, who then only answered in riddle form; I was worn out just sitting on an air-conditioned bus.

The temperature was in triple digits by the time we arrived in Delphi. The June sun glared insistently overhead, glancing off the ruins that were once the prosperous and beautiful mecca. I loved being here. I imagined the priestess sitting on her tripod stool above the cracks in the earth from which the potent, mind-altering vapors, which transported her into a prophetic trance, emanated. I loved imagining what it must have looked like in its glory: the marketplace; the paths lined with stones; the bright, white marble exteriors; the statues of the gods looking down on the sojourners from impressive heights; the money changers and the food vendors and the priests as they strolled the grounds. I loved walking along the timeworn dirt pathway that serpentined up the hill and touching the still-visible outlines of the vendors' stalls carved into the hillside.

Just up above the Temple of Apollo was the omphalos: the center of the world for the ancient Greeks. The word "omphalos" means "navel." The omphalos is the point at which the upper and lower worlds meet. The oracle sat at this point, where the worlds of spirit and humanity touched, receiving petitioners and offering them the veiled, prophetic answers to their queries about future fortunes. I wished that I could ask her a few questions right about now.

Of course, the original omphalos was long gone and had been replaced by a stone replica. It could have been a contemporary piece of modern art: an ovoid, smoothly shaped rock about three feet tall, perched unremarkably near the top of the hill overlooking the ruins. Everyone wanted a picture of himself standing, touching, or making a gross gesture at the center of the world. It's amazing what sort of pull this rock—this myth—still exerts on its visitors, how much we all want to feel connected to something larger than ourselves, to locate ourselves in relationship to something wiser, something eternal.

I looked up after taking a picture of the omphalos, trying to locate Richard. I found him standing below me, looking out over the valley and the ruins. He was wearing a light blue seersucker suit and a straw fedora. He appeared to be happily taking it all in, tromping up and down the dusty hills with his East Coast summer attire, eyebrows climbing over his tortoise-shell glasses.

I wondered how it was possible for him to keep such equipoise, how he could maintain his sweetness and sense of humor. His first-born son was gone; his daughter-in-law, now with him, was a constant reminder of what had been lost, and still he supported me, took care of me, dragged me to see Delphi. He seemed indefatigable: always open, always good-natured and kind.

After a time, we all piled back onto the air-conditioned motor coach and wound slowly down the hill, past the site where Oedipus Rex was born—or died, or killed his father, or blinded himself (it's hard to remember). I did remember the interesting little fact that "pus" means "feet," as in "octo-pus" or "eight feet," so that alone made the trip worthwhile.

On the bus, there was a single father with his daughter. She appeared to be ten years old or so; he was balding slightly, in his forties and likewise widowed. They were from the U.S. and touring together. The father seemed interested in me. I tried to imagine what it would be like to have a ten-year-old stepdaughter. I felt too young for that, but I imagined that I could handle it.

We stopped for lunch at an outdoor taverna. Father, daughter, Richard, and I shared a table under a pergola in the back. Richard saw the flickers of interest, and he leaned over and whispered encouraging remarks in my ear, just as Barbara had done at the Derby. I appreciated his support and awareness, but it made me uncomfortably self-conscious. I resisted anything that would possibly implicate me as a traitor to his son or to them.

The truth was that I wasn't yet capable or interested in anything serious. It's hard to feel attractive or desirable when your world is turned upside down, and everything you know, everything you dreamed, everything you planned is stripped away in one night. You lose your bearings and your sense of self. You begin to imagine that you must look the way you feel: tired and swallowed up.

Widowhood is a black hole. All the air, all the life is just sucked right out, and all that is left is a huge, gaping void where your life used to be. *Whoosh ... gone.* So when the nice guy on the bus leans over and wants to talk to you and you feel the energy and vitality of life again, it's like climbing out of the void and seeing a star twinkling in the distance: it's not home, it's not a new beginning yet, but it's hopeful. It felt good to know that I could be desirable and that I was still attractive, even if it was to a balding man who was old enough to have a ten-year-old daughter. It made me feel that perhaps all was not lost.

The next day Richard and I were back on tour—on foot this time—climbing the ancient Acropolis to the Parthenon. It was visible at night from our hotel, illuminated in a strangely Vegas-like presentation with changing, colored floodlights. Physically being at the Parthenon was surprisingly moving. Unlike so many other experiences where there is a general disappointment in seeing a famous object in person ("I could've stayed home and enjoyed it more" sort of thing), the Parthenon grabbed my imagination. Even crawling with the ubiquitous throng of tourists, I was moved by the enormity and history of it.

Even more, I felt a radiant energy, a power like that at Delphi but stronger, more massive in scale. It no doubt had something to do with the sheer colossal size of the Acropolis, which was part of the original intention and design of the structure; but it also related to the fact that this was a temple built for a female deity, the mighty and glorious Athena. Originally, the temple housed a massive, radiant golden image of the goddess, now lost to antiquity.

I looked up at the columns, tilting my head back to take in the incredible size of the structure. At my adamant insistence, Richard had succumbed to hiring a personal guide, one of the many locals who wait at the base of the hill for an opportunity to make some cash while imparting their well-rehearsed narrative. We made a serendipitous choice in an embodied human Athena: an extremely knowledgeable and delightful middle-aged native with beautiful, long, dark, wavy hair and a wide-brimmed hat, who slowly guided us through the history of the place. Her vivid and detailed descriptions, including the copious mythology that is imbued in all of ancient Greece, brought the tumbling columns and rock-strewn ground to life.

She pointed out all the hills of the gods and goddesses of the Pantheon, visible in the distance from the Acropolis. We learned what the vestal virgins did, and how the white bones of the temple before us were once painted in brilliant hues. Having always loved history and stories, I found myself in a delightful reverie, seeing past the plodding pilgrims and treeless vistas to a time thousands of years past. The Athens of today is crowded, hot, and polluted, but the Athens of my musing was covered with green, rolling hills and temples dotting the landscape and toga-clad teachers. For a few hours, I completely forgot about my mean, little life and was engulfed by the larger beauty and mythology surrounding me.

As we made our descent, we walked an ancient, winding, pedestrian pathway down to the city. Another amphitheater spread out below us on the right, crumbling now but its outline still visible. The path wound down to an unusual and welcome car-free, tree-lined area, where there were beautiful shops and places to buy maps of the old city. I bought a blue platter painted with bright, emblematic lemons and enjoyed the last moments of a welcome serenity.

The rest of the afternoon was devoted to a searingly hot sojourn, by way of taxi, to the Athens National Museum, the urban tangle of jumbled buildings and black, paved streets, hideously exaggerating the already blistering temperature. As we drove, I looked out the window just in time to see an enormous, six-foot-long, smoking cigarette perched on top of a small, square, newspaper kiosk. It was making slow circles above the little building, puffs of smoke wafting out of the tip every few seconds. It looked like something out of a Greek Disneyland, except instead of a huge, revolving hot dog, it was a giant cigarette.

I was completely captivated. I turned around, craning my neck to stare at it through the rear window as we drove past. The Greeks either had not heard or simply did not care about the deleterious effects of tobacco, as evidenced by the cigarettes I saw in every other person's mouth and this display in the middle of the madness of Athens. I admired the honesty of it, the disregard for conventional wisdom and political correctness.

There is a pervasive attitude in Greece that, if I were to give it a voice, might say, "I created democracy. I gave you language. I gave you classical mythology," and then turn away with a look of bored disdain and take a long drag on its cigarette. It was arrogant and *defiant*. Maybe that's what I liked. It was strong and in your face and defiant: the opposite of me.

The museum itself was a nightmare, due largely to the fact that it had no air conditioning; however, the central drawback to the place—apart from its sauna-like properties—was that, strangely and inexplicably, there were no descriptions for what we were looking at, which made maintaining interest through hundreds of amphora and thousands of armless, headless, anatomically correct figures somewhat challenging. One would expect to find something, anything—a name or a date—but it was, in effect, an enormous, hot attic for ancient Greece: objects without context; objects without stories; objects, therefore, without meaning.

The following day, we left Athens and met Andrew's Aunt Jane and Uncle Stephanos in Piraeus, a 2,500-year-old port city. We boarded an ugly, hulking ferry that would take us to their home on the island of Spetses. As we moved away from the cacophony of Piraeus and into the archipelago, I stood at the railing of our colossal craft and stared out at the tiny dots of land sprinkled in the sea, some so small that they had room only for a small, plain chapel perched on the bare stone; others, larger and more treed, provided private sanctuary for the ultra-rich.

We stopped for lunch at the island of Hydra, a place so rocky and steep that there were no cars, just sad, little donkeys that meandered slowly up and down the cobbled lanes, wooden saddles sitting on their miserable, worn backs. I rode one of them out of curiosity. The saddle hurt my bare legs, and I felt hugely guilty for burdening him with my unnecessary weight, just so I could have the experience.

I wandered on foot along the shopping area, looking in the store windows, gazing at the gorgeous gold for which Greece is famous: bright, gleaming pieces of soft, twenty-carat jewelry. The old designs were especially alluring, and I spent quite some time choosing a set for myself, consisting of a simple, gold collar with a small sapphire set in the center and matching earrings and ring.

As I looked at the jewelry, I talked to the shopkeeper about my husband and showed her my sapphire engagement ring. Like all people to whom I told my story, she was deeply sympathetic and kind. Richard came up behind me and admired my choice. I introduced him to the shopkeeper, who offered him very sincere condolences. Richard appeared both moved and uncomfortable. He pulled out his wallet and insisted on buying me the entire set.

When we re-boarded the ferry for Spetses, I sat in the window seat next to Barbara and showed her my jewelry. Barbara wore eyeglasses that darkened when they were exposed to light, making it impossible to see or read her eyes. The overall effect was slightly alienating; it was like looking at an enormous fly. She glanced sideways and down at my adornments and then quickly looked up and away.

"I think jewelry is a waste of money," she stated flatly, staring straight ahead. "I'd much rather have something useful."

She looked down and opened the package on her lap to reveal brightly colored, floral table linens. Then she turned away from me and to her right to speak to Richard, who was sitting across the aisle from her. I sat awkwardly on the plastic seat beside her, silently wishing that she would move to another seat, wishing that I were somewhere else, and wondering why she said these sorts of things.

Was she angry? Was it because Richard had bought me jewelry? Was it because her son was dead and I was alive and sitting beside her? Or was it that she simply did not realize how rude she sounded? Whatever it was, I knew that it had nothing to do with me, but I seemed to be receiving the brunt of her unhappiness.

I retreated to the comfort and confines of my private thoughts, thoughts that calmed and amused me. It occurred to me that linens were a strange choice, particularly for someone like Barbara: all flowery and ultra-feminine when Barbara was anything but.

Barbara was an enigma. She could be kind and generous in certain moments, like inviting me to join them on this trip or offering me sets of her china, but more often she acted either uncomfortable or disdainful around me, as if I were strange and inadequate. Everything I said to Barbara seemed to be met with either disregard or disagreement. It unnerved me. I constantly felt wrong and awkward in her presence.

I imagined that this was how Andrew felt much of his life. He always suffered under the impression that he was somehow wrong and a disappointment. His very conception was wrong and disappointing: an unwanted accident. Barbara liked to say that Andrew had arrived two months early. I could never tell whether this statement was made in jest, or whether it was an attempt to mask the truth of an unplanned, unwed pregnancy.

We landed at Spetses, a lovely little island frequented primarily by other Greeks. We made our way by foot to Jane and Stephanos' house up the hill, suitcases coming via moped behind us. Their home was one of four among which they divided their time, and Jane was busy opening curtains and settling in, talking with the housekeeper.

The house—intelligently built, as are all homes in hot climates—was beautifully cool, with walls two feet thick and blue shutters on the windows to block the Mediterranean sun. I was physically and emotionally exhausted from the trip and from the psychological flotsam and jetsam generated by the journey, and I fell into a long, deep, desperately needed sleep in my darkened room, away from everyone, lost in my dreams in the soft, cool, enormous bed that I wanted never to leave.

"Time to get up! You can't sleep all day."

Barbara's voice woke me out of my peaceful oblivion. It was a high, penetrating voice, distinctive and very insistent. I sat up on my elbows, trying to get my bearings in the pitch-dark room. The door was slightly ajar; I could just make out Barbara's head, poking through tentatively.

"Okay," I croaked, only barely conscious, unclear as to the day, the time, or the reason she felt that I should be up and about.

She closed the door and I sat up, wrapping the sheets around my naked body.

*Why couldn't I sleep all day?* I wondered.

I was irritated, and I wanted to say something, but I couldn't. I didn't want to be difficult; besides, I'd invited myself on this trip. Not to mention that these were still my in-laws, and I loved them, quirkiness and emotional repression and interpersonal tensions notwithstanding.

Accommodating these tensions and the lack of affect was hard on me. It was very difficult to feel as awkward and uncomfortable as I did with Barbara, unsettling not to have my bearings with her after four years. I just couldn't seem to find her sweet spot, and I wore myself out trying.

At lunch later that day, I was seated beside a neighbor, a woman with whom I felt instantly at ease. She ran a small copy shop just around the corner and up the dusty road from Jane's house. The woman was pretty and warm and solicitous, and spoke English fluently. She and I were engaged in a convivial conversation, a welcome sociable interlude. She asked about my horseback riding, and I was telling her about the fall I'd had in March and how I'd been immobilized for almost two weeks.

Barbara was sitting across from us, listening attentively. She interrupted me mid-story.

"Well," she said, "it wasn't *really* two weeks ..."

Her tone clearly indicated that she thought I was exaggerating, lying even. She was looking at us over the top of her glasses, like a prosecutor eyeing a witness on the stand.

Barbara turned to the guest, who was seated beside her, and proceeded to tell *her* version of my story. I was dumbfounded. My new friend seemed equally uncomfortable. Barbara hadn't been there, hadn't seen me lying in bed whacked on four different painkillers, unable to bathe or even stand without screaming in pain; she hadn't witnessed the emergency-room visit and the ambulance and the six weeks of physical therapy.

I was livid that she would humiliate me like this in public. If I'd been a cartoon character, there would have been sparks flying from my eyes and a little, dark cloud circling over my head. I couldn't let her do this, practically accusing me of lying. My incensed pride over-rode my usual deference to her.

"Actually," I said assertively, "I *was* in bed for ten days. The horse's hoof crushed the nerves in my low back."

Everyone was quiet. Barbara stared at me, smiled a small, thin-lipped, forced smile, and turned back to her companion.

Greece was turning out to be one of the lonelier experiences of my widowhood. I felt far worse being here that I did at home. I was out of my element, limited in my expression, and required to be more civil, more active and more pleasant than I wanted to be. I understood that Barbara did not like to deal with emotional topics, but this ... this was just plain mean.

I wanted to go home. I was sorry that I came, sorry that I had asked to come. It seemed to me that Barbara did not want me there either. It was hard to feel that she did not respect or like me. I felt slightly stuck. There was no one my age or even of my generation here, and nothing to do but take walks and be seen but not heard. It felt like an unspoken gag order had been imposed on me. Barbara wanted us all to be up and active—not expressing anything personal or dwelling in emotion. This was most definitely not my style. I am a dweller, an expresser. We were at an emotional impasse, neither of us able to be anything other than what we were.

I caught only one, small glimpse of a softer, more vulnerable side of Barbara as we all went for a walk one morning to a café by the water. She was walking ahead of me, as she always did, talking with Jane. Walking by myself behind them, I tried to inconspicuously catch what they were saying. Barbara was describing an empty feeling she was experiencing in her body. She gestured to the left side of her torso, just under the ribcage. She said that she had felt it since Andrew's death—a sensation of an actual, physical hole inside her body.

I was intrigued, overhearing this confession. It was the first time that I had heard her speak of the loss in a personal way. Even though she was not confiding this to me, I was glad to hear it and grateful to feel, at long last, some emotional presence. For the first time, I felt real compassion and empathy for Barbara. Before that moment, I could only guess, could only assume that she must be devastated, must be grieving somehow, somewhere, because I never once saw it, never heard it, never felt it.

Nicole's admonishment echoed in my head: "You cry in private."

I had understood this to mean that I should not cry in public, which she undoubtedly meant. But perhaps it was also her way of telling me that, just because I didn't see Barbara cry, it didn't mean that she didn't express herself. That was a very foreign concept; not only did I cry myself a river in my solitude, I cried streams and ponds and puddles everywhere else, too. I couldn't help it.

I watched Barbara walking ahead of me. She was wearing a plain, blue, cotton shirtdress, buttoned all the way up, flat shoes, no make-up, and little jewelry. I mused about Barbara from the consulting room in my brain. Feeling lonely and bewildered by both the spoken and unspoken conversations surrounding me, I tried to distance myself by looking at Barbara psychologically. Doing so helped me to depersonalize, and it summoned my compassion.

Perhaps, I theorized, she was uncomfortable in her skin, like Andrew. Perhaps it was a form of self-protection, like a snapping turtle in its shell, well armored and defensive. It occurred to me that what I was seeing was a very wounded woman.

I imagined a story that went: "This is a woman who was never made to feel good about herself, who was trapped by a narcissistic mother, and who found refuge in her mind. This is a woman who feels lonely. This is a woman who doesn't know how to relate warmly to people, particularly women."

This story sounded frighteningly familiar.

We arrived at the café and drank our coffee, with me silently listening to the conversation, and then we walked down to the bay. We followed the water's edge around the town to a small cove where Stephanos' new boat had just been completed and where it sat, precariously, in its crude, wooden mooring. It was a beautiful, classic Greek-style boat—a *kaiki*, about thirty feet long. We stood by as a ragged collection of men and boys—laboriously and with much gesticulating, yelling, and delay—pushed it out of its makeshift launch and into the water. Stephanos stood on the deck of his new ship, yelling down instructions and corrections in Greek. We cheered and waved as Stephanos began his maiden voyage, standing proudly at the helm.

By the time he returned from his virgin voyage an hour later, Stephanos proclaimed his utter boredom with the boat, tossing his hand in the air as if to say it was already passé. The boat had been Stephanos' latest project and diversion.

Stephanos had strong opinions about everything, most of them negative, and he held a particular disdain for all things American, including his wife, whose money supported them. He appeared to know a great deal about everything, but he didn't seem to actually do anything. I had the distinct impression that even Richard, who loved and was loved by everyone he met, had a certain distaste for this man's ease in allowing his wife's inheritance to carry him through life.

We all took a sail together on the new boat, out into the bluest water I had ever seen. Jane had made a picnic consisting of saltless bread, wine, ouzo, and cheese, and we ate as we bobbed on the sapphire water, staring down into the clear depths. I jumped overboard to swim, luxuriating in the water's warmth and beauty; I felt self-conscious in my bikini, the only adult child among my in-laws.

Clearing the table that evening after a late supper of ubiquitous Greek salad, ouzo, and fish, I found myself in the kitchen, alone with Jane for the first time since arriving. Jane was an extremely sweet woman, tiny and sprite-like with a fairy's countenance. She moved in quick, flitting movements; her speech was soft-spoken and rambling, her thoughts seemingly partially elsewhere. I could imagine why:

Living with Stephanos could send anyone into an alternate reality. She seemed to ignore Stephanos' rants, as if she didn't hear them at all, and cleaved instead to Richard. She clearly idolized her brother, staring at him adoringly and holding him lovingly. She seemed almost an innocent—as much girl as woman.

To my complete surprise, Jane spontaneously began to tell me, in a very natural way as she bustled around the tiny kitchen, about a letter that Andrew had dictated to her for his parents, after his death. I stopped, stunned by this casual revelation, and looked at her. I had no idea to this point that Jane was spiritual in the least; there had been no hint of it, naturally enough, among the family. If they knew of her metaphysical leanings, it certainly would not be something they would ever discuss. I was immediately captivated by the mysterious and mystical nature of this communiqué. I was aching to hear from Andrew, hungry for word, for some breadcrumb of information tossed over the veil from the other side; now, here, in a minute kitchen a world away, was an unexpected morsel.

Desperate for real conversation and yearning to talk about Andrew, I pounced on the opportunity, eager to hear more before being dragged back to the land of surface pleasantries. Standing together at the stove, Jane explained how Andrew had come to her and what he had told her.

I asked if he had said anything about me, and she told me that he had simply and only said, "Kate will be fine."

That was disappointing. I didn't feel fine. But, as Jane explained, it was his parents with whom he had unfinished business and his parents who needed to hear from him. It made sense to me that he would try to provide some comfort and closure for them, perhaps even ask for and offer forgiveness.

In the midst of this much longed-for conversation, Barbara burst through the swinging door into the kitchen and looked questioningly at us. I was still reeling from Jane's revelation, still caught up in the perceived nearness of Andrew.

Barbara was unhappy. She instructed me to come back to the table, saying that I should not hide away in the kitchen. She clearly felt very uncomfortable with me being alone with Jane. Barbara seemed to be monitoring me for any signs of intimate conversation, which, like an unattended campfire, might spontaneously erupt into a wildfire, consuming us all with flaming emotion. She was the self-appointed park ranger and she was on me like a hawk. I found it not only supremely irksome, but also quite bizarre. All I wanted to do was to be able to speak openly about the one person whom we both loved and missed; the person who had brought us together; the person who had broken our hearts.

I left the kitchen and begged off for a walk alone. I headed down the winding road to an ice cream shop near the shore, desperate to get away from the confinements of family and the tacit requirement that we not speak of anything personal or sad.

The shop was completely open to the warm, night air. I sat in the furious glare of the fluorescent lights, looking out at the darkness, listening to dance music coming from some party or bar down the dirt road. I watched couples walk by, watched the good-looking young men who did not watch me. It was depressing to be so utterly invisible.

*Why did no one even so much as give me a passing glance?* I wondered. *Here I am: a young, single, blonde woman, sitting alone in the middle of the Mediterranean. What's the problem?*

Then I realized, all at once, that *I* was the problem. I had a great, big sign on my forehead, an energetic neon sign that flashed "Grieving Widow." Even though part of me wanted male attention, and even though I needed to feel beautiful and attractive, my entire being was radiating a message that said, "Keep Clear."

I wanted to be pulled out of my sadness, to be saved, but no one and nothing could do that for me. There was no rushing this process. I wasn't ready for a new chapter in my life, nowhere even close to ready; and with that realization, I felt myself sink under a heavy shroud of despair and resignation. I felt trapped, buried alive. I hated where I was, hated the mandatory isolation, but I was stuck in it for a while—how long, I did not know. Recognizing this loathsome truth depressed the hell out of me.

Uncle Stephanos rolled by on his bicycle in the dark, lit cigar hanging from his mouth. He waved cheerfully at me, carefree and happy on his way to have a drink somewhere. I stood up and walked out of the fluorescent glare and into the dark night, back to the house, listening to the waves lap at the shore.

As I walked, I thought about an ancient Greek ritual that I once read about. I could not recall where or when; for all I knew, it might yet survive in some remote, rocky, little village somewhere in the Aegean. The practice was this: On the first anniversary of a loved one's death the older women of the village make a pilgrimage to the cemetery, singing and wailing their lamentations. Once at the grave, they unearth the remains of the beloved, removing the entire skeleton. The wife, or mother or sister, washes and cradles the bones, singing to them, before oiling them and gently placing them in a community ossuary, which will be their second and final resting place. The entire process is part lamentation, part remembrance, and part release.

I was completely awed and shaken by this ritual: To be so intimate with death, so comfortable with the smell of it, the feel of it, fingering the earth and the bones and the shreds of flesh; to look it in the face and hold it lovingly in your hands. What strength these women had! What love and courage to be able to look life and death in the face! Unearthing the bones was the confirmation of the inviolable finality of death. By this ritual, mortality was made manifest. There was no resurrection, no reclamation or return to a former happiness.

I didn't feel strong enough or brave enough to be initiated into this circle of women. I didn't want the bones. I didn't want to see them or look at them or feel them. I didn't want to deal with death anymore; I was tired of it. I wanted to get as far away from it as possible. I was more than ready to leave this hot, parched country where tears didn't flow and the dead weren't discussed. I needed to jump into the cool water of quiet sadness where my tears could fall unseen and unchecked.

I needed to come home.

# 27

B ack in my house on the hill in Ashland, the thought recurred that I needed to be alone, as much as I hated it. This was a realization, not a desire; I certainly didn't want to be alone, but something seemed to be telling me that it would behoove me to learn to become comfortable in this imposed solitude, to face the gnawing feelings of emptiness and anxiety that seemed to swallow me whole.

On a trip to Bali, some years prior, I had been drawn to the brightly painted, wooden carvings of dragons that were found everywhere on the island. One of the young, saronged artists in Ubud, whose work I admired, told me in his beautiful, halting English that images of demons and dragons are placed at the entrances to the temples to test those who would desire to enter. Only those who can endure their own doubts and terror, and rise above them, can pass through, into the sacred center.

That metaphor and imagery had not left me. I had the sense, when I would slow down enough to acknowledge it, that I needed to pass into that sacred center, that I needed to face my twin demons of fear and loneliness. I knew it, but I did not want to do it, even as it beckoned to me. Knowing something and embodying that knowledge are two very different things.

I sat looking out at the dark night, the velvet weight of stars holding me hostage in my brightly lit kitchen. I stared out at the blackness, at a total loss as to what to do with myself. After wandering around the hushed house for twenty minutes, restless and anxious like a lost spirit, I dragged out a large sketchpad, sat down in the window seat, and began coloring large, dark-blue swaths on the paper. On top of the blue, I made little yellow stars; in between the stars, I wrote the word "lonely" over and over, until it covered the page.

I sat and stared at my work. There it was. I felt no better, no different having externalized it. What I needed, or at least what I desperately wanted, was for someone to call me, someone to drag me out to a movie or dinner, someone to bring over a pizza and sit with me, someone to tether me back to the world of life and blood and living things. It didn't need to be a lover; a friend would suffice: a real, live, flesh-and-blood friend.

The only friend I had nearby was Nicole, and I grabbed the phone and called her. This was a mistake. She laughed at me, and chastised me for not being able to be lonely without doing something about it, without calling her. That pissed me off. What did she expect? I was thirty-four years old with nothing to wrap myself around. I'd tried to integrate myself into the land of the living, but it was always challenging. The unrelenting sense of loneliness—shrouding me wherever I went, whatever I did—was proving more pernicious than the grief.

I longed for Ainslie, wished that she could come over to be with me. All of my friends and colleagues and former clients were in San Francisco.

*Maybe I should go back to that,* I thought. *Finish my licensing and open a practice.*

I opened the cabinet underneath the window seat where I sat and pulled out the animal puppets I once used with my young clients. I stuck the life-sized skunk onto my hand and stared into its dark, pointed face, thinking about my former life, remembering the sweet faces who'd confessed their thoughts and fears to my animated hand. I thought about five-year-old Dylan, whose mother had been killed in a car crash. I had told him that he could always love his mother, and that she was always with him.

He had replied in his quiet, rolling Irish brogue, "I'll love her until the Earth melts."

I'd spent the fall before Andrew's death painstakingly assembling my licensing application, completing it the afternoon he was killed. I had walked in the house and dropped the pristine, three-inch-thick photocopy onto the table, pleased to be finished with it after three months of meticulous, tedious work. That was just after three o'clock in the afternoon. Three hours later, thoughts of study and exams and building a practice had evaporated on impact.

*No,* I thought, *there was no way I could study for my counseling license, not now, not even if I wanted to, and I didn't.*

I had no concentration and little energy or wisdom to offer anyone. Perhaps more importantly, I had no desire. Some months before, when I was not even thinking about my counseling practice or about much of anything, I had heard a voice in my head—a sure, even, clear voice—that said, simply, "You will not practice therapy." Hearing that voice, that message out of nowhere, I had stopped what I was doing and listened carefully.

"Okay," I said aloud, acknowledging the message, and then I waited, holding my breath for the rest of it. It told me what I *wouldn't* be doing, and I waited to hear what I *would* do. But that was the end of the oracular pronouncement. I told Nicole about this communication; she looked at me askance before changing the subject.

The truth was that, in my heart, I hadn't really wanted to continue my therapy practice since before Andrew and I were married. I loved my colleagues and my clients, and nothing about it was wrong exactly, but it never felt quite right either. I had the sense that I was close to something but just not quite there, not quite seeing it. But having devoted six years and thirty thousand dollars to being a therapist, I had kept going—until Andrew died. Now, everything had changed. I was in another place, another country, alone with the dragons and the quiet and the bones.

As the days and nights stretched out, I mulled over Andrew's life and his death, slowly taking it all apart. I thought about our life together. I brooded about my continued, stubborn existence. I poured over every fragment, every piece, examining and feeling it repeatedly. I pushed my fingers into the earth, reflecting on the bones of loss and pain and fear, contemplating the forces of life and death. Sitting at the mental graves of my father and Andrew, I tried to come to terms with what it all meant. It meant *something.* My long hours with Nicole didn't help me with this exhumation; the extent of her analysis was that his death was "hideous." Meaning was something I had to uncover on my own.

Slowly, as I ruminated and examined the fragments of my life, I realized that I was on a much larger journey than I had initially imagined. It was a journey through widowhood, certainly, but that was just the first layer. Below that was an older layer of melancholy and depression; deeper still lay the unmourned loss of my father. And underneath all of it was the primal sediment, the archetypal bedrock: *Who am I and why am I here?* That question was waiting for me, waiting to be asked and answered.

The urge to settle in and take an accounting of what I unearthed stood in direct opposition to my desire to escape that very call. Even as I poked through the sediment, I wanted to run from it. I'd had enough. I was sick to death of death. Had I not explored enough, dug around enough, suffered enough? I'd already spent seven years in therapy, talking about all of it; what more was there to say? Ruminating on death and loneliness and the meaning of it all seemed increasingly self-indulgent and fruitless. More to the point, I was tired of it. I wanted fun. I wanted happiness.

I did not want the bones.

I was feeling entirely impatient with the process. *Perhaps that's a positive sign,* I thought. Impatience usually signals that something is ready to shift.

⊜⊜

I began to feel, on many more days now, single and not just widowed. Single was a very different feeling than widowed; "single" means looking around, being curious, thinking past the immediate present. It was a positive sign and a welcome, if surprising, interlude from the isolation and obsession that is early widowhood.

But "single" also insinuated the loathsome necessity of dating. I'd never liked dating, not even in high school when everything was relatively simple and no one had a messy relationship résumé. "Dating" meant sifting through the pile of sand for the one, lone jewel that may—or may not—be lurking somewhere near the bottom. This prospect felt both slightly exciting and tremendously tedious—unless, of course, I went my mother's route, which was the Yellow Brick Road to Burger King.

My mother had the habit, when widowed, of latching on to even the paltriest of attractions, molding and bending herself to fit whomever was at hand (age, attractiveness, sexual orientation, or marital status notwithstanding). Watching her hanging on a man who quite clearly did not care for her always made me feel embarrassed and sad. So desperate was she to be loved that she would attempt to create love wherever and with whomever she could. The result, not surprisingly, was that she often found herself hurt, spurned, disappointed, or with someone who could never meet her insatiable hunger to be validated as a person.

I was—and I knew it—in precipitous danger of becoming my mother. With the exception of Andrew, my one and only requirement in a potential partner had been that he was interested in me; questions of his suitability or integrity were secondary, if they were considered at all. I was grateful to be loved and quick to settle for security, real or imagined: the unfortunate, unconscious fallout from my early experience of loss.

I had not dealt with this particular little habit, had not grappled with the father hunger, the attempts to fill the hole his death had created in me, had not yet fully embraced the fear. On an intellectual level, I understood that I had "abandonment issues," but I hadn't fully integrated how my father's death during my formative years had affected me.

Instead, I tried to circumvent the grief that loitered around the edges of my life, erroneously thinking that understanding the origins of my longing was the equivalent of healing it. To the outside world, I appeared to be a very confident and strong little girl, and later a confident, strong woman; yet, mostly unbeknownst to me, a tremendous void always waited to be filled—a void created by fear and loneliness, which had no shape and no name; a void that became a black hole which pulled, with tremendous gravitational force, any prospect for love and security into its gaping maw.

This basic state of insecurity formed my Achilles' heel. I could see my tendency toward inappropriate men, but I saw it only as a vague lack of self-esteem, something that needed a good pep talk. The problem now, however, was not simply poor choices. Now, at the advanced age of thirty-four, I felt old and used up, marked by divorce and widowhood: unattractive disadvantages, I feared, to have on my dating résumé. I felt certain that I was in mortal danger of never finding anyone with whom I could spend my life. I was getting too hungry.

To ward off the danger of becoming my mother, and in the hopes of avoiding any future disasters à la Keith or Satele or Derek, I decided to put pen to paper and describe the sort of man I wanted. I would create a list of prerequisites for a potential mate: my personal guidelines for dating. In this way, I reasoned, I would avoid the pitfall of desperate loneliness; I would avoid a fast-food romance, a relationship based on emotional starvation. In the past, I'd been too passive; this time, I would be proactive and cautious.

I made my list into an art project one night, getting out my sketchpad and really going to town. Turning over the page covered with "lonely," I created a wish list of anything and everything I thought my future mate ought to be. I decided that he should be older, preferably widowed so that he would be mature and understanding of my situation. He should be financially well off. He should have self-awareness. He needed to be compassionate, kind, loving, and able to access his emotions. He had to be intelligent, of course, with a wicked sense of humor. While I was at it, I decided that he should be tall, six feet at least, good-looking, and well dressed—maybe some gray at the temples.

I was enjoying my future lover and beginning to feel excited about the possibilities. This exercise was far better than digging in the bone pile. It felt good to be looking forward rather than back; it felt good to take the reins. I liked this. I decided that I should take it to the next level: I would take my specific requirements and put them in an anonymous ad. That way, I reasoned, I would have a chance of attracting what I wanted.

Internet dating had not yet arrived in 1998, and personal ads were just beginning to transition from newspapers to computers. I placed an anonymous newspaper ad and waited. Soon enough, the recorded phone responses flowed in. None of them were even remotely intriguing; some were pathetically funny, most all were just plain sad. Certainly no one came anywhere close to being a real candidate. There were obviously a slew of other desperate souls out there.

My spirits flagged as I realized, for the thousandth time, just what a unique and wonderful person Andrew really was. Issues or no issues, he had so much to offer, so many attractive qualities, so much talent and intelligence and humor and sensitivity. The pool of intelligent, charming, attractive, sophisticated, psychological, successful, available men appeared to be completely dried up. I would never find a partner in this provincial place. Clearly, I would have to fish other waters. I went back on-line and began searching the San Francisco personal ads, imagining that I would find a more urbane and sophisticated pool of men there.

Then, Dr. Dan appeared. His ad said that he was a psychologist (good), had "penetrating green eyes" (provocative), and loved to dance (a plus). Intrigued, I emailed him. He emailed back. After a couple of weeks of writing back and forth, I drove down to the city, sight unseen, to meet him. Walking into Peet's Coffee & Tea on Fillmore Street in the late afternoon for our rendezvous, I recognized him immediately and my heart sank; he did have green eyes behind the glasses, but any possibility for attraction ended there.

I tried to bolster my disappointment by exhorting myself with quickly recounted platitudes: *Don't judge by appearances. Looks aren't everything. Give him the benefit of the doubt.*

Besides, there wasn't much I could do at this point. It was too late to pretend that I didn't recognize him; we'd already spotted one another. I ordered my coffee and we sat down to talk. When he told me that he had a strange fascination with the Japanese horror figure Mothra, I weighed the possibility of making an escape by pretending to go to the restroom and sneaking out the back door. In hindsight, that would have been the kinder decision for us both, but it felt mean and I couldn't do it. I'd driven all the way here to meet him, and we had prearranged a night of dancing at his favorite club that evening.

We walked across the street and up the hill to his office. He asked me where I'd parked and I pointed across the street to my black BMW.

"That figures," he said.

*What the hell is that supposed to mean?* I wondered. His derisive, dismissive tone irritated me. I already imagined where the rest of this encounter was headed, but I didn't know just how bad it would be.

Dr. Dan picked me up at my brother Chris' house after dinner, and we drove to the SOMA district to an old, brick warehouse. We walked inside the cavernous space that had been converted into an enormous, modern, dance club. Quickly, he led me to a staircase near the back of the room which we climbed holding hands. At the top was a long, narrow landing, leading to a door with a small plaque: this was a modern day speakeasy. The door opened to another time and place. Here, the music harkened back to the fifties, as did most of the dancers' attire.

Dan immediately disappeared by himself onto the dance floor. Left standing alone and at a loss, I went to the bar and ordered a drink. I sat there for an hour, watching the dancers jitterbugging and sweating, feeling equal parts irritated and bemused, wishing that I had made the bathroom break when we were at Peet's. Dan popped in sporadically to gulp some water, and then he was back on the floor. Exasperated, I finally went out on the floor by myself after a kind woman took pity on me and offered to show me some steps.

I gamely tried to enjoy myself without my date but, after a few minutes of inept solo dancing, I was done. On one of his pit stops, I told Dan that I wanted to leave and asked him to take me back to my brother's house. This clearly irritated Dan. He resented being taken from his good time and seemed distressingly unaware of his rudeness, to the extent that he suggested, as we drove, that we go back to his place. I turned and stared at him with fierce incredulity.

Chris met me at the door as Dan peeled away.

"Mothra's out," I said.

My brother laughed heartily as he put his arm around my shoulder and closed the door behind us.

A month later, I went back to San Francisco, this time to meet Peter—an entrepreneur with whom I exchanged a long volley of emails and phone calls and a picture before deciding to meet in person for Thanksgiving; after my disastrous date with Mothra, I thought better of waiting until a holiday to meet. In a spontaneous burst of inspiration, I flew down to San Francisco before Thanksgiving, just for a day, to surprise Peter. This would accomplish three things: first, I would see him in person; second, it would give me some insight into his character to see how he responded to my surprise; lastly, if we were not a match, it would spare us both from having a miserable holiday ... and it was something to do.

I was delighted with myself as I boarded the plane for the one-hour trip to the city. I was excited to see what would happen and pleased with my spontaneity. I crawled into the window seat marked 1A and found myself seated next to a handsome, Italian-looking man, who looked to be in his forties. He was wearing a sport coat and had a winning, Tom Cruise-sized smile.

As the plane taxied and lifted off, we began to talk. Sam worked in Hollywood but lived with his family in the obscurity of southern Oregon, commuting as needed for his work. Sam was very interested in me and in my story. He seemed particularly to like my idea of surprising Peter.

"If it were me being surprised, I'd love it!" he joyfully exclaimed.

This encouraged me greatly. I continued telling my story, emboldened by the positive response and the interest. I told him all about Andrew and about my list of requirements for a man, and how I was trying to be more discerning. I felt very mature as I said all of this, really on top of things.

Sam listened, attentive and thoughtful. "It's good to have your list," he agreed, "but you ought to leave room for someone different from what you imagine, someone wonderful, to show up. If you hold on to your list too tightly"—and here he made a tight fist for emphasis—"you might never meet him. It's good to stay open."

I looked at Sam, studying his face. He was smiling softly, his eyes pleasantly wrinkled, looking at me gently and knowingly.

"That's true," I said, nodding. "I'll keep that in mind."

We landed just before eight in the morning. After getting Sam's number and promising him a follow-up report on the outcome of my adventure, I grabbed a cab and drove up toward San Francisco, into the Castro District and to Peter's house. I paid the driver and looked at the place from the sidewalk; I was not impressed. I walked up the stairs and knocked on the door, inhaling deeply. I waited about thirty seconds, trying to discern what was happening inside. I heard conversation and footsteps, and then the door flung open. Peter stood, wearing a big, blue bathrobe. He was toweringly tall and overweight. He reminded me of Alfred Molina, only less attractive.

Peter was not delighted to see me. The look on his face was something of a cross between shock and irritated incredulity. After an awkward moment, he asked me in, introduced me to his assistant, and excused himself to dress.

I quietly looked around the Lilliputian-sized house; it looked like a cheap Vegas motel. Once again, I thought about canceling it all right then, but that would look strange. It didn't seem right or kind to bust into someone's house after flying 350 miles, and then just walk out. I wanted to, but I couldn't.

*Just like Mothra*, I thought ruefully.

I glanced around more, looking in the kitchen. The place was pure, unadulterated gaudiness: all mirrors and navy blue paint and bright plops of red and orange scattered here and there. It looked like an old, painted hooker.

Peter emerged a few minutes later, seeming more receptive, and suggested that we go to his office so he could make a few calls and clear his calendar. His mood seemed lighter. We climbed in his Range Rover—the only car that fit him, he said, being such a big man—and drove downtown. At least he hadn't lied about having money.

The office, such as it was, consisted of a large, completely empty floor of a mid-century building. There was one old, metal desk, sitting in the middle of the industrial carpeted room, with a phone and a computer sitting on top. Wires and cords ran down the side of the desk and snaked across the floor. A sad, dying plant tilted wearily next to a wall.

I looked out the windows cheerfully as I waited. I might have expected to be feeling uncomfortable right about now, but I was having fun. I felt very calm and composed. I wondered what, exactly, he did for a living; it seemed slightly suspicious.

We left and drove across town to the Marina District and walked along Chestnut Street, window-shopping. It was readily apparent that there was no attraction on either side. All the emails and conversations faded into oblivion as we tried to make the best of the morning. At noon, we stopped for lunch at La Méditerranée on upper Castro Street, back near his house. We made idle conversation, but there was little to talk about. Peter seemed irritated and bored by me, and I thought he was something of a fraud, being neither handsome nor sophisticated. I understood why he had placed an ad and why he might still be unmarried at almost fifty.

Despite the awkwardness and mutual lack of attraction, Peter—like Mothra before him—now wanted me to go back to his place. I marveled at this ability to divorce sex from interest. It's arguably a valuable skill, but one that I don't possess. Perhaps he thought that he deserved something for all his trouble that morning, for canceling his workday and having to deal with me. I thought that the best thing to do was to abort the relationship before we invested any more time in it, and I said so.

My experiment now over, I left the restaurant and walked back onto Castro Street. I felt oddly ebullient, as though I were free and had checked something off my list. It felt good to be done with Peter, good to be alone: *That* was a new one. I strolled among the throngs of gay men who call the neighborhood home, looking at the shops and enjoying my free time and the warm sun until it was time to go back to the airport. I was relieved that I had not waited until the Thanksgiving holiday to meet Peter in person; I'd saved myself a lot of time and trouble by making this impromptu visit. The whole thing struck me as very funny, from start to finish.

The droning hum of the Boeing 737 provided a backdrop to my thoughts as I flew home late that afternoon. I thought about what Sam had said to me on our flight earlier that morning, about his affirmation of my spontaneity and his oracular message of not closing the door on unexpected guests. I couldn't wait to call him and tell him how it went. I hoped he knew something that I, as yet, did not.

PART FOUR

## TAKING FLIGHT *or* THE OTHER SIDE OF NIGHT

*At cycle's end, the monarch begins to fly. The butterfly looks for flowers with nectar to drink. Its job is to reproduce, but this job is not easy. A butterfly cannot repair wing damage, so it must be careful to find shelter in storms. A butterfly cannot regulate its body temperature, so it uses its surroundings to maintain body heat. At night, it roosts—taking shelter from the cold. During the day, it basks—resting its open wings to catch the warmth of the sun. With this final cycle, it rests, mates, and new life begins.*

# 28

I arrived back home as the sun was setting behind the west hills, unlocked the front door, and sat on the floor in the den. Bentley waddled in, his white, plumed tail slowing fanning back and forth. He jumped up on the green velvet sofa and looked down at me with his large, unblinking eyes. The sun was coming in at a slant through the window, low and warm. It was completely quiet.

I sat there for a while, leaning against the wall, and closed my eyes. A quiet calm surrounded me and there, for the first time in a long time—maybe for the first time ever—a visceral experience of peace came over me. In this state of tranquility, it occurred to me that I was done: done looking, done trying, done running from my fears and loneliness. *Done.* It was time to face my dragons; time to finish washing the bones.

A strong gentleness enfolded me, and I experienced what could only be called "grace." I'd never felt it before. There wasn't a trace of angst or disappointment or fear that I had felt for years: no self-judgment, no desire, and no resignation—just peace. A clear, quiet awareness entered my consciousness.

*I don't need a relationship. I'm okay.*

I was alone, on my own, but for the first time, that realization did not ruffle me. The fear was gone. I preferred being quiet and alone to the obsessive, fruitless hunt for a man to make me feel complete. I might feel sad and lonely, but that was okay, and I was okay and I was going to be okay. I did not just believe this, or wish it; I knew it. Something in me had shifted.

I dug my fingers and toes into the pale, green carpet, enjoying the feeling of the wool on my skin. There, in my quietude on the floor, I had the distinct impression that the circumstances surrounding my widowhood—leaving city and work and friends—was purposeful; that God, or the universe, or whatever it was, intended that I use this time of solitude to face myself, to release the distractions and take a long, hard look at my life; to "wrestle with the angel" until it blessed me.

From that broader perspective, this was the ideal situation. Freed from the necessity of work and without close friends or a relationship to distract me, there was only me—me and this sense of something more, something I could not name but simply felt. Now, for the first time, facing these dragons, this angel, this pile of bones, did not seem fearful or onerous. It felt ... *sacred*, like an initiation into something splendid and magnificent. I had the sense that something or someone was waiting for me, waiting for this moment. I had crossed through the temple gates.

This wasn't the first time that I'd had this thought. Even at the age of eight, I had felt that there must be a reason that I had lost my father so young when other kids hadn't. I sensed that there must be a purpose, a message in it. Although I could not articulate it at the time, I remembered feeling the impetus to understand what this purpose was. I remembered thinking that, if I could share what happened to me with others, they might feel more comfortable sharing their difficult feelings and experiences with me. It was a kind of opening, a doorway that connected my inner world with the larger world that surrounded me.

I had the same feeling a few days after Andrew's death—that there were reasons and blessings contained in this traumatic shifting of life-as-I'd-known-it. I'd wandered into the guest room where we watched that last movie together and, sitting on the blue futon where we last sat, I had thanked Andrew out loud. I thanked him for freeing me from what could only have been a terrible, Hobsonian choice. I thanked him for freeing me to find the kind of love I needed and wanted. I thanked him for loving me, and I felt relief and happiness for him that he no longer had to suffer. Even then, even in the midst of an almost unbearable sadness, a greater consciousness, albeit small and transitory, managed to penetrate the pain: *Something good will emerge from this.*

Now, for the third time, this larger awareness was arising, reminding me that there was work to be done, that all was not lost. It encouraged me to hold on, to keep going, even when I had no idea where I was headed. These moments of illumination were a portal to an expanded consciousness. Even when they were clouded by the mundane exigencies of daily life and emotional storms, they provided a connection to an unwavering wisdom and strength. Their presence told me that there was something more.

Sitting now on the floor of the den, almost two years after being widowed, everything seemed to slow to a calm stillness. My brain, normally racing like a coked-up ferret, became quiet and clear. I turned my face to the lingering warmth of the sun, which had now set behind the mountains. It felt good to stop moving, to stop trying to fill the void. I'd struggled for almost two years to keep my demons at bay: my demon fears of loneliness and sorrow, of insecurity and sadness, of melancholy and depression.

The anxiety and the quiet fear were lifting, being replaced by a growing awareness arising from within this calm center. I realized, in that moment, that I had been wrestling with the angel far longer than these past two years; I'd been struggling since I was eight years old. I saw, too, that the angel with whom I was wrestling was not trying to kill me; it was trying to *save* me. Nothing in my outer world had changed; my vision had just adjusted, and I was seeing my life in a new way, with greater clarity and deeper perspective.

Awareness leads to seeing; this is a well-known phenomenon. You decide that you want to buy a Vespa, or get pregnant and, all of a sudden, everywhere you go you see pregnant women riding Vespas. It's not because there's been a wild proliferation of Vespas and pregnancies; it's that your mind has focused its attention and is looking for these things and become open to seeing them.

Now that the doorway of awareness was opened, a new knowledge was arising, spawned somewhere deep down inside of me, in a place that is invisible and untouchable. I knew, all at once and with complete certainty, that everything that had ever transpired in my life was meaningful. Everything was connected. Everything had purpose: my father's death, Andrew's death, Bentley, everything—whether I liked it or hated it, whether it was painful or joyous—was imbued with purpose and meaning. Once I stopped flailing around and sat down, still and open, this became very apparent.

I crawled up onto the couch next to Bentley and stroked his soft hair as I leaned back on the velvet cushions. In this welcome stillness, I realized that this was the moment that had been waiting for me—the moment that I had tried to fend off for more than two decades—but I was no longer afraid. The angel I wrestled and the dragons I faced were one in the same: they lived in the void created by my father's unmourned death, waiting for me in the dark shadows of my deepest fears and greatest pain, waiting for me to arrive at this threshold.

I had assiduously avoided such reconciliation, fearing that, if I looked into the void of my grief and pain and sorrow and anger, I would disappear forever into that dark night. The terrible irony was that, in trying to avoid the dark oblivion, I had run directly into it. It wasn't grief and sorrow that isolated me after my father died; it was *not* grieving, *not* expressing that had put me into the isolation of my cold cocoon—a cocoon from which I had never fully emerged.

Loss is difficult for everyone, but it is particularly formidable and terrifying for a child. Children are not equipped to deal with the thorny truths that death foists upon a person. My father's death forced my awareness of a new and terrifying truth: *Nothing is certain.* This truth reached down into the core of my being and stirred the existential angst that dwells within us all. It left me perpetually on guard, vigilant, and frightened. Terrible things *can* happen, and they frequently do.

Had my trauma been addressed at the time, my fears might have been allayed, and I might have avoided the descent into decades of depression and isolation, but they were not. No one in my family knew how to grieve, how to work through such a tragedy. There was no mourning, no talking about feelings, no therapy to guide me through the darkness, no one to listen to my fears or explain my mixed feelings. We buried my father, unwrapped the Christmas presents, and went back to our lives.

In the absence of any of these sorts of cushions, my anxieties went underground. To the outside world, I seemed fine: I was first chair in the orchestra, the lead in the play, an honor student. But suffering doesn't show up in sackcloth and ashes. It seldom rolls around moaning on the ground. It no longer dresses in black for a year or hangs a wreath on the door. It looks like a normal eight-, or eighteen-, or thirty-two-year-old person. It shops for broccoli and smiles at the cashier. It gets up in the morning, gets dressed, and goes to school or work. In fact, very often, the only way you see suffering is if you look really hard, if you ask the right questions ... if you *care*.

In my second year as a private school counselor, I worked with an eight-year-old girl whose father had died very young and very suddenly. Each week, I would look at her sweet, open face as she spoke of missing her father, and when she left I would cry. I cried for her loss, I cried for mine, and I cried because I was giving something to her that I had so desperately needed for myself. I cried because I realized, for the first time, how terrible and how inconceivable it was that no one had ever spoken to me about losing my father; that no one, seemingly, had cared. The silence surrounding my loss sealed the wound his death inflicted without the benefit of the love and understanding that might first have served to clean it out.

I carted this unconscious sadness and pain and suffering around with me for a couple of decades like a hermit crab, imagining that I was mostly okay. But, unattended, my wound festered. Grief and suffering have no expiration date; they can drag out for a lifetime, infecting your entire existence. My unexpressed grief appeared only in disguise, revealing itself as an addiction to perfection; as the need to be in a relationship in order to feel whole; as low-grade, chronic depression and melancholy.

Years of therapy helped me to peer into the dark places. I began to understand the damage that had been done by shoving all my grief and mourning into the closet. I began to see the glimpses of the internal damage spawned by unattended loss, and the ways that damage played out in my life, most obviously in my relationship choices. I knew why I cried for my clients and why I'd been drawn to the practice of psychology; I entered the field for the same reason that most people enter it: I was deeply wounded, and I wanted to heal that wound.

The first time I went to see a therapist, during my brief, ill-fated marriage to Satele, I knew none of this. When I sat down in Dr. Bob's dark, orange shag-carpeted office and he asked what had brought me in, my response was not that I was dragging around a gunny sack of grief about my father's death and had absolutely no idea who I was or what I was doing with my life.

I had looked at Dr. Bob with great earnestness and replied, "I want to learn how to get my husband to stop drinking."

In graduate school they called this "the presenting problem," in contradistinction to "the real problem." It takes a long time to get to the real problem, the Moment of Truth. Usually, the real problem is buried deep down, unattended and perhaps forgotten—and for a very good reason. It's tender stuff. It's painful. You have to work your way down to it, slowly, repetitively circling and spiraling around it. This slow, steady descent is necessary to prepare you to face the thing you've been avoiding all along. It's the emotional equivalent of preparing for a triathlon: you can't just jump in and expect to be able to survive. You have to be in shape. You need strength and endurance.

That was how I began to *re-member*, to put myself back together, at the age of twenty-seven, before I knew anything about anything. That day in Dr. Bob's office I started poking in the dirt, tentatively exploring the surface of my life. Three years of this exploration, coupled with my graduate work, enabled me to begin to thaw the outer edges of my frozen state. I explored the shame and sadness about my relationship with Satele, and I began to constellate a fledgling sense of self.

When I met Andrew, it felt like a reward for having done that work. His kindness and love were a balm for my sad spirit, his love standing in stark contrast to the chaos I'd been through with Satele. I had no idea how much more I had to exhume from my interior until Andrew's death broke my life wide open and emotions—long buried and hidden deep in the unseen folds of my heart—erupted and flowed hot and strong. The fear, the insecurity, the sadness, the depression, the anger, the longing—everything I had ever suffered or avoided suffering, was waiting for me.

In the pristine, fall days that followed my return from San Francisco I enjoyed a tranquility that I never imagined possible. To my delight and surprise, I was no longer particularly sad or overwhelmed. *I'm okay.* That phrase kept running through my mind. *I'm okay. Everything's okay.* It was the first time in a long time that everything had felt okay.

All my chasing after men suddenly seemed very adolescent and laughable, but that was okay too. I'd done what I felt I'd needed to do, and now I was finished. It seemed like a last gasp, a last fitful flailing of a dying habit. I was ready for something else, for another way of being. I was ready to simply allow life to unfold as it would, ready to stop trying to plug some imaginary hole in the great dam of my inner being and just let everything go with one, great whoosh: the past, the fears—all of it. I was ready to let it come rushing out and release the pressure, ready to let it find its own level inside of me.

I continued to think about Andrew, but more often the thoughts were happy ones, not just the eternal looping of the death and my loss. Andrew had kept his promise: he had not left me after all. I missed his corporeal presence like hell, but it felt good to be able to have him present in spirit and in my thoughts without being dissolved by sadness.

I thought back to the day when Nicole told me that Andrew was gay. Her tossed-off remark had torn me apart for a week, causing me to question whether Andrew had even loved me, or if I had been a foil for him, a ruse, our marriage a sham. I had set myself in opposition to Nicole's certainty and frantically called Ainslie, demanding that she tell me if Andrew had been gay.

She had said, calmly, "No, Pea. Andrew wasn't gay."

This statement had soothed me, but the question lingered. Now that I was in a stronger, more beatific state of mind, my thoughts returned to this niggling question. I needed to understand what I believed, to come to my own truth. I needed to do this before I could move on, because the past is not just the past; it's the present and the future, too. Was Andrew gay? Did he really love me? What exactly was our story? I needed to know, for my own peace of mind and heart. I was ready to allow the truth to reveal itself to me.

As I stared out at the eastern horizon from my kitchen, I calmly reviewed our entire relationship, from our first meeting to his proposal to our last good-bye. I recalled the conversations where he told me his innermost thoughts and feelings. As I culled through my memories I felt an overwhelming sense of love.

One thing was already clear: Andrew's spirit was dealt a fatal blow long before his plane hit the ground that December day. He had already given up hope of ever finding a peaceful resolution to his inner dilemma and, in that giving up, he'd denied his soul. He had tried, in good faith, to fit himself into a constricted, "acceptable" definition of himself: Andrew as male, as masculine, and only that. He had tried to disregard what his body and mind and spirit were telling him, tried to disregard his pain and suffering. He tried, but it was a Sisyphean task. It was never really a possibility; he could not escape who he was nor could he live a lie.

Torn between the person he felt himself to be and the person that could be accepted by others, Andrew had been trapped between a rock and a very hard place. The problem, as I saw it now more dispassionately and with greater perspective, was not that he cross-dressed or wanted to be a woman; the problem was that he could not comfortably express or live who he was. His inability to do this was the source of his suffering; it is the source of all suffering.

It was also true that I had, unconsciously and inadvertently, contributed to his suffering because I had not accepted him either. I did not embrace the whole of him. For selfish reasons, I wanted him to be a normal man. I chose to believe his efforts at normality and his wishful thinking because it made my life seem perfect. I chose to overlook the signs that, in retrospect, were clearly there—showing me, telling me that he needed something else.

I thought about the time that Andrew and I had flown down to Carmel for the day. We stopped at a restaurant and sat at a patio table under an eve, drinking a glass of wine. A light rain was falling, evaporating into the scent of wet concrete.

"I have this vision," Andrew said in the same, slightly distanced way someone shares a dream from the night before. He was sitting across from me, looking out at the rain and talking softly, in a sort of reverie. "I am flying a plane. I put it on autopilot and walk to the back, to an open door. I stand in the doorway and scatter your ashes. I watch the ashes being swept into the sky, and I wait for the plane to fly into the side of a mountain."

The imagery was disturbing, though at the time I'd thought it tragically romantic. I imagined his vision was of us far in the future: the lover unable to live without his beloved. It was only now, three years later, that I understood the meaning in the message. It wasn't *my* ashes that he scattered from the plane: it was Sonia's. When that part of him was sacrificed in order to lead a more acceptable life, Andrew could not continue. He had lost too much of himself to survive.

I caught my breath as the meaning of his prescient vision finally sunk in.

*Of course,* I thought. *Of course. He already knew.* Or part of him already knew; his unconscious knew. When Sonia died, he would have to die, because they were one person. It was an unconscious foreshadowing of his death.

Everything is meaningful.

A sweet, deep sadness came over me—not at his death but of the suffering of his life. Andrew was not gay, not that it really mattered. He was in the wrong body. It was as simple and as complex as that. I knew that the love Andrew and I shared was real and honest, if ill-fated. This love underlay all else, surviving beyond everything that buffeted our marriage, surviving his death. Love is everything: It is beyond circumstance, immutable and eternal.

Twenty minutes of solitary reflection settled me into a deeper and more peaceful understanding—twenty minutes and two years of contemplation and questioning, of washing the bones. It no longer mattered to me whether Andrew had wanted to be a woman. Loosed from the bond of marriage our love became uncomplicated. It returned to its natural state of being: complete and unfettered.

# 29

I was sitting in the den, watching television, when I heard the phone ring. It was not the usual ring, clear and loud; it was an anemic, garbled, halting sort of ring. I stared at the receiver, unsure whether to pick it up, whether what I'd heard was an actual call coming in. It managed another faltering, muffled ring before I turned off the television and stood to answer it, still unsure what exactly was happening.

"Hello?"

There was no ring tone, no static. There was nothing. No, not nothing, exactly; there was something, but I couldn't discern what that something was. The sound coming through the receiver sparked with electricity.

"Hello ..." I said again, and then held my breath, listening, straining to decipher what I was not hearing.

The silence was alive. It was as if I were connected to someplace out of a Dr. Seuss book, where tiny Whoville residents were gathered, shouting into a large, funnel-shaped contraption to get my attention, their muffled calls arriving inside large, floating cotton balls. My brow furrowed in concentration; goose bumps erupted on my arms and legs, and then I knew.

It was Andrew.

This conclusion lacked all reason and rationality. It was a fantastic, delusional breech of logic that could easily be explained away as a wish. I tried to explain it away. But I wasn't thinking about Andrew at that moment; I wasn't drinking or pining or doing anything that even remotely related to such an occurrence. I simply *knew* that it was Andrew, and I knew that he was making his continued presence known. It wasn't that I wanted it to be him; it just *was*.

I hung up the receiver, still holding my breath. Clarity flared, bright white and fresh, illuminating a dawning awareness inside of me. This was an affirmation, a gift. I finally had begun to understand, to see beyond the immediacy of my personal pain, to step back and take in the larger picture. Now that my clouded emotional fog had lifted, Andrew could make contact. Calm and receptive, I could finally hear him.

*It's okay. Everything's okay. Andrew is okay. I am okay.*

In the days after Andrew's death I'd cried inconsolably, asking—pleading—for him to come to me, to tell me that he was all right, to tell me anything. Someone told me that I couldn't hear him because I was too sad. That seemed so unfair and just plain wrong; that's when I most needed him. But now I understood; it made complete sense. I had been weighed down by the leaden heaviness of an unfinished grief; a blanket so dense that nothing could penetrate it.

The words of the living room oracle returned to me for the thousandth time: "Energy cannot be created or destroyed. It only changes form."

All of a sudden, I thought about a man whom I had met at the farmer's market that past summer. He'd been walking around in shredded pants, his long, white hair and sky-blue eyes shaded by an oversized straw hat. Beside him, on a rope lead, was a large llama, similarly decorated with a hat and blanket and crystals of various colors. I heard him telling someone that the llama had the highest vibration of any animal other than a dolphin and, because of that, it could communicate with people.

I began to think about this idea of vibrational energy and communication. I was thinking about energy never disappearing, and I was beginning to piece together an outlandish and alien notion: People never die.

I thought of Chief Seattle's words: "There is no death, only a change in worlds."

Slowly, a much larger picture began to come into focus, as if the camera on my life were moving from an extreme close-up to a wide-angle panorama of the whole of existence. I had emerged from the cocoon I created two years prior—the cocoon that had cushioned and protected me against the horrors of dissolution and death. Surprised to find myself alive, I sat, slowly flapping my wings. I wasn't gone; Andrew wasn't gone. We both, in our own ways, had been through a change in worlds.

When a caterpillar spins into its cocoon, most of its cells panic at the impending mortification, rushing to commit a sort of Jim Jones-ish mass suicide, liquefying and becoming caterpillar soup. Some of the caterpillar's cells, however—poetically called "imaginal cells"—recreate themselves, evolving into something radically different and unexpected. These surviving cells shift their genetic configuration, morphing into a butterfly.

One of the dangers inherent in grieving is becoming lost in your personal pain. It's very easy to take death as a personal affront. It is, after all, an enormous, breath-stripping blow to your being. Crushed by the tidal force of pain and anguish, it feels easier to succumb than to bear up under it. It feels easier to quit, to rush to your own death. Your world has ended. The "you" you have known has died.

Grief is a slow, sticky business, but it does flow, albeit at the speed of a glacial thaw. Complicated grief, however, is grief that is frozen solid. Complicated grief occurs when you resist grieving, or when you resist emerging from your grief. In both cases, there is a refusal, consciously or unconsciously, to flow with the difficult and painful feelings. In the first case, you resist death; in the second, you resist life. In both cases, you are paralyzed.

Andrew's Aunt Julia never got over the loss of her husband because she never allowed herself to fully grieve. Her beliefs and her culture kept her from fully feeling and expressing her anguish when it was boiling over inside of her. She had slammed down a lid on that pot and only occasionally did it begin to rattle, betraying its continued presence. That's what happened that day in the car, when the pain pushed up the lid and the grief boiled over onto the front seat. She had resisted her grief for years, and it was still there, waiting for her. Until she acknowledged her grief, she could not return to full participation in the life that awaited her.

The flip side is to take up permanent residence in your grief. Like Queen Victoria and the suicidal caterpillar cells, you decide that your happy life is over for good. You lay out the deceased's clothing every day, wear black for the rest of your life, and tell everyone you meet that you are a widow, that you were left, that life is hard. You reduce yourself to the single-faceted identity of "victim." You turn black in your cocoon, refusing to emerge, refusing to let go of an old identity that is no more.

This resistance is natural and very human. There is a good reason that the feelings of grief and the process of mourning are considered a dark night of the soul. In that night, you lose your bearings and your vision. Your life becomes a fierce boiling. Losing someone precious stokes the fires under the pot of personhood, the boiling melding the disparate elements of existence into an altogether new entity, one that is deeper, richer, more sublimely refined than the raw elements that compose it, and it hurts like hell.

The fierce boiling of loss—with its ingredients of pain, grief, anger, doubt, fear, and love—is not something one jumps into willingly. It is an unbidden, unavoidable abduction. The doorbell rings or the test results come back and, in a single, suspended moment, life is irrevocably changed. You are pushed into the pot. And, just like the caterpillar undergoing its unbidden, cocooned deliquescing, the pain of boiling will not end until either something new is born or you die.

The only choice you have—and it is a crucial one—is whether you will allow yourself to be transformed by the terrible boiling. You can choose to submit to the frightening process or you can try to fight it—refusing to face the feelings, deciding that you are a victim of cruel fate—and allow the fierce boiling of life to simply boil you away, leaving only bitterness and dry, dark remnants of what was once a vital aliveness.

In turning yourself over to the ordeal that is grief and mourning, you die a conscious death. You endure the dark hours and weeks and months, knowing that something potent and meaningful is happening. You begin to see signs and hear whispers of oracles: hawks, phone calls, wisteria vines, and tombstones—the imaginal cells—speak to you. In time, you begin to sense that you have not disappeared for good; you have not died. You look different, you feel different ... and you are. You have new capacities, a new spaciousness that could not have shown itself absent the boiling.

What Julia and others told me was true: I would never get over my losses, but neither would I carry them around like some sort of ghostly Jacob Marley, weighed down by the chains of loss and an incomplete grief. Those chains remain locked around your heart and encumber your life insofar as you do not allow yourself to grieve and feel and make sense of life and the loss. It is a choice whether you live in the loss or live in life. It doesn't always feel like a choice, but it is.

# 30

I sat in my lovely house on the hill in my pile of bones, looking at them and putting them back together like so many Lincoln Logs, piecing together the truth of my losses. My experience was unique and sad, but I was not marked for sorrow; that was a fiction I'd made into my personal mantra. The truth was that I had been very happy, and I had also been very sad. That is the nature of life.

When I was first widowed, my overriding thought was that I could not survive it, and I did not wish to. But the thought that I couldn't go on without Andrew was simply not true. It felt true, but it wasn't. I *had* gone on without Andrew, to my dismay and surprise. Losing him hurt beyond any sort of pain that I had ever felt or could have imagined. I hated it, but it did not end my life; it ended that particular chapter of my life—a chapter I liked a great deal, a chapter I thought would be the whole story.

Death is a letting go, not only of the person you loved but also of the person you were and the life you imagined that you would have. This compound loss pushes you into the pot of reality, where youthful fantasies are boiled away. But in facing the pain and disappointment of a new existence, one begins to find solid ground. You can't build a new life until you root yourself in the truth of where you are and begin to marshal your inner resources—begin to allow the surviving imaginal cells to transform you into an entirely new creature.

It takes enormous strength and courage to go through this process and to do it well, which is to say, fully, completely, and with some amount of grace. Grief and mourning are universally unwelcome guests. They are the family you can't stand; the ones you hope will never visit. But they always come, and they stay far longer than you want them to. They upend your routine and shadow you constantly, making it difficult to breathe, to eat, to sleep, or to focus on anything but their noxious presence.

As with many unwelcome things, however, grief and mourning come bearing gifts—gifts that you do not receive unless you tolerate their long stay, unless you sacrifice yourself to their fierce demands. It's imperative that you let your emotions rip while they're fresh, while they're bubbling over and tearing your insides apart; to get it out while it's raw and everyone is gathered around you, ready to hold you and feed you and cry with you. If you do not invite your grief in when it first arrives, it will sit at the edges of your heart and fester and rot. It will steal your life. It stole mine.

It's entirely unnatural not to grieve. Repressing powerful emotions serves only to shove all the energy that is hemorrhaging out of your soul into a small, dark corner of your psyche where, one day, it will seep out and throttle you, which is precisely what happened to me.

I did not know how to grieve, how to express my many confused thoughts and feelings at the loss of my father. My grief was locked into a few minutes of a cold, December afternoon, watching my brother place the box containing my father's ashes into the ground. I took my suffering and balled it up, tucking it in a dark corner of a deep cabinet. I did not integrate my sadness and pain, did not make meaning of it. I cried a lot over the years, but that's not the same as grieving. Grieving is a working through, a metabolizing of emotions and the new reality of life without the beloved. It's feeling. It's washing the bones.

Lacking any intimate or ritualized guidance through my suffering, grief took up residence at the edges of my life, reminding me of its presence through depression, anorexia, chronic loneliness, perfectionism, and the pernicious need to have someone—anyone—in my life to make me feel whole.

Andrew's death pushed me right back into my ungrieved loss, his sudden departure mimicking my father's. The blow reopened the primal wound, making it wider and more apparent, exposing what I had hidden away. I had to see what was waiting for me. I needed to unearth the bones and weep.

My sadness did not entirely dissipate as I poured over these runes, but my fear did; so too the wrenching, all-consuming pain.

My father hadn't left me, and neither had Andrew; they had died, and that is a very different thing. They were following the course of their own, fateful trajectories. The fact that I was subject to the fallout of their journeys was not accidental, but neither was it personal. Their deaths changed me, affected me in ways both subtle and profound, but so had their lives. Finding this less personal perspective completely altered my experience of loss. I was still part of the drama, but I was just one actor among many: not a one-woman show.

Coming into awareness of the interconnectedness of life, and abandoning the idea of coincidence for the more encompassing concept of synchronicity, lifted an unseen weight from my heart, shifting me out of fear and victimhood. Not only was I not the next Job, I was, in truth, very fortunate to have had these experiences, as wrenching as they may have been, because traversing that terrible terrain had led me to this moment. I wasn't special or singled out or destined for a life of loss. My world was contained within greater worlds, a sort of Russian nesting doll of realities. There was so much more to life than the limited reality of what was immediately apparent. I had no idea what was next, but I was ready to simply *allow it to happen.*

Proof of this shift into a new, more expansive perspective came during a routine doctor's visit in mid-November. As I sat in the waiting area, filling out paperwork, I came to a section asking about my personal status. I paused and considered my choices: "single, married, separated, divorced, widowed." I began to smile, and then I laughed out loud. I was all of the above. They didn't have a category for that, but they needed one. This awareness of my new, expanded status brought no shame, no sadness or grief; on the contrary, it made me feel wise and strong. I was a survivor. I smiled as I put pen to paper and circled all five words.

I was all of the above.

# 31

I awakened on Thanksgiving morning and looked down at Bentley curled up by my feet; I felt both peaceful and extremely grateful that he was the only male sharing my bed with me. I got up and threw on some jeans, a warm jacket and hiking boots, stopped for coffee, and then drove with Bentley out to the barn. No other cars were there when we pulled in.

I grabbed the two big plastic bags of carrots I'd brought and carried them with me to the barn. Setting them down, I rolled back the large door. The pungent smell of hay and horses met us as Bentley ran into the wide center aisle, excitedly searching for horse droppings, and standing—paws braced on stall doors—to meet the soft noses of his large friends.

I walked behind him, glad that nobody else was there. The barn was still and cold, the only sounds the snorts of the horses. I went first to Sammy, who greeted me wide-eyed and impatient for his carrot. I hugged his dusty, warm neck, rich with the scent of sweat and earth, and kissed his long, hard face. I made my way down one side of the long aisle and back up the other, stopping at each stall to offer a carrot and to stroke a nose. This was already a happy Thanksgiving: no travel; no family dramas; just quiet alone time with the animals.

I walked out into the thin, bright sun. Bentley scurried to join me; his furry, white mouth caked with horse manure. He was in his bliss.

I smiled as I slipped into the driver's seat of my car. Bentley hopped onto my lap and perched with one paw on the armrest, cupped in my elbow. We headed back toward town, and then turned off onto I-5, heading north to my mother's house.

My mother was in the midst of nervous preparations as I walked in. She was having a gathering of friends in a few hours for a formal Thanksgiving meal. I had chosen not to join them but I wanted to see her and help with last-minute details. Bentley climbed up the back of the sofa and onto the kitchen counter, where he lay down, assuming his usual perch away from my mother's ill-bred bulldog, Buddy. I cleaned off Bentley's face and poured myself a glass of champagne.

"Will you please get David's china down for me?" my mother asked. I dragged a chair over to the refrigerator, climbed on top of the familiar, 1960s Formica counter, and began to hand down the once-a-year china. "Have you seen the table?"

My mother took great pains with her holiday tables. Celebrations always gave her frustrated artistic talents a furlough from their long imprisonment. Of all my childhood memories, the birthday and holiday tables were among the most accessible because of the happy times they evoked and because my mother took pictures of them every year, pasting them in her voluminous photo albums and labeling them with care.

Each time we pulled out an album, she would point at these pictures and say, "Look at that table. I always celebrated every occasion."

I climbed down from the counter and went into the dining room, which was only ever used on high holidays—Valentine's, Thanksgiving, Christmas—and occasionally, birthdays. Normally, throughout my childhood, we ate at the counter or at the family table that my father had fashioned from an old door and some wrought-iron legs. We were not allowed to touch the teak table for fear that we would set down a glass and leave a mark, or drop a blob of cranberry sauce, permanently staining it. Even now, red wine was barred from all dinners.

"It's beautiful," I said, and I meant it.

My mother looked pleased. It was good to be with her, just the two of us. We talked more easily than we usually did, my detachment from the celebration calming her and lending me a certain dispassionate view of both my mother and the event. I now understood her pride at expressing her creativity and at maintaining a sense of beauty in the midst of a difficult, twenty-five year marriage to my father, and I appreciated her efforts.

Once everything appeared ready, my mother began to gear up for the first arrivals.

"You should leave before the guests arrive," she said.

I knew my mother well enough to understand that she didn't want my dressed-down appearance to mar her formal event, so I took her subtle clue and, without donning my usual resentment, tossed on my jacket and opened the front door. Two of my mother's guests stood on the doorstep.

"Hello," I said, and smiled. "Please come in. I'm just leaving."

"Where are you going?" A large, strong hand gripped my arm. "You can't leave!"

The voice was emphatic; it bordered on panic. It belonged to an imposing, six-foot-two, large-framed, mostly bald and, based on my experience from living many years in San Francisco, flamboyantly gay man. He was dressed in what Ainslie would call "casual smart" attire: turtleneck and slacks and an overcoat draped over one arm. What really caught my attention, however, were his eyes: enormous and round, open so wide that I could see the whites all the way around the blue irises. I looked at him, his hand still clutching my arm.

"Why not?" I asked.

"You're the only other person here remotely close to my age."

He dropped my arm and waited for a reply. His septuagenarian female companion, led by my mother, disappeared into the living room.

"Sorry, I'm not staying."

"Why not?" he pressed.

I tilted my head down, raised one eyebrow, and asked, "You haven't heard my sad story?"

"No. What's your sad story?"

The intensity of his stare and those enormous, bulging eyes were slightly disconcerting. I drew in a long breath.

"Well," I said, finding it hard to imagine that anyone in my mother's circle didn't already know all the lurid details, "I lost my husband two years ago in a plane crash, and my father died at Christmas, so the holidays aren't particularly celebratory for me."

"Oh, then you should come and be part of the opera," he said, enormous frogeyes staring down at me. This non sequitur caught me by surprise.

"Oh no," I said immediately and emphatically, shaking my head.

"Why not?"

He looked genuinely perplexed at my answer, as though anyone would be delighted to jump at such an opportunity.

"Well," I replied, inhaling slowly, "two reasons. One, I can't sing; and two, I hate opera."

"That's okay! You can help with the sets!" He was irrepressible. "I'm the artistic director, Doug Langdon," he explained, extending an enormous hand.

"I'm Katherine," I said, my hand disappearing inside his.

The man was doggedly persistent and charming in a dramatic, over-the-top, operatic sort of way. I could easily imagine him as a director. I could also imagine him wearing a feather boa.

"We have a performance New Year's Eve," he added.

This statement clinched the deal. New Year's Eve is the worst night of the year for the single and lonely, closely followed by Valentine's Day.

"Okay," I smiled. "I'll help with the sets. Anything to have something to do on New Year's Eve."

"Good!" he boomed. His large face, framed by a goatee, beamed. "Now don't leave me here alone," he stage-whispered.

He was nothing if not engaging, but again I demurred.

"I can't have dinner dressed like this," as I gestured at my jeans and hiking boots.

"Borrow a dress."

I appreciated his tenacity; it felt good to feel enveloped in such buoyant energy.

"Okay, okay," I laughed. "I'll stay."

Two weeks later, I showed up on my appointed Thursday afternoon at the First Presbyterian Church for rehearsal. After helping him plunder the Shakespeare Festival's set department, Doug had talked me into having a non-singing role, called a *supernumerary*, for the opera's Christmas production of *La Bohème*. It was almost two years to the day that Andrew had been killed, but I was neither undone by this fact nor consumed by it. I was beginning a new adventure, trying something completely out of my box. It felt good. Not exciting, but ... *normal*.

I walked upstairs, following hand-printed signs that directed singers to the rehearsal space. Bentley, gamely dressed in a blue knit sweater, trotted ahead of me into the carpeted room. I'd been expecting a gathering of local retirees, but this is not what greeted me. I was, along with Doug, one of the older people there.

I waited with Bentley on a small, velvet fainting couch in the corner as the room slowly filled, listening to conversations and examining my fellow performers, some of whom I recognized. Doug was exuberantly proclaiming his love of one particularly rotund singer's skintight, black vinyl pants. When everyone had arrived, Doug began quick introductions.

"Okay, everyone. This is Katherine, who will be one of our supernumeraries, and Bentley, who will also be appearing on stage."

I raised my hand to identify myself, and Doug continued with oversized gestures.

"This is Stephan, our tenor from Portland; Susan, our Mimi; Tristan, our recently engaged baritone, playing Schaunard." Tristan's fiancée Gabrielle, who was singing in the choir, smiled from the sidelines and waved her newly engaged hand in the air to signal her ownership. "This is Trisha, our recently married, lovely Musetta. And this," he stretched out his arm dramatically, "is the very single Michael Stevens, our Marcello."

The very single Michael Stevens rolled his eyes as he glanced over at his colleagues. He was thin and tall, dressed in a plaid shirt and tan corduroy pants. He had very short, graying hair and a goatee. The introduction was not lost on me or anyone else in the room. Doug looked over at me, lifting his eyebrows in an exaggerated way, giving the broadest of hints. I looked down, slightly embarrassed but also amused at the transparency of his matchmaking.

Doug began blocking the first scene, placing me directly behind Michael. He looked all of twenty-two, despite the gray hair. I stood in my spot, staring at his neck, which was covered with freckles. I wondered, in an abstract, offhanded sort of way, if the freckles continued down his back or were just on his neck. He wasn't redheaded; it seemed strange. Then I wondered why I was wondering this at all.

I continued my musing as Marcello, arms crossed in front of his chest, opened his mouth and began to sing. A round, deep, powerful sound suffused the room. I felt a chill sweep down my body and the hair on my arms stood up. Michael's voice penetrated my core, reverberating inside of me, making me catch my breath. When I had said that I hated opera, it was before I heard this.

I stood silently awestruck, listening to the soaring melodies, thinking how pale and angular the English language sounded in comparison to the undulating sensuality of Italian. Michael/Marcello stood, serious and focused, occasionally pressing two fingers against his ear to hear himself.

"A rich, creamy baritone," Doug later enthused in a slightly sickening gush. "You'll be able to say that you knew him when."

The next evening, following the rehearsal, I asked a few of the singers, whom I had identified as friends of Michael, if they would like to join me for drinks. We met up at a local British-style pub and sat around a table in front of a roaring fire. Thousands of tiny, white Christmas lights festooned the bare tree branches outside, illuminating the black night that was visible through large, brick-framed windows. Sitting here, I became aware of my own joy. I heard myself laughing and joking.

I was having fun.

My companions hailed from Portland, three hundred miles away. They were all young, aspiring singers; all talented; all poor; all seduced by the possibility of finding fame on larger stages in bigger venues.

*Two weeks*, I thought. *I have two weeks to enjoy this before it all disappears.*

Their presence felt like a gift, an unexpected holiday for me, and I intended to make the most of their time here. The ambient noise in the pub was tremendous: happy and convivial. I joined in the banter at the table, maintaining an awareness of Michael in my peripheral vision. He was listening to the conversation without saying much—a trait that, perhaps out of my psychological leanings, I found intriguing; it left me wanting to know more.

During one conversational volley, I heard Michael make an aside to no one in particular. It was a dry and sharp-witted remark, and it seemed that I was the only one who had heard it. I leaned back in my chair and looked over to where he was sitting at the end of the long table. We made eye contact.

"I heard you," I said quietly.

He smiled, pleased at the acknowledgment.

"Let's play darts," I said to the table, issuing a general but pointed invitation.

I stood and Michael stood as well. We grabbed some darts at the bar and took our drinks over to the brightly lit corner where three dartboards hung on a long wall. A couple of the other singers joined us. Michael and I began a friendly competition, tossing the darts in turn as we engaged in an increasingly suggestive repartee. Feeling intoxicated less by the alcohol than by the joy of companionship and flirtation, I came up behind him and wrapped my arms around his waist. He lifted both arms in surprise, hands clutching the darts.

"Let's see if you can get a bulls-eye with a little distraction," I teased.

Michael eased back into a relaxed position. Seeming to enjoy my flirtatious overture, he turned his head and looked over his shoulder at me.

"Alright," he smiled.

He pulled back his arm and tossed the dart, missing the board completely. He emitted a good-natured groan as the others laughed.

"That wasn't fair!" he said.

"Totally fair. You owe me a drink," I said.

The next day, there were no rehearsals. I stood in my kitchen in the early afternoon, looking at my phone, debating.

*What the hell,* I thought. *I have nothing to lose.*

I picked up the receiver and called the inn where Michael was staying.

"Hi, it's Katherine." I said when he came to the phone. "I wondered if you'd like to see a movie with me this afternoon."

"Oh. Thanks, but I better not. I think I'm going to work on my music today. Thanks anyway."

"Oh," I said, surprised and disappointed. "Okay. I'll see you tomorrow then."

I hung up, confused. Had I utterly misinterpreted our flirtation the night before? Had I come on too strong? It seemed like the epitome of irony that, having at last come to a point where I was not seeking a relationship, where all I wanted to do was have a good time for a couple of weeks, I was being rebuffed. *It's just a movie*, I thought, *two lousy hours. How much practicing can a person do in a day?*

At rehearsal the following day, Michael seemed curiously distant. I fought the feeling of disappointment that was insinuating itself on me. I tried to feign indifference, to tell myself that it didn't matter and I didn't care, that I would still have fun, but something had shifted and I couldn't quite get myself back to the feeling of lighthearted joy.

Tristan and his fiancée Gabrielle were giving me a ride home after rehearsal, my car having been rendered useless by the heavy snowfall earlier in the week. As I climbed into the backseat in the church parking lot, the opposite door opened and Michael got in. I shrank a bit. I wasn't sure how to act or what to say, and I remained quiet as we drove the eighteen miles back to Ashland, listening to the singers dissect the rehearsal.

Twenty minutes later, we pulled into the circular driveway of Michael's bed and breakfast. He had mentioned during our ride back that the heat in his room had gone out the night before. I'd offered him my guest room—a last effort to see if I had, perhaps, misconstrued his silence—but he declined. Michael got out and leaned down to say goodnight to everyone.

"I'd better go in with you," Tristan said to Michael, "just to make sure the heat's back on. We wouldn't want you to freeze."

As the two men crunched through the snow, Gabrielle pulled down her sun visor and began to apply some lipstick. Staring at me in the mirror, she paused in mid-application.

"Well, what do you think of Michael?"

"I think he's great, but he doesn't know I'm alive," I said, as I stared out toward the inn.

I winced, hearing these words escape my mouth. We sounded like a couple of freshman girls, talking at our lockers.

"Oh, I think you're wrong," she replied in a singsong, I-know-something-you-don't-know sort of way.

Her question and her statement both surprised me. I wondered if she did indeed know something that I didn't.

"Really? I don't think so." My reply was half-question, half-demurrer.

"He told Tristan that he was attracted to you."

Just then, the men returned to the car. Michael opened the door and bent down.

"The heat's not working again. Is your offer still good?"

Tristan's face was next to Michael's as they peered in at me, waiting for a response.

"Sure," I said, trying to sound offhanded.

*Don't get excited,* I thought. *He probably actually wants to use the guest room.*

Tristan drove us through the downtown, all lit up for the winter holidays, and up the icy hill to my house. Michael and I got out, and we waved goodnight to Gabrielle, who waved and smiled coyly as they drove off. I still had no idea what was happening; the signals were too mixed to decipher. We crossed the snow-covered bridge to the front door. I unlocked it, greeted Bentley, and invited Michael inside.

"Come on in. I'll get some sheets and a blanket. The guest room is there."

I pointed toward the den on the right. I went downstairs to grab some linens and a spare pillow from the closet. I brought them up, and we made up the sofa bed.

"Are you tired, or would you like a drink?" I asked when we finished, trying to gauge where we were.

"A drink would be good."

Buoyed, I showed him to the living room and lit a fire. Then I went to the kitchen and poured two small glasses of Grand Marnier, the only thing I had in the house. I carried them to the living room, handed him a glass, and curled up in a corner of the white sofa, a couple of feet from where he sat.

Michael seemed somewhat reserved, but he was easy to talk to. A relaxed rapport unfurled as we spoke. He was just twenty-seven and had been in only one long-term relationship, yet there was a maturity about him, a calm presence that I found appealing. His intelligence and wit and gray hair belied his youth and relative lack of life experience. It was a new and strange experience for me to feel attracted to someone absent any concomitant sense of desperation or desire to make it into something more. It felt relaxing. It felt good.

I woke up the next morning, quietly rolling out of bed to avoid waking Michael, and tiptoed upstairs to the kitchen. I smiled as I passed by the unmessed guest bed, and recalled the night's intoxicated passion. After a couple of hours, I heard him walking up the stairs. He came tentatively into the kitchen in his stocking feet.

"Good morning," he said.

He walked over and gave me a light kiss.

"Good morning," I replied with a smile.

A long-forgotten mixture of pleasure and embarrassment seized me as we embraced. We held each other for a minute. He was taller than Andrew had been; I liked that my head rested on his chest when he held me.

"Want to get some coffee?" I asked.

We spent the rest of the week together, driving to the remaining rehearsals and performances, making love in the mornings, going out for drinks late. On New Year's Eve, following our last performance and the after-party, Tristan and Gabrielle and Michael and I all went out dancing, and then drove back to my place in the early morning hours, the men singing dueling Figaros in the car as Gabrielle and I held our ears to dampen the overwhelming sound.

When the furious two-week interlude was over, Michael returned to his life in Portland, leaving me with a wistful hollowness that filled the space the brief affair had inspired. The combination of camaraderie and creativity of those two weeks had stimulated a longing that my quiet, peaceful life just could not satisfy, and the revivification of passion and romance had left an aching impression on my heart. I'd gotten what I wanted and what I needed. It was fun. It was over.

I was fine.

When I checked my email a couple of days later, Michael's name appeared in my inbox.

"Operagod," it read. That was an over-the-top sort of moniker for such a reserved guy, I mused. I clicked on it and read. His words took me off guard; he wrote eloquently and with surprising passion.

*Who is this?* I wondered. *Was this the quiet, subdued person I met?*

I was captivated by his wit and outpouring of feeling in the same way that I had been arrested by the sound of his powerful voice that day in the church.

A volley of emails ensued and, with each one, I was again delighted and surprised. His writing expressed a surprisingly deep and emotionally rich interior that was intimate, playful, and suggestive. He made me laugh. As much as I had enjoyed him during our time together, I was beginning to feel something more as I read his words. I wondered if there were something here and how it could possibly develop with three hundred miles between us.

# 32

It was now mid-January. I stood on an early Friday afternoon in my kitchen, in the spot where Michael and I had kissed, restlessly staring at the smooth, bright, oak floors. I had just reread one of his emails, and I was thinking. I had nothing in particular to do, no one to be with. I was totally free. I called my new friend Cybelle, whom I'd met at the barn. I'd already told her all about Michael.

"I'm thinking about driving up to Portland," I said.

"When?"

"Right now. What do you think? Should I do it? Is this asinine?"

"No, you should go," she answered. "Why not?"

I hung up, giddy. In all the years I'd lived in Oregon, I'd never been to Portland. I called his number.

"Hello?"

"Hey! It's Kate. What are you doing?"

"Laundry. What are you up to?"

"Nothing," I said. "I'm thinking about coming up to visit."

"When?"

"Right now."

"Right now? Today?"

"Is that okay?"

"Sure, yes," he said.

He gave me directions and told me to be careful, which I liked. I threw my things in a bag, hopped in the car with Bentley, and got on the freeway for the four-hour drive north. For the first three hours, I remained high with gleeful self-pleasure. I plugged a Chris Isaak tape into the cassette player and sang along: "What a wicked game you play, to make me feel this way..." I had no idea what the outcome of the visit would be, but I liked driving alone with somewhere to go and an adventure waiting. I liked the anticipation.

Michael greeted me at the door of a second-story apartment in a large, wooded complex. It was already dark and starting to rain as he showed me in. It was strange to see him in this environment, away from friends and from the drama of an opera. A dying philodendron drooped from atop an oak bookcase. There was a sofa and a chair, a small dining table and a stereo. A vase of mixed flowers sat on the kitchen counter, a welcome for me that Michael had bought at the grocery store across the road.

We quickly fell back into our comfortable rapport, learning more about one another. We ate Thai food and walked through Washington Park. I loved being back in a beautiful, urban setting. Unlike small, sleepy Ashland, Portland felt vibrantly alive.

I lay next to Michael on his hard futon the following night, listening to the rain and the wind outside. The storm made the rain spout on the other side of the bedroom wall clang and screech. It was strange to be in what looked like a college dorm room; it brought the disparities in our age and life situations into sharp relief. Our lives were so different, yet we melded so easily. I pondered the possibilities, and the potential problems.

Sunday morning as we dressed, Michael made a comment in the midst of casual conversation that caught me the wrong way.

"There's always something to laugh about. You've got to find something to laugh about at least once a day," he said offhandedly.

"I think that's pretty naïve," I retorted.

Michael remained relaxed but adamant.

"Even on a bad day, there's at least one thing to laugh about."

"You've obviously never been through anything very difficult in your life," I said.

"Well, you have to laugh to get through."

"You know, the day my husband was killed, I just couldn't find anything to laugh about," I replied tersely.

Michael looked at me, his face serious.

"Well," he said, "that's understandable ..."

He had inadvertently just poked at the still-tender wound I carried and tapped into my musings about our compatibility. His innocence sent me on an internal tirade. Suddenly, the whole relationship seemed impossible. He didn't get it. He could never understand me, could never imagine the depth of despair I'd been through, could never have the compassion I needed. He was too young, too naïve. The two weeks we had enjoyed together in Ashland were just a happy fling; a small, whirlwind romance created by the surreal atmosphere of a theatrical production. It wasn't real life. *This* was real life.

We stood, quiet and uncomfortable in the tiny bedroom.

"I haven't been through what you have," he said carefully.

"No, you haven't."

We fell quiet again, neither of us knowing what more to say. We went out for coffee and I told him that I should probably get back before dark.

I drove back down Interstate 5, thinking, Chris Isaak quiet in the glove box. Michael's statement and attitude had upset me. I thought he was savvier than that; it was disappointing. On the other hand, what did I expect? That he would be perfect? That every potential partner would have to be widowed to have empathy? That they could crawl into my skin and feel what I felt? That they should even try? What would that serve?

This post-widowhood relationship business wasn't going to be as easy as I had imagined. It wasn't like the kind of dating I did before being married. This was a whole other operating system. This was Widows 2.0.

I looked out at the pastures dotted with sheep, and the hills, sheathed in a dark blanket of leaden clouds. I hadn't anticipated how a new relationship would bring up certain feelings, how I would compare everything I did or heard or felt to what it had been like with Andrew, or how it resonated with my experience. I hadn't thought about the inevitable rush of forgotten memories—how virtually everything I did with a new partner would conjure up a memory of Andrew or something we did together.

*What would it be like if our roles were reversed?* I mused.

As the new partner of a widow or widower, you're supposed to be kind and understanding about their loss and the life they had with someone else, the person before you; after all, they never stopped loving them, and they've been through the wringer. Still, I imagined that it would be hugely tiresome to compete with an invisible rival for someone's affections, not to mention exhausting trying not to offend hidden sensibilities. For someone like Michael to date me was a courageous thing to do, now that I thought about it: courageous, or ill-advised.

It was hard to know what to think. Was Michael not mature enough, or was I being unduly defensive—or both? I decided that I owed Michael an apology, regardless of whether we saw one another again. After all, it wasn't his fault that he hadn't lost a spouse, that he hadn't been through that particular ordeal. I couldn't expect everyone to tiptoe around my wound. This return to love was just going to be more challenging than I had imagined. When I got home, I immediately opened my computer. I clicked on my email, opened a blank page and began.

"It would be a shame to throw everything away on a misunderstanding," I wrote. "I think we have something good here. I'd like it to continue."

In May, after more visits and many letters, Michael came back down to Ashland to perform in *La Traviata*, and again we shared the stage and my bed. This time, when the show closed, Michael stayed. We decided to have a trial run at a real relationship.

⸙⸙

Five months later, we sat on the deck of my house in the crisp, blue-white air of late autumn. Grizzly Peak had the first dusting of a powdery snow on its crest, and the swath of oaks and maples running down the hillside warmed into a woolen blanket of crimson and gold. I walked out the glass door from the breakfast room into the bright, thin light, and sat down on the chaise beside Michael. He set down the paper that he was reading. His green-brown eyes, always soft and persistent, looked at me.

"I can't stay here any longer," he said quietly. "I love you, but there's nothing for me here. I have no opportunities; I'm too far removed from everything." He paused as I took in the implications of his announcement. "Whether you stay or go," he continued, carefully, "I have to leave. I need to go back to Portland. I'd like you to come with me."

He spoke with a definitive calm, in a way that said he'd been thinking about this for a while. We'd talked about Portland many times while sitting over coffee. I would ask him about various neighborhoods as I looked at the real estate listings in the Sunday paper, half-toying with the idea of what it might be like to live in an urban setting again, and in a place without a past. The idea was at once appealing and disconcerting.

I liked Ashland, nestled between rolling hills and blue-green mountains. I loved my house, which looked to the eastern horizon and seemed to touch the clouds that floated just above it during the winter. I loved it even more since Michael had been here with me. All the pieces of my little life coalesced with his presence, creating a dreamlike whole that satisfied and comforted me. I'd immersed myself in my contentment and closed my eyes to everything else, including Michael's career.

The inevitable necessity of Michael's return to the world sat with us now in the cold, October sharpness; his unexpected but inevitable announcement grounded my five-month flight of fancy. For the last five months, I had picked up where my honeymoon with Andrew had left off, subtly slipping into a relationship that felt both comforting and comfortable. I had not wanted to think beyond my current contentment, so I didn't.

The languorous life that had evolved through the summer and fall had nothing supporting it: neither of us had lives apart from one another, no jobs or social connections. We barely existed, except to each other. I could see that Michael's prodigious talent was going to waste, yet to argue for his languishing potential was to argue for my own loss.

Hearing Michael's sobering statement presented me with a dilemma: Should I stay in Ashland, alone in my pretty little life, or should I risk letting it go in the hope that this relationship would continue to evolve? I was up against the conundrum of love and loss.

Stymied, I went to see Nicole, hoping that she might clarify the situation enough for me to make a well-grounded decision. I sat on the black futon in the small, familiar room in her apartment and rearranged the pillows to make myself comfortable. She sat down slowly, her arthritic body sharp and cautious, wearing her usual long sweater and leggings. Bianca jumped into her lap, panting as Nicole stroked her, her two black, marble-like eyes staring at me.

"So, how are you? Is everything okay with you and Michael?"

Her voice rose at the end of each sentence, the small lilt indicating a question behind her questions.

"Michael says that he needs to go back to Portland, that there's nothing here for him."

"He's right, honey. He should go," she replied quickly, not waiting for me to finish the rest of the story.

I knew that she'd been waiting for this moment, hoping for it. The way she said it was absolute, as though it were all patently obvious, as though the story were familiar and the ending already written. She gazed steadily at me, her darkly lined eyes penetrating. It was the stare that she gave me when she was waiting for me to wake up and get something.

I was irritated that we weren't having a discussion; that she wasn't being a good friend, let alone a decent therapist—someone who would ask questions that would lead to well-considered answers. She clearly had her own thoughts on the matter and wasn't interested in hearing mine.

"Michael needs to go," she said, "and you need to stay."

My jaw tensed.

"He's not for you, honey. You've had your fun and it's been nice, but now it's time for it to end."

I looked at her tautly. Suddenly, I was eighteen and she was my mother, telling me not to go with this boy, that it would ruin my life, that he wasn't good enough for me—she who had fawned over him; she who had said nothing until this moment. I was now pulled not just between my home and Michael, but also between Michael and Nicole. I felt the heat of betrayal rush through my body.

I was angry that she wasn't helping me; angry that she thought she knew what was best for me; angry that she had predetermined what sort of life I should live; angry that she had summarily dismissed the man whom previously she had given only praise. Her quick and dismissive response surprised me, but it also galvanized my rapidly rising anger into a strong, sharp rebuttal, one that went straight to what I knew to be the heart of the matter.

"If Michael were rich, you wouldn't be saying any of this."

I spoke the words calmly, rising to her argument, sure in my mind of her motivations. Nicole leaned back in her chair, her drawn-in eyebrows rising as she stared me down.

I was right. I stood up and walked out through her living room and down the stairs to the front door. I drove home hotly, shoving the stick shift into gear as I accelerated out of the parking lot and up the hill, enjoying the sound of the powerful engine and the feeling it gave me. I tore around the corner of my house and into the garage, and sat there listening to the engine wind down, thinking and trying to cool off before I saw Michael.

I loved Nicole. I'd loved her despite her unorthodox methods and her overindulged opinions. I loved her strong will and her ability to navigate all sorts of people. I loved her openness to new experiences and her self-confidence. I loved driving her into the mountains in my BMW for hamburgers and iced tea in the Greenspring Mountains, high above Ashland. I loved that she thought I was funny, and laughed when I impersonated Jerry Lewis. I loved her for being there when agony and fear were closing in, and I had no one else at six o'clock in the morning.

This time, though, she had overstepped an invisible boundary, and she had lost me. I could feel it. I'd been willing to forgo a real, therapeutic relationship because what we shared provided so much of what I needed. But neither friend nor therapist had the authority to dictate my heart, particularly with such a superficial dismissal.

Still, that night as I lay in bed next to Michael, I thought about what Nicole had said. I thought about my list of requirements for a relationship, few items of which Michael met. And I thought about Sam, from the flight to San Francisco a year earlier, and his reminder that what I sought might not come in the package I expected. I thought about Andrew, and our love, and the problems that existed along with that love. I thought about the two years of loneliness that I had just exited and what I had written in my journal a few months after Andrew died: that if I ever found real love again, nothing and no one would prevent me from embracing it—not fear, not money, nothing.

My choice was simple but not easy. A future with Michael was not certain; my house was. I did not want to act out of desperation; neither did I want to be foolish. I wanted to be smart in every way: smart in my head, smart in my heart.

To love again was to risk losing that love. That's the inherent dilemma in embracing a real life. Ultimately, as I lay next to a sleeping Michael, I realized that it didn't matter whether I chose to stay or go. What mattered was the reason behind my choice. Lying there in the dark, I arrived at the real question: Did I choose love or did I choose fear? Love and fear were the dragons positioned at this new threshold of my life; dragons that I needed to face if I wanted to see what treasures and trials lay within.

Seeing it this way, I knew what I needed to do.

⌒ ⌒

Are you ready?"

Michael was in the driver's seat, looking over at me, waiting for my okay. The moving van had left, and now it was just us, parked in front of the house, and Bentley silently curled in the backseat. The rain beaded and rolled down the passenger window as I stared out at the place of my solitude and protection. The winter rains had stripped the trees of their color, but the yellow leaves of wisteria still clung to the bridge leading to the front door, and the red berries of the hawthorn hung courageously to their long, black branches. I was sad but sure.

The week before, I had taken the stone heart that a friend had given me after I was widowed and buried it in the yard under a tree. I was done with my heavy heart and grateful for all that love and grief had given me. I stared at the spot where I had buried that leaden, gray heart in the earth, allowing the feelings of soft sadness and anxiety and gratitude to sit with me in the silence of the raindrops. Life was right here, in the car with me—a new life, an uncertain one.

"I'm ready." I said. "Let's go."

This being human is a guest house.
Every morning a new arrival.

A joy, a depression, a meanness,
some momentary awareness comes
as an unexpected visitor.

Welcome and attend them all!
Even if they're a crowd of sorrows,
who violently sweep your house
empty of its furniture,
still, treat each guest honorably.
He may be clearing you out
for some new delight.

The dark thought, the shame, the malice,
meet them at the door laughing,
and invite them in.

Be grateful for whoever comes,
because each has been sent
as a guide from beyond.
Welcome difficulty.
Learn the alchemy True Human Beings know:
the moment you accept what troubles
you've been given, the door opens.

Welcome difficulty as a familiar comrade.
Joke with torment brought by a Friend.

Sorrows are the rags of old clothes
and jackets that serve to cover,
and then are taken off.
That undressing,
and the beautiful naked body underneath,
is the sweetness that comes after grief.

—Rumi

Made in the USA
San Bernardino, CA
27 November 2013